## About the Author

The late Marshall Wolfe was educated at Williams College, USA, and Oxford University, where he was a Rhodes Scholar. He joined the United Nations Secretariat in 1946 shortly after it was founded. From 1963 to 1978 he served as Chief of the Social Development Division of the United Nations Economic Commission for Latin America (ECLA) in Santiago, Chile. While at the ECLA, he developed a reputation for his willingness to question some of the conventional wisdom on development. In the 1970s he entered into a joint venture with the United Nations Research Institute for Social Development (UNRISD), the ECLA and UN Headquarters to develop an ambitious 'unified approach to development analysis and planning', becoming the principal drafter of its preliminary report.

He is the author of various papers on development, mainly published in *CEPAL Review*, as well as co-author (with Matthias Stiefel) of *A Voice for the Excluded: Popular Participation in Development* (Zed Books, 1994).

G000139660

# ELUSIVE DEVELOPMENT

## Marshall Wolfe

ZED BOOKS LTD
London & New Jersey

UNRISD
Geneva

*Elusive Development* was first published by
Zed Books Ltd, 7 Cynthia Street, London N1 9JF,
UK, and 165 First Avenue, Atlantic Highlands,
New Jersey 07716, USA, in 1996.

Cover designed by Andrew Corbett
Set in Monotype Garamond by Ewan Smith
Printed and bound in the United Kingdom
by Biddles Ltd, Guildford and King's Lynn

Earlier versions of sections of this book appeared in
M. Wolfe *Elusive Development,* UNRIFD/ECLA,
Statistical Publishing House, Budapest, 1981, and in
*CEPAL Review.*

A catalogue record for this book is available from
the British Library

US CIP data is available from the Library of
Congress

ISBN 1 85649 379 2 cased
ISBN 1 85649 380 6 limp

# CONTENTS

# CHAPTER I

# WHY 'ELUSIVE' DEVELOPMENT?

## A sceptic's apology

Certain institutional imperatives and a personal reaction to those imperatives have shaped this book. The institutional imperatives derived from the efforts of United Nations organs in their early years to secure, for the 'social', equal status with the 'economic' in development policy; then to prescribe a 'unified approach to development analysis and planning' or to point the way to alternative 'styles of development' responding better to human needs than the processes heretofore passing for development. These efforts, through continual changes in terminology and emphasis, have assumed prior consensus on certain values of human welfare and social justice, on 'development' as an identifiable phenomenon essential to the realization of these values, and on the rationality and benevolence of certain entities – the international organizations, national governments, voluntary associations, public opinion – jointly striving for development so conceived and capable of acting on developmental prescriptions.

I participated in these efforts during more than thirty years within the United Nations Secretariat, mainly through studies designed to answer some variant of the questions: Are national societies approximating more closely to the professed values of human welfare and social justice? What can the entities named above prescribe or do to bring real trends into closer correspondence with these values? In my struggles with these questions I assumed that to make any contribution towards an honest answer was a worthwhile task. This conviction, however, has been only precariously reconcilable with the ritualism and evasiveness visible in the ways international discourse has commonly posed and answered the questions. The institutional imperatives to identify 'progress' that took at face value the 'national achievements' reported by governments, and the normative declarations approved by those governments, clashed with observable reality. In this reality, 'development' emerged from complex and confused struggles at the international, national and local levels; the strivings of the different centres of power and social forces had consequences which differed from what any of them had wanted or expected; and the capacity of institutions and individuals making up the state to exercise foresight or guide national change processes in any coherent direction was problematic.

The studies were addressed mainly to governmental participants in

United Nations meetings, planners, social programme administrators, and other presumed makers and executors of development policy rather than to social scientists or the general public. In the minds of this intended audience, questions of values and broad objectives had been resolved already, through their formulation in the Universal Declaration of Human Rights and numerous resolutions endorsed by the representatives of practically all states.

The same audience was unreceptive to explorations of questions of theory. It supposed that such questions had already been answered satisfactorily, or that the answers could wait, or that raising the questions would endanger the international consensus on the meaning of development. In formal terms, through instructions to the Secretariat, it requested factual information and practical prescriptions, although it made little use of either.

The fate of international studies responding to these requests demonstrated the superficiality of concern with the 'practical'. An intergovernmental body might direct the Secretariat to prepare a report for its next meeting on how to satisfy all human needs. Half a dozen functionaries would strain to do so. The result, which might be expected to have a reception equivalent to that of one of the great documentary landmarks of human history, would be tepidly approved or criticized and would disappear without trace into government archives and the storerooms of the issuing organization, rarely remembered even by other functionaries preparing subsequent 'practical' reports. It might receive a brief mention in the more conscientious newspapers when it appeared, but scholarly journals would not trouble to review it.

In the writings in which I was able to express a personal reaction to the institutional imperatives, I evaded literal responses, and instead tried to distinguish, in terms meaningful to the intended audience, the full range of problems that must be faced when proposing relevant prescriptions. Thus, I reformulated the questions posed above in the following terms: *If* one really wants development responding to the values of human welfare and social justice, and *if* national societies and the international order present quite different patterns and trends, what can be done and by whom? To whom does one address advice? Who is entitled to give advice?

Confrontation with such questions might well be unsettling to the more literal-minded believers in the developmental articles of faith and also to the wider circles that depend for status and livelihood on the perpetuation of the bureaucratic structures and ritualized meetings based on these articles. For nearly half a century the promotion of development has been an industry in which supply has created its own continually diversifying demand for 'experts', in which conferences beget conferences and declarations beget declarations, in which major 'problem areas' incorporating different conceptions of developmental priorities continually hive off organizationally, receive symbolic recognition in 'years' or 'decades', inflate themselves to cover all aspects of 'development', and spawn infinitely ramifying coordinating mechanisms.

The same questions might well seem naive, lacking in theoretical grounding and misleading as guides to action to social scientists and ideologists who have never taken seriously the suppositions of potential international harmony and compatible social class interests in development. From their point of view, why should anyone, for reasons other than mystification, expect existing states – instruments of dominant social classes or transnational power centres – to introduce styles of development oriented to human welfare and social justice? Can a valid response be anything other than the identification of social forces capable of transforming the society and the state? Does not the inter-governmental and governmental machinery of development studies, meetings and socially oriented declarations deserve Tolstoy's taunt that the ruling classes would do anything for the people except get off their backs?

By the 1970s, the eclecticism of international discourse, the heterogeneity of the regimes participating in it, the pervasive dissatisfaction with what had been done in the name of development, and the quest for policy innovations had increasingly blurred the dividing line between developmentalist and revolutionary ideologies, and brought about an ambivalent receptivity to radical questioning of the articles of faith. The realities of the world, too harsh to be camouflaged by discreet reports, continually pressed the international organizations in this direction, while institutional continuity, vested interests in ongoing programmes, and governmental admonitions to be 'practical' continually forced them to try to pour the new wine into their old bottles, to assume that all states meant well, and that practically all ideological positions were ultimately reconcilable. Thus, forms of social action that had emerged painfully from revolutionary struggles in specific national societies were discussed as if they were promising prescriptions that might be adopted at the will of any regime along with a selection from the more conventional tools of social action. One outcome was the proliferation of what I then labelled 'utopias devised by committees'.

The explorer of development might find himself in an uneasily eclectic position for reasons other than this institutional bias. The state, in its real manifestations in the world, was obviously far from being the rational, benevolent, autonomous entity that international deliberations and development prescriptions, particularly in their earlier stages, seemed to assume. 'Development', under whatever interpretation, was not necessarily a central preoccupation of the forces controlling states or contending for power. At the same time, in a good many national societies, the state was asserting a degree of autonomy and an apparent capacity to determine the direction of social and economic change that could not have been predicted from the previous balance of social forces or the country's place in the international order. This tendency became more pronounced as the international order itself fell into crisis after crisis and the previous ties of dominance and dependence were strained or broken.

For better or worse, developmental voluntarism came to the fore in widely differing national societies and under widely differing leaderships. Various 'agents of development' asserted their right and duty to set their societies on new paths. The outcome of their choices, whatever the intentions behind them, seemed ambiguous at best. Technobureaucratic regimes put off social justice objectives to a remote future or simply compelled the population to swallow the agents' assertion that they were being realized. Voluntarist miscalculations under populist and socialist regimes led to the further impoverishment and oppression of the masses that were supposed to benefit.

However, it seemed premature to conclude that the structural situations in which agents trying to manipulate the state found themselves ensured that whatever choices they made would turn out badly. Could the state achieve a measure of autonomy and use it to do more good than harm? Under what circumstances? Could international interpretative and normative activities, linked to the formation of a confraternity of would-be agents of alternative styles of development, increase the likelihood of positive outcomes? Could the more cautious prescriptions for state action to satisfy basic needs and eliminate extreme poverty do more than foster conformity with systems of exploitation that must eventually perish? Did the more radical and egalitarian proposals, demanding, for example, de-linking from the global economic system and extirpation from poor countries of transnationalized consumer societies for affluent minorities, risk giving fuel to 'terrible simplifiers' who might replace a bad social order with a worse? I was unable to answer such questions to my own satisfaction.

The alternative political approaches that subordinated action by the state to transformation of the structures of power controlling the state and of the consciousness of the people exploited or excluded by current styles of development were more attractive but no more verifiable as means to 'authentic development'. Efforts over the past century to identify social classes capable of transforming their societies and to devise strategies for them had had no incontrovertible successes. It did not seem legitimate to contrast the real shortcomings and hypocrisies of existing states with millennial post-revolutionary expectations. Moreover, the proponents of these approaches commonly went to the other extreme from the developmental prescription-mongers in disregarding the practical questions of how styles of development corresponding to their values might be constructed once power had come into the hands of social forces really wanting such development. Class struggles were real enough, and the possibility that in certain conjunctures the classes whose interests conflicted with the existing order would assume the roles expected of them could not be discounted. The weight of evidence suggested, however, that the capacity of these classes to act coherently would continue to be weaker and their dependence on the state greater than the ideologists aspiring to mobilize them would admit.

The major influences on the content of this book have been my experiences since the early 1960s in the United Nations Economic Commission for Latin America (usually known from its Spanish initials as CEPAL); my participation during the early 1970s in a research programme centring in the United Nations Research Institute for Social Development (UNRISD) and aiming at a 'unified approach to development analysis and planning'; and my intermittent involvement between 1979 and 1993 in an UNRISD research programme on 'popular participation in development'.

The first experience exposed me to a clear-cut advocacy position on development evolved by CEPAL since the late 1940s. This position emphasized the planning of state action within a capitalist framework to accelerate economic growth and influence the distribution of its fruits. The thinking behind it was primarily economic, preoccupied by capital accumulation and industrialization, but increasingly incorporated social concerns on its own terms, both as means to the end of higher productivity, and as human welfare justifications of the striving for development. Within this setting, economists challenged sociologists and specialists in sectoral social programmes to identify and prescribe for 'social obstacles' to development.

The experience also exposed me to the radical questioning of 'developmentalism', inspired by Marxist as well as religious ideologies, characteristic of the non-official intellectual climate of Latin America and increasingly represented within CEPAL during the 1960s.

It exposed me, lastly, to the real processes of economic, social and political change in Latin America that in the main confounded the expectations of developmentalists as well as revolutionaries, confronting both with the apparent consolidation in most of the region of a 'peripheral capitalism' dominated by transnational enterprises and global finance capital, imitative, repressive, wasteful of human as well as natural resources, juxtaposing ostentatious consumerism and mass poverty.[1]

The second experience gave me a different vantage point for observation of the variants of pragmatism, determinism and utopianism that emerge when a multidisciplinary and multinational team tackles the what, why and how of development. Chapter 2 describes this experience in some detail, with its genealogy in previous United Nations efforts to prescribe for development, and the different 'approaches to a unified approach' that sought common ground during the course of the quest.

Chapters 3 and 4 attempt to set out, in an objective and classificatory way, the heterogeneous social and political structures and the links between national centre (or state) and social unit (or local group) that enter into policy making and policy frustration. These chapters are intended to demonstrate to seekers for technocratic or normative–utopian development prescriptions the intractability of certain features of the real world that they might otherwise disregard. These chapters are obviously vulnerable to criticism in their pretension to cover a very wide range of national and local phenomena, without sufficient digestion of the enormous body of theoretical literature and empirical studies of these questions, and without distinguishing clearly between the basic and universal on the one side, and the conjunctural and localized on the other.

The main justification for returning to the history of the 'unified approach' is that the United Nations family of organizations has re-embarked on similar quests under the labels of 'social integration' and 'integrated approaches' leading up to the 1995 World Summit on Social Development, with typical institutional amnesia about the past.

The third experience, entered into after my retirement from the UN Secretariat in 1978, took me away from the world of economists, planners, specialists in social programmes, and international bureaucrats prescribing for development, to the world of peoples being incorporated into the real processes of economic growth and societal change with little or no control over the terms of their incorporation; of their organized efforts to participate in 'development' or, more often, defend themselves against it; and of the ideologists and activists aspiring to guide, mobilize, or 'conscientize' them.[2]

The present text is the third to be published under the title *Elusive Development*. In each version the more obsolescent or repetitive chapters have been dropped, others rewritten so as to camouflage past illusions, and more recent efforts added to grapple with the old questions, in a process similar to that of the man who kept the same pocketknife but with three new blades and two new handles.[3] The economically or techno-cratically oriented conceptions of 'development planning' to which many of my earlier arguments were addressed are by now as obsolete as 'real socialism'.

This version follows upon my retirement to a village in Vermont and participant observation of parish-pump politics and issue-oriented group activities, experiences throwing new light on the gap between broad policy prescriptions and the ways in which limited achievements emerge from the interplay of values, priorities, prejudices and apathies.

## A wastebasket for commonplaces

Throughout my inconclusive struggles with the development Proteus, I have tried to purge my arguments of certain commonplaces of international policy-oriented discourse. Contributions to this discourse that in other respects radically challenge the conventional developmental wisdom continue to fall back on these formulas. Since these are symptomatic of reluctance or institutional inability to face the full implications of the failure of the real processes of economic growth and social modernization to respond to the hopes invested in them, it may be well to point them out here.

1. *'Growing awareness'* or *'increasing recognition'*: these are among the most venerable and overworked formulas in documents on social questions, and are well represented in discussions of other aspects of development. They generally express the user's hope of lending an aura of consensus to his own conviction that something ought to be done, while evading the identification of agents able and willing to act effectively. The continuing revolution in communication media indeed makes more people than ever before aware of a wide range of urgent problems, but the predominant response seems to be growing bafflement and increasing apathy.

2. Use of the *first person plural* to indicate that the user arrogates to himself representation of all persons of good-will, or of the masses refusing to suffer any longer their poverty and exploitation. This use of 'we' has become particularly prominent in the declarations of semi-official and unofficial international advisory groups and conferences, in which 'we' (lumping together officialdom, social scientists, public opinion and the poor) are assumed to share awarenesses and demands that would in reality seem subversive to some of the parties spoken for, inadequate and ingenuous to others, and incomprehensible to the majorities that are preoccupied with survival rather than 'development'. In a condescending variant, 'we' are supposed to be the unenlightened public that is responsible for the social injustices and environmental menaces that the user is denouncing.

3. *Warnings of catastrophe* for the international order or the national societies unless they transform themselves promptly. These formulas, closely related to the growing awarenesses, are directed to the centres of power and wealth to persuade them that it is in their own interest to lead or at least acquiesce in radical reforms and renunciation of privileges. The centres of power are by now quite accustomed to paying lip-service to the importance of the warnings, but probably continue to feel in private that they can shift to others the price of whatever catastrophes may come and that the alternatives offered are neither convincing nor convenient. Renewed confidence in the market as sole legitimate determinant of the future relieves them of responsibility. Moreover, experience indicates that national societies as well as the international order itself can continue to function, however irrationally and unjustly, modifying but not transforming structures whose imminent collapse has been predicted for many years, and even reconstitute these structures after real catastrophe has come upon them.

4. *Personification* of 'countries' as actors, as in the assertion that 'countries' have a right to 'choose' their styles of development, free of external pressures. The structure of inter-governmental organizations composed of formally sovereign states has made this an unavoidable fiction, but it has obscured the reality made plain in other passages of the same declarations: if styles of development are chosen at all, the choices are made by organized social forces within countries that must try to impose their choices on the rest of the society by persuasion, neutralization or coercion, and that must manoeuvre within constraints imposed by the country's place in the international order.

5. *Division* of the personified countries into two groups – rich and poor, developed and developing, central and peripheral, First World and Third World, North and South and so on – with the 'real socialist' Second World up to the 1990s generally considered a rival model for the rich, developed, central category. The division corresponds to certain real characteristics of the world order, and it had an instrumental utility in promoting joint action by the 'developing' or 'poor' countries, but it has been misleading in several important respects:

— It fostered a supposition that the countries of the first group had found the path to permanent gains in material well-being and social harmony, and that their evolution and the economic laws derived from it offered a model for the rest of the world. One might expect this supposition, one of the earlier articles of faith of developmentalism, to have been too cruelly refuted since the 1970s by events in 'capitalist' as well as 'real socialist' countries to serve even as an inspiring myth. Nevertheless, the supposition seems to have consolidated itself in the former countries in a 'culture of contentment' paradoxically coexisting with inquietude over the unmanageable accumulation of menaces and perversities in the system.[4]

— It fostered a supposition that each category of countries is homogeneous in essential characteristics, with common interests and problems. In fact, both categories are extremely heterogeneous in their power structures, resource bases, population characteristics and roles in the international order, at the same time that the globalization of economies and cultures is binding the first category more closely to the second. Political ideologies and 'development' policies have become somewhat more uniform within and between categories, but this uniformity will not necessarily persist. Formulas assuming that the 'poor' countries and the 'rich' countries can take uniform positions *vis-à-vis* each other, whether of cooperation or confrontation, aid or exploitation, obscure the real complexity of the alternatives for alignments and ties of domination or self-defence.

— The dichotomization of countries, like the 'we' formula, fostered a supposition that the dominant forces of the 'poor' countries shared in the poverty, or at least in a determination to do something about it. In fact, the spokesmen for most of these countries had no personal reasons to envy the incomes and lifestyles of their counterparts in the 'rich' countries and this, as press comments in the latter countries demonstrated, weakened the credibility of their appeals for a new international economic order. The same international reports that personified the poor countries and attributed to their leaders a determination to eliminate poverty presented evidence that increases in the wealth of these countries and in the operational capacity of their governments generally had no positive impact on the poverty of the masses.

6. International discourse has continually referred to '*social actors*' expected to '*play roles*' in development. This image suggests a drama in which the actors have roles defined for them, based on development dramas already performed elsewhere or on eschatological visions concerning the destiny of classes and societies. One might imagine a stage on which certain actors, convinced that they need a script to give sense to their performances, have tried to play roles that are incompatible with the scripts preferred by other actors on the same stage, or have strained to combine incompatible roles in their own performances. Meanwhile, the majority of participants in the drama of development – from the dominant as well as the dominated classes – have improvised and reacted to continually changing opportunities and shocks, paying little heed to the scripts.

## Existential development

The exploration of approaches to development undertaken in this book will encounter many different actors 'playing roles' within many different combinations of opportunities and constraints, in pursuit of an objective that is continually being redefined, falling back on verbal and organizational rituals for lack of ability to foresee and control the course of events, and sometimes violently rejecting reality for its failure to conform to their conceptions and values. One finds, internationally and nationally, a renewed affirmation of the need for different, more comprehensive, ideally 'integrated' approaches to development, combined with real concentrations of power, resources and public attention on aims that are either irrelevant to such approaches or obviously incompatible with them.

The legitimacy and relevance of the present exploration depend on the supposition that the present international rethinking of development is not altogether a mystification, condemned by the societal and institutional positions of its practitioners to offer solutions that will always be too little and too late, but that mystification is bound to creep in, through the conscious or unconscious need of the practitioners to *appear* to be facing challenges boldly while really evading them. If the exploration stimulates some of the actors in development to think harder about what they are doing and wonder whether they should not be doing something else, the purpose is served.

The practitioner might well retort: 'What positive, practical proposals do you have? Are you not really insinuating that the audience you address is irredeemably incapable of doing anything worthwhile?'

This book, of course, does not set out to demolish previous 'How to Develop' prescriptions and then propose an infallible new one, nor does it reject previous societal candidates for the honour of leading the way to development and then nominate different agents who can do the job. It really points to an existential approach to development, in which the actors should come to terms with an awareness that theirs is a possibly Sisyphean task of trying to impose a measure of value-oriented rationality on realities that will remain permanently recalcitrant to such rationality. Or one might return to the hackneyed image of the blind men and the elephant; possibly the elephant they are trying to describe does not exist beyond their ability to imagine it and 'integrate' their fragmentary images.

All societies that survive will have to strive to 'develop' in the sense of enhancing their capacity to function over the long term for the well-being of their members. None will ever reach a safe terminal state of 'being developed'. Apparent success may, in the long term, lead into a trap of relative incapacity for policy innovation, as a good many 'over-developed' as well as 'developing' countries are now demonstrating. From this point of view, all national societies at all points in time confront a certain range of accessible alternatives with different combinations of advantages and disadvantages. The capacity of their dominant forces to choose specific alternatives depends not only on objective conditions but also on their subjective appreciation of these conditions and the momentum of what has already been done. Choices or failures to choose are continually closing doors and opening different ones.

Ideally, the striving for development should embrace the whole human race, but the international participants should attach a positive value to diversity in styles of development, if only for the sake of experimentation and cross-fertilization, as long as these styles do not diverge grossly from the international consensus on human rights and values. Within these limits, each society should be free to evolve its own style and count on the cooperation it needs to do so. In practice, however, the actors trying to realize this ideal need to pay careful attention to external constraints and the internal forces linked to these constraints, and try to manoeuvre within the limits of the practicable. (Even definition of the boundaries within which 'choice' can be meaningful is difficult in view of the hetero-geneity of formally sovereign states within the world system.) The meeting of needs through international cooperation remains precarious, inhibiting and in great part illusory. The actors cannot dispense with such co-operation, but neither can they lean on it, especially when they leave the conventional paths. As the crises of the 1980s demonstrated, the sources of financing have straitjackets waiting if the actors are overconfident or unlucky.

Recognition during the 1970s of the legitimacy of alternative styles of development and the possibility of value-oriented choice was a step forward from previous conceptions of development as a process uniform for all countries, following its own laws, to be discovered and obeyed under penalty of permanant backwardness, but it raised more questions than it answered: Who was entitled to choose a national style of development and adjudicate the gains and losses? Could styles of development corresponding to international norms for social justice, within the limits of austerity and sacrifice set by national resources supplemented by problematic external cooperation and narrowed by foreseeable external sabotage, ever be acceptable to the articulate and organized social groups whose acquiescence would be essential? Would even the political leaders, ideologists and planners who were calling for more equitable and autonomous development accept the implications for their own lifestyles? Would national societies in the real world be able to achieve the degree of consensus and rational organization called for except at a price that would distort each initiative into something different from the image of the just and free future society informing it at its beginning?

## The present and the future

If one tries to summarize the main features of the 1990s and the present stage of efforts to describe and prescribe for the imaginary elephant, the paradoxes of economic and cultural globalization stand out. Interdependence and intercommunication have become even more pervasive and multidimensional than could have been expected in the recent past. The imperatives of participation in the world system, together with the perverse outcomes of national experiments in socialism and populism, seem to have ruled out deliberate de-linking and state-managed quests for alternative styles of development. The same trends, however, have generated new forms of diversity between and within countries and divergent prospects for societal evolution or disintegration. These prospects derive partly from a differential capacity for advantageous incorporation in the global order, and partly from contradictions that threaten the long-term viability of the order itself.

The technical capacity of international organizations, states and other institutions to inform themselves about what was happening has increased enormously, while confidence in their ability to digest the information and intervene in pursuance of clear purposes has eroded. This general 'crisis of responsibilities' manifests itself quite differently according to region and historical background.

In the 'rich' countries of Europe and North America one finds the majority 'culture of contentment' described by Galbraith contending with a 'culture of insecurity', a 'culture of complaint',[5] and a 'culture of exclusion'. A sense of unlimited possibilities for rising consumption and technological innovation coexists with an uneasy awareness of a wide range of menaces, dysfunctions and inequities. Alienation from the political system and the state coexists with organized pressures on the state to 'solve problems' and protect group interests.

In most of East and Southeast Asia one finds aggressive participation in the world market and dynamic economic expansion. Millions of people are emerging aggressively from poverty into 'cultures of opportunity'. The forces controlling states try to reconcile profit-oriented individualism with social discipline. Problems of population increase, environmental degradation, exclusion from livelihood of the rural people least able to cope with the market economy, and political corruption trouble these forces, but responses are subordinated to the safeguarding of economic dynamism. China, once the utopia of advocates of egalitarian, participatory development, has become the most extreme and paradoxical example of these trends.[6]

In Latin America one finds a precarious recovery from the debt traps and economic crises of the 1980s, with deepening contradictions between resurgent political democracy and increasing concentration of wealth accompanied by insecurity or impoverishment for the majority. State policies are constrained by market imperatives enforced by lending agencies, on the one side; and by endemic corruption, political stalemates and the inability to eliminate arbitrary violence by military and police agents of the state, on the other.

In most of Africa, one finds long-continued economic decline and majority impoverishment; collapse of state schemes for original styles of development followed by generally ineffective efforts to apply the structural adjustment prescriptions of lending agencies; increasing irrelevance to the needs of to the global order; alienation of people from states perceived as repressive and corrupt; and in a good many cases state disintegration into endemic civil conflict.

In the Middle East, one finds a paradoxical combination of regional self-identification on the basis of culture and religion with intense rivalries between states and groups within states. As elsewhere, the outcome of state-managed development policies has been remote from growth as well as equity objectives. Minorities have gained, while majorities have remained in poverty or been excluded from previous sources of livelihood. Here a relatively systematic and region-wide political–religious reaction against the 'modern' state and the norms of the global order itself has emerged, in contradictory combinations with state efforts to intervene aggressively in the global order through control of oil exports.

In the successors to the 'real socialist' states of the recent past, one finds traumatic transitions from a period when the state assumed all-inclusive responsibilities for managing development and enforced assent to exaggerated claims of achievement. Here more than elsewhere globalization has meant a wholesale rejection of the past, an embrace of market forces, private enterprise, pluralist democracy and consumerism, accompanied by radical delegitimization of state power, on the one hand, and the persistence of economic and political power centres deprived of ideological justification, on the other. While the experiences of the successor states in managing these reversals have differed widely, the reversals have notoriously generated insecurity, widening inequalities, exclusion of part of the active population from employment, and disintegration of the pre-existing safety net of social services and subsidies. The sequence of events, and the inability of new, largely imported, rules of the game to achieve a reasonable degree of consensus, have stimulated a ruthless pursuit of self-interest and a flaunting of consumerism among minorities; and sullen resentment, scapegoating, xenophobia or hopelessness elsewhere in the populations.

## Pluralist democracy

Affirmation of pluralist democracy as the main source of legitimacy of the state has accompanied globalization, in spite of incongruities with other dimensions of this process. Open political competition and contested elections have emerged in more countries than ever before, although a good many national regimes continue to function in flat contradiction to this norm. International linkages among issue-oriented and interest-group organizations (human rights, environmental and gender protagonists, trade unions, and so on) as well as political parties point to a kind of globalization of democratic strivings contesting global market-dominated policy imperatives.

At the same time, the implantation of a uniform model for pluralist democracy clashes with the weakness or absence in many parts of the world of supportive institutions of the civil society and with different national traditions and expectations concerning political power. The apparent extension of democratic choice to national majorities has co-incided with a shrinkage in the capacity of the state to respond to or reconcile conflicting demands with resources, most striking in the countries subject to structural adjustment programmes but visible almost everywhere. Governments and political parties are more resigned than previously to multiple constraints and veto powers from lending agencies, potential investors of capital, the military and the middle classes terrified of inflation and hostile to taxation. The majority might well feel that it is invited to enjoy democratic choice only as long as it refrains from making use of it to advance its own perceived interests. The label 'low-intensity democracy' seems appropriate for the pattern of promise and frustration.[7]

From the standpoint of the quest for 'human development' or 'sustainable development', the affirmation of pluralist democracy has other implications inseparable from those summarized above. In the 1970s and earlier, a good many advocates of alternative styles of development as well as advocates of state-guided capitalism were prepared to endorse mobilization regimes directed by vanguard parties and charismatic leaders as more promising and even more democratic agents of development than parliamentary regimes.

Different advocates identified certain countries as 'good examples' of development under democratic–authoritarian auspices: China and Tanzania were coupled as examples of egalitarian, communitarian, anti-bureaucratic mobilization; Yugoslavia as an example of workers' management and ethnic harmony; Mexico as an example of political stability and sustained economic growth under single-party direction. These and other 'functioning utopias' have proved to be mirages. One is back to Winston Churchill's characterization of democracy as the worst form of government except for all the others.

Pluralist democracy, according to one recent exploration of its relevance to the world of today, implies a juxtaposition or balancing of the representation of the interests of majorities, citizenship and limitation of power through fundamental rights:

> To be democratic, a political system must recognize the existence of inescapable conflicts of values, and thus not accept any central principle of organization of societies, neither rationality nor cultural specificity ... Everything that affirms or imposes a one best way ... a norm of conduct identified with the universality of reason, is a menace for democracy.[8]

A compatible approach insists that 'outcomes of the democratic process are uncertain, indeterminate ex ante'; and it is 'the people, political forces competing to promote their interests and values, who determine what these outcomes will be ... Democratization is an act of subjecting all interests to competition, of institutionalizing uncertainty.'[9]

Such formulations imply that, to the extent that democratic values and procedures influence human affairs, people will be able to make meaningful political choices, defend their perceived interests and set limits to the dictates of technocrats, bureaucrats, ideologists and concentrators of economic power. They even imply that the majority has a right to be wrong in the eyes of these diverse agents of policy. They do not altogether exclude the legitimacy of normative approaches to development, but imply that these should enter the political arena without pretensions to infallibility.

In any case, infallible voluntaristic prescriptions for development are now less formidable rivals to democratic choice than is the seemingly irresistible but precarious momentum of the world system itself. Under its imperatives the practice of democracy at the national level risks exhaustion in resentful impotence.

A composite description based on several real national situations may help to clarify the paradoxical necessity and elusiveness of pluralist democracy in the world today.

Certain states meet conventional criteria for nationhood and also for formally democratic procedures. They have periodic elections, vigorous inter-party competition, varied and autonomous institutions in the civil society, and free communication media reaching the majority of the population. At the same time, their capacity for coherent policy-making has been semi-paralysed by institutionalized corruption; the exercise of arbitrary violence with impunity by the military, police, landowners and mafias; economic processes that are dynamic but anarchic, generating environmental devastation and persistent high inflation; and a gap in power, wealth and access to education and other public services between social classes so wide that much of the population is excluded from democratic participation except in the form of electoral manipulation. To the groups holding political and economic power, as well as to the large middle strata striving desperately to achieve 'modern' standards of consumption, the excluded are invisible while passive but pose a threat of anarchy if they make demands.

In such a situation, various political movements and issue-oriented organizations involving minorities among the middle strata as well as among the excluded have their own conceptions of responsibilities for democratic social integration and are struggling heroically to make them effective. Some of these conceptions focus on modernization and demo-cratization of the state, while others distrust the state, avoid participation in national party politics, and look to widening autonomy for new localized social movements within the civil society. The national regime representing the state claims wide responsibilities for development and social justice, but in practice can hardly go beyond opportunistic crisis management. The state as public sector and the array of provincial and local administra-tions have components that function effectively and democratically and others undergoing disintegration or in the hands of self-serving cliques. For the groups struggling to modernize and democratize the society, including important elements within the public sector, participation in international discourse on these questions, information on comparable problems and tactics elsewhere and, of course, material support are important. At the same time, it is hard for them to reconcile their per-ceptions of the urgency of societal transformation and redistribution of wealth and power with the self-limited open-ended conception of pluralist democracy summarized above. Such actors have probably had their fill of universalistic ideologies and policy prescriptions from abroad during past eras of state-managed development optimism, the Cold War, and subsequent debt traps and structural adjustment programmes.

A good many other national patterns could be distinguished within the world system of states, from stable welfare states with long traditions of pluralist democracy, now grappling with the suspicion that visions of higher levels of consumption and greater social equality with each generation were mirages, to states controlled through terror in the hands of cynically predatory armed forces. None of these patterns, of course, can be static. Economic and cultural globalization and the division of humanity into a system of interacting states that are formally equal in rights and similar in responsibilities have not made their potential future evolutions more uniform. If anything, the intensity of global interactions along with the precarious implantation of pluralist democracy make the range of possible futures more diverse.

Humanity is entering into an 'information economy' or 'information age' according to various recent expositions. One salient aspect is 'the ever-growing role played by the manipulation of symbols in the organization of production and the enhancement of productivity'.[10] This dimension of globalization introduces unprecedented and continually changing relationships between systems of production, distribution and consumption, on the one hand, and requirements for human labour and educational qualifications for labour, on the other. Even the more optimistic prognoses for the information age point to a future of intense destabilization, rather similar to Marx's summing up of capitalism in the *Communist Manifesto*.[11] It is not clear how any 'development policies' accessible to states or the world system of states can cope with the marginalization of increasing numbers of people and whole countries that are superfluous or unable to qualify themselves to enter it.

Other aspects of the information age are equally unsettling *vis-à-vis* self-limiting pluralist democracy. People throughout the world have access to more varied information (and disinformation) than ever before. The requisites for keeping up with the information revolution become more formidable, both because of the dizzying rapidity of changes in media – from press to radio to television to videotapes to computer networks – and because of the diversity of messages. People from all classes and backgrounds are in a sense excluded from confidence in being able to grasp the implications of the scientific, technological, economic, political, cultural, demographic and environmental transformations of the world today, while they are bombarded by presentations, interpretations and warnings concerning them accompanied by stimuli to consume. While the distribution of sources of information is naturally uneven, some modern media penetrate even remote and 'traditional' rural communities.

For some people, the information age means an unprecedentedly wide range of choices in lifestyles, gender and age group identifications, and an equally wide range of causes that can be embraced so as to achieve a sense of influencing change and warding off menaces. For others, it means an unprecedented range of possible survival strategies, all of them subject to unforeseeable risks. For still others, it offers vicarious satisfactions in the form of exhaustive information on sports events, the private lives of celebrities and so on, to the practical exclusion of more unsettling information. Brazilian and Mexican soap operas have become the most appealing aspect of the information age to millions of people in very different cultural settings. The flood of unsettling information and cultural stimuli also generates xenophobic and fundamentalist reactions that make use of the same techniques for dissemination. Among young people it supports the globalization of continually changing youth cultures or anomic frustration and resort to violence.

In such a world, the supposition that some rational, benevolent but unimaginative entity is waiting to receive Good Advice and then act on it is hardly tenable. Nor is the supposition that a conspiracy of power-holders, responsible for the lamentable state of humanity, is waiting to be exposed and vanquished. One must face the prospect of permanent struggle with challenges changing into different challenges. One must try to keep in balance the recognition that ideas have consequences and the recognition that these consequences emerge in the midst of confusion, perversion, myth-making and human preoccupations only precariously related to the values that inform discourse on development.

## Notes

1. The later diagnoses of Dr Raúl Prebisch, principal architect of the CEPAL position and no friend to revolutionary socialist alternatives, support this picture. See Prebisch, 'A Critique of Peripheral Capitalism' (1976) and 'Socioeconomic Structure and Crisis of the System' (1978). Latin America is now emerging from the economic and political crises of the 1980s in many respects transformed but with its variants of peripheral capitalism seemingly more consolidated but as wasteful and inequitable as ever.

2. The findings of this team research programme under the auspices of UNRISD have been published recently: Stiefel and Wolfe, *A Voice for the Excluded* (1994).

3. The first version was published in Spanish under the title *El desarrollo esquivo: Exploraciones en la política social y la realidad sociopolítica* (Fondo de Cultura Económica, México, 1976, and in Portuguese as *Desenvolvimento: para que e para quem?*, with a foreword by Fernando Henrique Cardoso (Editora Paz e Terra, Rio de Janeiro, 1976). The second version was published jointly by the UN Research Institute for Social Development and the UN Economic Commission for Latin America in 1981.

4. 'What *is* new in the so-called capitalist countries – and this is a vital point

– is that the controlling contentment and resulting belief is now that of the many, not just of the few. It operates under the compelling cover of democracy, albeit a democracy not of all citizens but of those who, in defense of their social and economic advantage, actually go to the polls. The result is government that is accommodated not to reality or common need but to the belief of the contented, who are now the majority of those who vote.' (Galbraith, *The Culture of Contentment*, 1993, p. 10.)

5. Hughes, *Culture of Complaint* (1993).

6. For a recent expression of bafflement at the implications of China's trajectory, see Kristof and Wudunn, *China Wakes* (1994).

7. Gills et al (eds), *Low Intensity Democracy* (1993).

8. Alain Touraine, *Qu'est-ce que la démocratie?* (1994) (my translation).

9. Adam Przeworski, *Democracy and the Market* (1991).

10. Manuel Castells, 'The Informational Economy and the New International Division of Labor' (1993).

11. 'Society, community, family are all conserving institutions. They try to maintain stability and to prevent, or at least to slow, change. But the organization of the post-capitalist society of organizations is a *destabilizer*. Because its function is to put knowlege to work – on tools, processes and products; on knowledge itself – it must be organized for constant change ... It must be organized for systematic abandonment of the established, the customary, the familiar, the comfortable, whether products, services and processes, human and social relationships, skills or organizations themselves.' (Drucker, *Post-capitalist Society*, 1993.)

# CHAPTER 2

# THE QUEST FOR A UNIFIED APPROACH

## Neglected history

This chapter is a contribution to the history of 'social' ideas in the United Nations; a history neglected and therefore repeated up to the present for reasons that will emerge in due course.

In February 1971 a team organized jointly by the UN Research Institute for Social Development (UNRISD), the UN Economic Commission for Latin America (CEPAL) and the Social Development Division of the UN Headquarters Secretariat met in Geneva to plan a quest for a 'unified approach to development analysis and planning' with a perspective of some eighteen months for the exercise. Resolutions approved the previous year by the UN Economic and Social Council and General Assembly specified the kind of social-justice-oriented development to be sought.

It is hardly surprising that the team did not produce a unified approach meeting the specifications of the resolutions during its life-span or that the subsequent efforts of UNRISD staff failed to synthesize such an approach from the materials it left behind. The shortcomings of previous development processes and policies were even more conspicuous at the end of the 1970s than at the beginning, and the range of contradictory attributes demanding 'unification' had widened: the reconciliation of technocratic rationality with popular participation, of continually expanding production and trade with protection of the environment, of continually diversifying human wants with priority to the satisfaction of basic human needs, posed questions that might be somewhat clearer than before but were as far as ever from plausible answers.

The unified approach project was one among many attempts to grapple with this recalcitrant reality. It was left behind by other explorations commanding larger resources and starting from more radical challenges to the conventional wisdom of development. Nevertheless, it helped to incubate ideas and slogans that have continued to evolve and ramify in sometimes unexpected ways in the international organizations and in different regional and national settings up to the 1995 World Summit on Social Development.

### Reporting on the 'world social situation'

The publication by the United Nations in 1952 of the *Preliminary Report on the World Social Situation* is a convenient starting point for a sketch of the prehistory of the unified approach. Naturally, such a sketch ignores many parallel or overlapping initiatives within and without the United Nations family of organizations. The UN resolutions calling for the preparation of this report assumed that the 'world social situation' was a definable reality that could be studied and reported on like the 'world economic situation', already the subject of annual UN reports. However, the resolutions left implicit the content and boundaries of the 'social situation'.

The small Secretariat team charged with preparation of the report could not start from a unifying concept. It confronted scanty and unreliable information for most of the world relating to an unmanageably wide range of questions that could be considered 'social'. It confronted political pitfalls deriving from the Cold War and the ongoing processes of decolonization. It also confronted bureaucratic pitfalls deriving from the compartmentalization of 'social' activities between agencies and units within agencies that the UN system had already achieved.

The team sought a manageably modest interpretation of its terms of reference: the report would focus on 'existing social conditions', dealing only incidentally with 'programmes to improve those conditions'. The 'social conditions' with which it would deal were to be practically synonymous with 'standards of living'; it would assess these as far as practicable through quantitative indicators.

The subject matter was to be broken down into 'social sectors', or 'components' of the standard of living, in practice delimited by the jurisdictional boundaries of the UN bodies dealing with these sectors and generally contributing chapters on them. In order to compensate to some extent for the resulting compartmentalization by sectors and worldwide generalizations by sectors, in which the social unavoidably became divorced from reference to specific societies, the report contained chapters on three of the world regions then beginning to be labelled 'underdeveloped': Latin America, the Middle East and South and Southeast Asia.

The UN organs that had requested the report received it favourably. It dispelled previous doubts about whether such a task could be carried to a coherent conclusion, it achieved an external reception unusual among UN publications, and it originated a series in which successive attempts to go beyond the self-imposed limitations of the *Preliminary Report* can be traced.

These efforts had a good deal to do with the way in which the 'unified approach' was eventually conceived and pursued. They were part of a conflictive evolution of ideas and organizational patterns in the UN Secretariat that reflected wider controversies under way in other international agencies, universities, research institutes and national governments. Personalities, struggles for survival and growth among bureaucratic entities, and stereotypes harboured by each of the parties concerning the others, to be sure, blurred or distorted the reflection. In very simplified terms, the following main positions can be distinguished.

On the one side were the economists who had dominated the authorized version of development thinking in the United Nations for many years, econometrically trained and and wedded to quantifiable laws and models. Some of these economists saw no reason to take the 'social' into account on any terms. Others saw allocations to consumption and to certain social services as important means for raising the productivity of the labour force. Still others were convinced that human welfare and equity, the values justifying the development effort, required some immediate attention to redistributive measures. However, they could come to terms with the social only through quantification compatible with their own techniques of drawing up national accounts, constructing models, analysing costs and benefits, calculating production functions and so on. If the advocates of social policies wanted a hearing they had to learn comparable techniques and provide quantitative data for them. Sound development policies, made possible by quantification of all the relevant factors, would eventually benefit everyone; enlightened self-interest would make governments and other societal actors adhere to them.

On the other side were the proponents of sectoral social activities, dominated by the experience of the United States, then at the height of self-confidence as dispenser of advice and aid to poor or war-devastated countries and itself advancing through haphazardly coordinated initiatives towards the construction of a welfare state. The activities in question were directed to the relief of poverty, the universalization of the basic social services found in the industrialized countries, the stimulation of community organization for social ends, and the propagation of the norms and techniques of the 'helping professions', in particular social work. These proponents took for granted that the forms of social action with which they identified were basic human rights, and that the norms and techniques, with secondary adaptations, would be suitable to peoples everywhere. If local resources were insufficient, external aid and training could fill the gap. They were as oblivious as the economists to questions of social structural change and power relationships, but were particularly oblivious to one question central to the latter, that of criteria for allocation of scarce resources.

The team responsible for the *Report*[s] *on the World Social Situation* found itself in the middle, seeking to understand the preoccupations of the economic quantifiers and the social sectoral specialists and to build bridges between them; increasingly sceptical concerning the pretensions of both, but inhibited in criticism by lack of an alternative frame of reference and by the Secretariat's distaste for internal polemics.

In their work, the term 'social development' gradually pushed aside 'social situation' with its static connotations but did not receive a more precise definition. 'Social development' became current as a counterpart to 'economic development'. Its users at this time identified it mainly with measurable improvement in standards or levels of living (the former term referring to norms, the latter to realities) and with government activities directed to this end. They issued two international surveys 1955 and 1959 concentrating on government plans and policies in. Afterwards, every *Report on the World Social Situation* was mandated to include 'programmes to improve conditions'.

The reports of the 1950s maintained a tone of qualified optimism. The social situation was continually improving, according to the statistical indicators, although the improvement was unevenly distributed and 'much remains to be done'. Governments were continually introducing new and improved social programmes. Practically all governments, by different paths, were advancing towards similar social goals, differentially hampered by misinformation, scanty resources and the shortcomings of the human agents of their purposes. The interests of 'developed' and 'underdeveloped' countries in a world future of rising levels of living were basically harmonious; aid by the former to the latter was an important reality, however poorly planned and insufficient. The social policies of all countries offered 'lessons' deserving study by their neighbours, although the flow of applicable lessons, and of experts to teach those lessons, might be mainly from the developed to the underdeveloped. The picture was of a predominantly rational and benevolent although highly imperfect world order.

By the early 1960s the reading of the statistical evidence and the evaluation of policies were changing significantly, although the conception of social development remained the same. The 1965 *Report on the World Social Situation* struck a note that was to be repeated with variations up to the present:

A picture of painfully slow progress in the developing countries emerges at the mid-point of the Development Decade. While some sectors of development (especially education) have continued to fare better than others, and some countries (and parts of countries) have advanced faster than others, it seems clear that, for the most part, the recent effort at development has fallen far short of hopes and expectations. Possibly some of these expectations were unduly optimistic; a more pertinent question is whether the development efforts, both national and international, have been sufficient – and in the right direction.

Progress has been limited both by external constraints and by internal political and social realities. Unfavourable trends in trade and problems of external financing have sharply limited the material resources for development in many of the poorer countries, while the implementation of development goals has been hampered in a number of these countries by political instability and dissensions, with frequent overthrow of governments amid charges of corruption; sometimes also by lack of the necessary political will for development, and frequently by persistence of administrative and social structures that fail to provide an organizational basis for change and development or to enlist popular motivation and participation. (p. vii)

In fact, the proponents of social development had begun to envisage development as a complex process of societal change and modernization, in which the 'economic' and the 'social' were separable only artificially and for purposes of analysis. However, their distrust of global theories and models (or their institutional inhibition against choosing any one theory of societal change), together with the kinds of information accessible to them and the intellectual habits generated by the sectoral organization of the reports and the negotiation of their contents with the bureaucratic guardians of the sectors, continually crowded them back into a narrower vision of social development: a vision made up of progress in separate components of levels of living, measurable through inescapably heterogeneous statistical indicators and promotable through equally heterogeneous social and economic programmes.

The social development proponents became sufficiently sensitive to the shakiness of the database of the elaborate statistical manipulations of the economists not to be tempted to follow suit with equally shaky social statistics. They considered but rejected as impracticable the objective of unifying the concept of level of living and measuring social development through a composite statistical indicator comparable to the national income or gross domestic product.[1] They made some use of the findings of sociological and anthropological field research but found in the theories then current in these disciplines no help towards an interpretation of social development matching the imposing structures built around economic development.

### Balanced economic and social development

Meanwhile, the idea of objective guidelines for allocations of public resources and better mutual support between economic and social programmes attracted the attention of national representatives in the UN deliberative bodies. During the 1950s various UN resolutions callled for 'balanced economic and social development' and asked the Secretariat for reports pointing the way to such development. The current debate between economists over 'balanced' versus 'unbalanced' growth strategies contributed to the popularity of the term, although the conceptions of what was to be 'balanced' had little in common. The resolutions conveyed a vision of social and economic 'fields' as distinct realities deserving equal shares of fertilizer. Some of the resolutions embroidered the imagery of 'fields' by urging that action in the 'two fields' should 'go hand in hand'. The Secretariat team responsible for the *Report*[s] *on the World Social*

*Situation*, after some years of speaking of 'balance' as a desideratum, began to tackle the question systematically around 1957, and presented its conclusions in the 1961 report, which began by stating:

> From a governmental point of view the question of balanced social and economic development is to an important extent a question of the pattern of public expenditure. There is no overall conception or theory of balanced development applicable to the expenditure policy of the economically under-developed countries at the present time; there are only fragments of a theory and 'common sense'.

The treatment of the question in the 1961 report maintained the cautiously empirical tone of the above quotation, summarizing a wide range of possible interactions between the 'social' and the 'economic' and of theories concerning such interactions. The report concluded that 'while it is theoretically not possible to state what levels of development in the various social components *should* go with given levels of economic development, it is quite possible to state what social levels *do* go with given economic levels', and that 'studies of actual patterns of development can assist the practical process of decision-making ... by providing evidence of social levels that can demonstrably be achieved at given levels of economic development [and] by providing evidence of imbalances'.

Between 1957 and 1964, thirteen 'country case studies' were completed and issued as background documents for the 'balanced development' project. Some of these studies were confident of the prospects for the national variant of planning, others exposed consistent failures on the part of political leaders and planners to foresee the resources that could be mobilized to achieve their purposes or the wider consequences of their efforts. The studies did not reveal any readily transferable techniques for balancing, and confirmed that juxtaposition of social and economic programmes in a development plan did not ensure either their integration or their implementation.

A good many of the studies confirmed implicitly that the size of allocations depended on some combination of bureaucratic inertia, the relative strength of organized pressures, the relative persuasiveness of advocates, or the hunches of political leaders, rather than on technical criteria. Moreover, in several of the countries political regimes and plans changed radically even before the Secretariat editors had time to issue the study.

### Norms and declarations

Within the United Nations during the 1960s at least two distinct approaches proceeded, if not hand in hand, in juxtaposition with the attempts to bring the multifarious activities relating to human welfare under a roof of 'social development', measure their progress, and balance them with economic activities. The more influential was the elaboration of norms for the economic development of the Third World, shaped by the kind of economic thinking described above, and symbolized by the first Development Decade. Interest centred on goals for investment, financial and technological flows from 'developed' to 'developing' countries, terms of trade and, as the expected result, rates of increase in the gross national product.

The second and more visionary approach was that of formulation of normative declarations on social and economic rights which, undeterred by the chasm between governmental votes for such rights and governmental capacity or will to honour them, culminated in the Declaration on Social Progress and Development approved by the UN General Assembly in 1969.

The approaches of development economists and proponents of sectoral social action evolved during the 1960s, although it is doubtful whether they came to understand each other much better. The economists became more inclined to recognize 'social obstacles' to economic development, at least as excuses for frustrated economic development plans and lagging dynamism, and to challenge sociologists for advice on how to insert missing ingredients and remove obstacles.[2] They became more interested in the contributions of education and health services to the upgrading of 'human resources' and tried to devise methods of quantifying such contributions which, it was hoped, would permit their incorporation into models and plans. Moreover, the dominant econometricians had to take into account more fundamental criticisms of the conventional wisdom from within the economic camp, in particular from Gunnar Myrdal in *Asian Drama* (1968).

### *Experts on social policy and planning.*

One manifestation, deriving from the pursuit of balanced development and leading directly to the unified approach, was the convening of a meeting of experts on social policy and planning in Stockholm in September 1969. This meeting was an attempt by the proponents of a broad but pragmatic conception of social development to strengthen their position by a common front with critical economists. More than half of the ten experts, selected by the usual criteria of geographical and political distribution, were economists who had already, in various ways, tried to incorporate non-economic factors into their thinking.

The central propositions of their report constitute an interesting demonstration of the ways in which the problem of rethinking development was generally conceived at the time, and shaped the terms of reference of the quest for a unified approach. 'The purpose of the meeting was to clarify further the role of social factors in development with a view to ensuring their adequate inclusion in development plans and programmes.' This proposition and the proposition that 'the economic approach to development analysis and planning had to be integrated with a social approach that was different in nature and would be more relevant to the problems of developing countries in the coming decade' were juxtaposed with less simplistic formulas:

> it is most necessary to view the development process as a complex whole, comprising economic elements *sensu stricto*, but also other social, as well as political and administrative elements. Any design for a development strategy, national or international, must cover all the above-mentioned fields if it is to be meaningful, internally consistent and capable of effective implementation.

Govermental and United Nations compartmentalization should give way to a 'more unified treatment', in which 'the idea of a single social system in which development occurs' should be 'taken seriously as its starting point'.

Misleading dividing lines between economic and social phenomena, and between economic and social development, were 'due in part to the rather narrow approach to the development process characteristic of past thinking in economics, which relied heavily on simplistic econometric models with highly aggregated variables', and in part to governmental and UN compartmentalization. An 'over-emphasis on economic growth rates of production has been based on the apparent ease of quantification in the concept of the national income or gross national product of developing countries': 'The dominance of economists among the social scientists, and the earlier development and easier quantification of their concepts, has meant that certain non-market aspects – those inappropriately labelled 'social' – have been neglected in approaches to development.'

The experts recommended that those aspects should be dealt with as 'neglected areas' rather than as 'social factors', but did not follow this recommendation in the remainder of their report.

The report endorsed one version of the 'dualist' label around which a great deal of ideological polemics and semantic confusion had focused during the 1960s:

> a meaningful approach to development planning must take account of the dualist structure of many developing societies – dualist in terms of the difference between modern and traditional sectors, differences within those sectors and differences between those participating in development and those left behind or on the margin ... The fact that development either leaves behind, or in some ways even creates, large areas of poverty, stagnation, marginality and actual exclusion from social and economic progress is too obvious and too urgent to be overlooked.

The report came down to earth by singling out one broad problem area as central to an acceptable development strategy: 'The major problem for the Second Development Decade is likely to be unemployment and underemployment. ... In the absence of vigorously enforced employment policies, the grim prospect of the Second Development Decade is one of rising unemployment, accompanied by increasing concentration of the worst aspects of poverty in the cities.'

The report juxtaposed the technocratic vision of development engineered from the top and the participationist vision of development emerging from popular initiative, but showed more affinity with the former: 'policies could and should be devised so as to activate wider social strata to increase their participation in the development process.' A major prerequisite for development is 'peaceful radical social change, as rapidly as possible': 'Peaceful domestic movements committed to rapid change should be permitted to flourish and, whenever possible, should be supported if they would help to promote a sense of participation and social engagement.' Finally, 'to achieve effective development planning, all planners should think in terms of all goals'.

The above quotations suggest certain papered-over differences between experts as to the nature of the 'social', but they also indicate a kind of compromise consensus on certain key suppositions that had already come under question during the 1960s. In miniature, they point to a number of conceptual problems that were to plague the subsequent quest for a unified approach.

First, the report assumes that a common process identifiable as 'development' is under way in the so-called 'developing' countries. This process is, almost by definition, good and necessary, although its present shortcomings, from the standpoint of human welfare, may be more easily demonstrable than its goodness. These shortcomings can be attributed in large part to deficiencies in government policies and these in turn to the dominance of economic planners with over-narrow conceptions and inappropriate tools. While the report voices many of the criticisms of economic growth and dependent modernization that were to become more insistent during the 1970s, it treats these as remediable defects.

Second, the report places unlimited confidence in the potential capacity of planners to take everything into account in an integrated fashion and reveal to policy-makers the one best way to do whatever they want to do. There is no trace of the various old and new disciplinary and theoretical positions that were questioning human capacity to plan comprehensively so as to reach predetermined ends or of the neo-liberal insistence, soon to become dominant in international development discourse, on the market as the sole legitimate arbiter of allocation of resources.

Third, the report does not entertain the possibility that the international organizations and governments to which it addresses itself, deriving from the power structures responsible for iniquities to which it points, might be neither willing nor able to undertake radical changes; that, indeed, they might look on their own requests for reports recommending such changes as a harmless ritual testifying to their good intentions. The report refers to the inadequacies of governments only in terms of Gunnar Myrdal's concept of the 'soft state' with 'insufficient power or will to carry out a number of desirable policies', and implicitly supposes that a 'hard state' could have such power and will.

### Mandate for a 'unified approach'

The UN Economic and Social Council and General Assembly approved the report of the experts in 1970 and decanted it into instructions to the Secretariat for further work. Their resolutions affirmed 'the need for a unified approach to development analysis and planning which would fully integrate the economic and social components in the formulation of policies and programmes at the national and international levels'. They laid down specifications for the kind of unified approach wanted. It must 'include components' designed:

a) To leave no section of the population outside the scope of change and development.
b) To effect structural change which favours national development and to activate all sectors of the population to participate in the development process.
c) To aim at social equity, including the achievement of an equitable distribution of income and wealth in the nation.
d) To give high priority to the development of the human potentials, including vocational technical training and the provision of employment opportunities and meeting the needs of children.

The above components were to be 'borne in mind in development analysis and planning processes, as well as in their implications, according to the particular developmental needs of each country'. The Secretary-General was to submit a report on the unified approach at the 'earliest possible date'. The General Assembly resolution, more specifically, requested him to 'evolve methods and techniques for the application of a unified approach to development, to be put at the disposal of Governments at their request'.

During the same year, the General Assembly approved an International Development Strategy for the Second Development Decade, the 1970s. The strategy was prepared mainly by the UN Committee for Development Planning, a permanent advisory body, set up in 1966, composed of eminent economists whose preliminary work for the strategy had been criticized in the report of the social policy experts as insufficiently human-welfare-oriented.

The report of the latter experts was apparently not brought to the attention of the Committee for Development Planning, for whatever reason. Thus, the 'unified approach' resolution and the International Development Strategy reached and passed through the General Assembly by separate channels. The strategy, like its predecessor, devoted most of its content to targets for economic growth, trade and financial transfers. However, the spirit of the times ensured that it would find room not only for a series of conventional and vague social sectoral recommendations ('developing countries will make vigorous efforts to improve ... will adopt suitable national policies ... will take steps to provide ...') but also an affirmation of the need for a unified approach somewhat stronger than that of the resolutions deriving from the experts' report:

> qualitative and structural changes in the society must go hand in hand with rapid economic growth, and existing disparities – regional, sectoral and social – should be substantially reduced. These objectives are both determining factors and end-results of development; they should therefore be viewed as integrated parts of the same dynamic process, and would require a unified approach.

The 'unified approach' had thus followed 'balanced development' into the international repertoire of aspirations that might mean many things to different persons.

## Methodological and institutional constraints

### United Nations research conventions

The preceding pages have suggested certain methodological and institutional constraints imposed on efforts by UN bodies to deal with the 'social' or with 'development'. The problem to be studied was usually defined through a resolution deriving partly from past reports of the Secretariat, and partly from the interests and points of view of the representatives of governments in the policy-making bodies. In practice governments rarely tried to impose a coherent ideological formulation through their representatives; they were generally content to seek recognition of their own achievements, counter criticisms and occasionally score off adversaries.

Definition of the problem usually preceded a request to the Secretary-General, as ultimately responsible for the work of the social units of the Secretariat, to produce a report containing 'practical' recommendations within a fixed period. These practical recommendations were to be addressed to governments, on the supposition that they would be willing and able to act on prescriptions couched in very general and qualified terms.

The conventions permitted considerable latitude in criticism of 'some governments', 'many governments' and so on, as inefficient, corrupt, shortsighted or compartmentalized, as long as these traits were treated as shortcomings remediable through good advice, and countries were not identified. Hypotheses that the problems addressed were not of a nature to be solved by the planning and actions of governments of whatever kind, or that typical existing governments would be unable to act on them because of the character and objectives of those governments, were ruled out a priori.

Research techniques, beyond the compilation and synthesis of available published information, followed a limited range of paths, usually specified in the governing resolution:

(a) A questionnaire might be circulated to governments asking for their views on the problem and their methods of dealing with it. The use of questionnaires distanced the Secretariat from responsibility for producing solutions to the more controversial questions, but had the disadvantage of eliciting incorrigibly heterogeneous materials (generally from a small minority of member governments) that had somehow to be 'taken into account' in reports.

(b) 'Country case studies' might be prepared through national institutions, individual consultants or members of the Secretariat. This technique offered a greater likelihood of obtaining fresh information and ideas in a relatively coherent form. However, the conventions demanded that the countries to be studied be selected for a maximum of geographical and political diversity, and selection depended on too many extraneous factors to permit clear definitions of what the 'cases' were supposed to demonstrate. Typically, the reports made only slight use of the country case studies because these were completed after the deadline, because changes in the circumstances of the country left them quickly out of date, or because they presented an unassimilable mass of detail.

(c) The governing resolution usually envisaged consultations with and contributions from appropriate specialized agencies and other units of the UN family having social responsibilities (such as ILO, FAO, UNESCO, UNICEF). The consultations might or might not be perfunctory, but overlapping jurisdictions and sensitivity to criticism of certain dogmas and programmes introduced additional inhibitions into the preparation of broad, ideally 'unified' reports.

(d) At some stage in the response to requests for reports and recommendations, a 'meeting of experts' was practically obligatory. The conventions demanded that the Secretariat select the experts, like the countries for case studies, for maximum diversity, within limits imposed by the Secretariat's contacts and information concerning their qualifications and availability. The role of 'expert', supposed to evaluate and improve ideas presented by the Secretariat, was ambiguous. If the selected experts exercised it vigorously, they exposed their own differences of background and viewpoint and complicated the Secretariat's task of producing a coherent 'practical' report. The more deeply an expert was committed to a comprehensive theory or strategy of his own, the less fitted he would be to enter into an unavoidably eclectic exercise.

In their combination, the instructions and techniques here outlined seemed to rule out the selection or construction of a single theory of social change on which to base an integrated strategy for social development. The instructions and techniques ensured that heterogeneous, incomplete and erratically selected information would have to be taken into account; that representatives of different ideologies and different terminologies would have to reach a lowest common denominator; and that their report would have to incorporate all proposals not radically unacceptable to other participants or self-evidently incompatible.

### The 'unified approach' research team

It was decided at UN Headquarters to centre the quest for a unified approach to development analysis and planning, once a grant from the Netherlands (later supplemented by grants from Canada and Sweden) made it possible to undertake such a study outside the routine of periodic *Reports on the World Social Situation* in the UN Research Institute for Social Development (UNRISD), located in Geneva. UNRISD was less bound by constraints and conventions than the Secretariat itself, but had a work programme deriving historically from the concepts of level of living, social development and balanced development that had evolved in the Secretariat.

The core of the research team that first met in February 1971 and engaged in discussions of preliminary drafts and conceptual papers during the greater part of that year was made up of the Director of UNRISD, who had taken a leading part in the evolution of UN social thinking since the *Preliminary Report on the World Social Situation*; the Chief of the Social Development Division of the UN Economic Commission for Latin America, where more politically oriented and conflict-oriented lines of thinking had been pursued for some time; an economist with experience in the Plan Organization of France and in the study of development indicators; a specialist in the study of decision-making processes; and an economist who had written extensively on development and served as policy and planning consultant in different parts of the world.

Other persons joined the team during the course of the year, contributed conceptual papers, or entered into discussions with the team: directors of national planning agencies, consultants on development planning, members of the UN Committee for Development Planning, and specialists in regional planning, in human geography, in econometric techniques and so on, who were expected to cover questions outside the competence of the team but relevant to a 'unified approach'.

Even the core members of the team had other responsibilities in the Secretariat, in other UNRISD research projects, in academic institutions, and as national development planning consultants. It was evident from the beginning that a team of this kind, with less than two years at its disposal, would not be able to reach a theoretical consensus or produce a comprehensive set of prescriptions for unified development. The team entertained the more modest hope of reaching agreement on certain central concepts, of clarifying theoretical or disciplinary sources of divergence on others, of stimulating new ways of thinking about development, and of producing two kinds of report.

The first report was intended to be a synthesis of central issues and unifying concepts, along with a few cautiously 'practical' guidelines; the second was to cover in some detail all those aspects the team considered relevant and important, in chapters to be written by individual team members and consultants, reflecting their different points of view, but given a reasonable coherence through discussions with the team as a whole.

In practice, budgetary limitations and the team members' other commitments made it impossible for them to continue their dialogue beyond 1971, and the texts that emerged remained too diverse in their 'approaches' as well as in their styles to add up to a publishable comprehensive report. In the later stages, a series of individuals within UNRISD struggled to impose order on a mounting accumulation of disparate materials.

### Studies of national experience

The team devoted a good deal of attention during 1971 to plans and negotiations for a series of studies of national experience, and eight such studies were eventually completed by national institutions or consultants, although only one of them by the intended deadline of May 1972. The specifications for these studies gave the executors considerable flexibility in pursuing aspects they considered nationally important, but sought a measure of uniformity by asking them to discuss the relevance to their national situations of certain preliminary hypotheses on emerging crises in development planning. Although the studies were small in number, the differences in their content and in the viewpoints of their executors deserve attention as indicative of differences in the real world of national societies to which the quest for a unified approach addressed itself.

Two of the studies dealt with Asian countries (Philippines and Sri Lanka) having extensive and bureaucratized social programmes, formal planning mechanisms and competitive party politics, with social service, consumption subsidy, job creation and public works accomplishments and promises critical to party success in elections. These studies were carried out collectively by institutions: a university school of public administration and a private socio-economic research institute staffed by persons having previous experience in the national planning system.

These Asian studies documented in detail the functionng of programmes and the deficiencies of coordination and overall policy guidance. Under conditions of political party competition for limited objectives, bureaucratic compartmentalization of social and economic activities, and diffuse dissatisfaction at the malfunctioning of the systems, but no immediate prospect of major changes in the distribution of power and the expectations of different interest groups in the societies, these studies could make various practical suggestions for improvements in policy formation and execution, but offered no hope of a radically different 'unified approach'.

Both texts indicated that the contradictions in the functioning of the societies were likely to become more pronounced in the future but that the deterioration would probably not overcome their basic stability for a long time. Meanwhile, planners had to try to understand political realities, adapt their proposals to such realities and help to educate political leaders and public opinion.

One study dealt with another Asian country, Iran, that was undergoing rapid modernization under autocratic leadership, with resources at its command vastly larger than those of most 'developing' countries, with formal planning machinery, but without open channels for the competition of interest groups and political movements. This study was carried out by a political scientist in contact with the plan organization. Its dominant note was intense frustration of several kinds: first, at the high social costs of the modernization process; second, at the limited and erratic use made by the 'patrimonial ruler' of the advice of technocrats and planners; third, at the precariousness of social stability resting on minorities only 'cynically committed' to the system and on a majority excluded and resentful. Here a certain unification of policy was present at the top, and bureaucratic, political and financial constraints were much less formidable than in the first two countries, but the human welfare objectives of the unified approach had a low priority, socially oriented planning could not count on a hearing, and transmission belts between the autocratic leadership and the society functioned poorly or not at all.

Two studies, carried out by individual economists, dealt with newly independent African countries, Kenya and Togo. Here formal planning machinery inherited from the colonial past was in the process of adaptation to new policy objectives; political competition was open but not intense. The tone of the studies was one of cautious down-to-earth optimism: policy formation had been erratic and planning had been ineffective owing to poor information, faulty administrative machinery and scanty resources. Gradual improvement in planning, adjusted to the capacities of the state, offered a good deal of hope as a means of making policy more coherent and more applicable. A radically different and more ambitious unified approach, however, was hardly advisable and would probably be impracticable for its demands on information and scarce qualified human resources. Another study, also carried out by an economist, of Trinidad and Tobago in the Caribbean sub-region, likewise focused on the modest potential of planning as a force for rationalization in a very small country emerging from colonial status with an excess of bureaucracy, intense factionalism and no clear political vision of the national future.

Two studies, carried out by individual political scientists, dealt with Latin American countries, Chile and Peru, that were then experiencing semi-revolutionary changes (since frustrated) within settings of considerable uncertainty concerning the real distribution of power and the capacity of the political regimes to transform the system of production and the distribution of wealth, incomes and consumption while simultaneously presiding over the emergence of new forms of political participation of the 'marginalized' masses.

These studies described the national planning mechanisms and the current social and economic programmes, but their attention lay elsewhere. Unlike the other studies described above, they could not treat the political and economic systems and the distribution of power as constant constraints on policy, for better or worse. In Chile and Peru, initiatives were under way (under the quite different auspices of a coalition mainly of Marxist-Socialist political parties and of a nationalist military government) to transform the systems and structures, against the resistance of other combinations of forces. Under these conditions, the problems of planners seeking to refine their methodologies and exert more influence over political leaders and sectoral bureaucracies receded into the background, although both regimes were favourably disposed towards planning.

The questions in the foreground concerned the character, degree of coherence and relative strength of the forces supporting and opposing structural changes in the control of land, industry and mineral resources; their tactics and ability to mobilize major sectors of the population; regime capacity to carry out the changes with a reasonable degree of efficiency under unavoidably conflictive circumstances; the possibilities for compromises or shifts in political alliances; the compatibility of changes with open political processes and with regime observance of laws weighted against such changes; the alternatives for future political regimes and forms of popular participation if the changes accomplished their immediate purposes; the finding of ways to enlist international support and neutralize the opposition of transnational enterprises and the US government.

In this series of studies the preoccupations of the executing institutions and individuals seem to have coincided with real differences in the national situations confronted. If the unified approach team had not dispersed by the time they were completed, their comparative examination could have provided a valuable corrective to the normative, universalistic and techno-cratic bias given to the quest by its terms of reference. They suggested that possibilities for human-welfare-oriented rationalization of policy were real but limited. For all their differences, none of the studies could envisage removal in the short term of the stumbling-blocks to a unified approach. More likely, the problems would evolve through the interaction of political, cultural and economic factors into other problems, not necessarily less formidable. Would-be agents of human-welfare-oriented development had to seek opportunities within these processes, rather than devise ideally comprehensive prescriptions.

### Differing approaches to a unified approach

Two documents set forth the elements of consensus reached in the unified approach quest while it retained a measure of interdisciplinary teamwork: *Report on a unified approach to development analysis and planning: Preliminary report of the Secretary-General, 25 October 1972* – his report was prepared by one member of the team and revised after comments from other team members; *Report of the Secretary-General on the Expert Group Meeting on a unified approach to development analysis and planning*, held at Stockholm in November 1971. Both documents were presented to a session of the UN Commission for Social Development in February 1973.[3]

A unified approach, according to the *Preliminary Report,*

> needs to make use of two complementary ways of looking at development: (i) development as a perceived advance toward specified ends based on societal values; (ii) development as the system of interrelated societal changes that underlies and conditions the feasibility of the advance.
>
> The first sense assumes human capability of shaping the future for human ends. It also assumes that the existing society has the right and the ability through general consensus, or through agents claiming to represent the best interests of the society, to make choices and enforce sacrifices in the name of development.
>
> ... The second sense assumes that development is an intelligible phenomenon susceptible to diagnosis and to objective propositions concerning the inter-relations of factors and the probable wider consequences of change in or action on key components of the 'system'.
>
> From the standpoint adopted here development is not a single uniform process or dimension of change and it cannot be assumed that 'development' means the transformation of the countries now labelled 'developing' into replicas of countries now labelled 'developed'. All national societies will be developing or trying to during the foreseeable future, and at the same time will be trying to cope with the contradictions and disbenefits that arise from their development processes. There is no reason to expect their efforts to lead to uniform futures, or to final resolution of their struggles in a blessed state of 'being developed'.

The *Preliminary Report* distinguished between the 'real style of development' ('what is actually happening in a given national society') and the 'preferred style of development' ('what the national political leadership, the planning agency, or some other significant political actor wants to happen'). It rejected the possibility of a 'detailed universal set of specifications' for development or particularized definition, but proposed a 'minimum criterion' for assessment of styles of development: 'the extent to which a style of development enables a society to function over the long term for the wellbeing of all its members'. Assessed by this criterion, certain styles might be viable but not acceptable, and others acceptable but not viable.

The criterion implies choices, explicit or implicit, with regard to:

(i) The extent and nature of national *autonomy*. (ii) The extent and nature of popular *participation*. (iii) The emphasis given to *production* in general, to specific lines and techniques of production, incentives and forms of control over the means of production. (iv) The *distribution* of the fruits of development and mechanisms for *redistribution*. (v) The encouragement or discouragement of specific forms of individual or collective *consumption* of goods or services. (vi) The extent and nature of *protection of the human environment*. (vii) The extent and nature of *protection of human relationships* contributing to solidarity, security, self-realization and freedom. These choices are complexly interdependent. If they are mutually contradictory beyond a certain point, the style will not be viable. If the choices are made in isolation from one another the probability is that they will be mutually contradictory to a dangerous degree.

The differing approaches that we shall now discuss emerged not only during the period of team activity but also later. Although positions changed to some extent in the course of discussion, and new insights emerged, one might conclude that each member of the team ended with his own 'unified approach', whose premises derived from his own ideology, discipline and previous experience.

Meanwhile, the international scene continually threw up additional major problems, approaches and slogans. The 1970s saw, instead of progress towards consensus on a 'unified approach', a continual diversification of interpretations of development, more ambitious international declarations aspiring to reconcile them, and also a mounting criticism of 'development', from several quite different viewpoints, as an outworn and misleading myth.

The following pages do not try to reproduce the positions of participants in the quest for a unified approach. Rather, the intention is to use these positions as a springboard towards a discussion of the different approaches that have continually confronted one another and entered into compromises in the international debate. All of those represented in the quest were, in one way or another, interventionist. Ironically, the only influential approach to development not represented was the one destined to become dominant during the 1980s: neoliberalism or reliance on market forces.

### Development economics re-examined and broadened

This approach assumed the centrality and at the same time the insufficiency of economic development theories and tools for diagnosis and planning applied to market or mixed economies. Economics offered the closest appproximation to a coherent view of development, but it had not yet 'taken into account' all the relevant factors. The approach also assumed the centrality of economists as advisers to governments. The unified approach must therefore be presented to economists in terms they could accept, incorporate into their methodologies and communicate to political leaders having their own preoccupations and limitations of vision.

This approach had several main components:

(a) An interest in sociological or psychological diagnoses of 'obstacles to development'. The supposition was that 'traditional' values, attitudes towards work and saving, class or caste barriers to mobility, child-rearing practices, extended family ties and so on stood in the way of a development process requiring accelerated capital accumulation and investment, continual technological innovation, formation of a disciplined and qualified labour force, and predictable responsiveness of the population to market incentives. This development process could progress faster and more smoothly once the social experts diagnosed the obstacles and prescribed how to remove them.

(b) An interest in educational, health, social security and other social sectoral programmes for their claims on public funds that might be otherwise allocated and for their contribution to economic growth through the improvement of 'human resources'. Quantification of this impact and calculation of the ideal size of allocations to social programmes were considered key desiderata in a unified approach, although difficult and perhaps impossible to achieve.

(c) A preoccupation with the measurable aspects of social justice and improved levels of living as the legitimate ends of development. The economists in question had abandoned the expectation current among many of their colleagues that these ends would eventually and more or less automatically derive from the maximization of investment and rates of increase in the national product. Employment policies, income redistribution policies and agrarian reform policies were all affirmed as essential components of a unified approach.

(d) A preoccupation with the improvement of quantitative methods for reconciling multiple objectives and guiding the selection of development projects. This was congenial not only to economists but also to most social sectoral specialists, in spite of their uneasiness at submitting to the predominance of economic justifications for social programmes. It promised them a means of ordering coherently what they were doing and also of obtaining a more sympathetic hearing in circles believed to have a decisive influence over the allocation of resources.

## Development planning rehabilitated and perfected

This approach derived from the preoccupations of planning practitioners in various 'developed' countries with market or mixed economies (France, in particular) and in a much larger number of developing countries. During the 1950s and early 1960s the number of countries possessing planning agencies and preparing fixed-term plans had increased dramatically. Even governments having no interest in such planning for themselves began to favour it for the 'developing' countries, if only as a means towards more effective use of their 'aid' to such countries: the support by the United States of ten-year economic and social development plans as a condition for aid under the Alliance for Progress is the most conspicuous example. The colonial powers had also left a heritage of 'development plans' and some rudimentary planning machinery in many of the newly independent countries. Courses training planners to fill the posts opened in the new planning agencies proliferated, and a body of professional planners with a vested interest in the success of planning came into being.

While the preoccupations of the planners coincided to a large extent with those of the development economists described above, they were more concerned with the legitimacy of their own function, their ties with politics, the nature and effectiveness of the transmission belts between planning and application. By 1970, experience had introduced a large measure of frustration and insecurity to mingle with the earlier claims for planning. The relevance of formal fixed-term development plans was beginning to seem doubtful. The planners could not help seeing that their prescriptions were being followed only sporadically, and that the results of such partial planning deviated widely and unpredictably from their objectives and their projections. Planners and economic theorists had less influence on the allocation of public resources than did alliances of industrial and construction enterprises, engineers and politicians, all of whom, for differing reasons, were wedded to large capital-intensive, highly visible, technologically advanced projects, however disruptive these might be to the environment and the livelihood of the people they were supposed to benefit.

Moreover, in the context of radical challenges to power structures at the end of the 1960s, a good many planners could no longer accept the role of neutral technicians at the service of the state behind which they had sheltered themselves when planning first began to be institutionalized.

Should they not serve the people rather than the state? But if so, how, since the state was their employer?

One reaction was to propose broader and more ambitious roles for planning. This reaction seemed to envisage a future social order in which planning would become an activity and source of guidance as pervasive as religion in some other social orders, with professional planners functioning as teachers and prophets, but with the laity as well continually learning and applying more comprehensive planning techniques and resolving their unavoidable conflicts of interests and values by integrating their plans.

The next two approaches to be discussed implicitly negate this vision of planning societies, although the vision itself might incorporate them as legitimate facets of the all-encompassing activity of planning.

### Pragmatic social and economic ameliorism

This approach gave priority to the identification of policies and measures that have worked, in the sense of demonstrably enhancing human welfare; to the consideration of how they might be made to work better; and to pragmatic criteria for their combination into mutually supportive packages.[4] The same approach dominated UN technical assistance in social questions, in which 'experts' set forth to apply methods learned in their home countries, on the supposition that they would be able to adapt such methods to the political and social setting of the country to be advised. (In practice, as often as not, the experts really set forth to advocate methods that they had never been able to apply in their home countries.)

The approach of pragmatic social and economic ameliorism had met with harsh and obvious criticisms over the years, but its proponents had plausible arguments on their side. After all, throughout the world human-welfare-oriented and human-resource-oriented programmes of many kinds were continuing to appear and expand. By now they accounted for sizeable shares of public expenditures and of the national product in most countries, irrespective of their structure and level of production, their political system or their distribution of power. Presumably some of them worked better than others. Comparative study, then, could throw light on the reasons and on ways of raising the general level of effectiveness.

The approach of pragmatic ameliorism was one of the two that persisted in later demands made by UN policy-making bodies for pursuit of a unified approach.

### Capacitation of national societies

This approach emphasized the building up of institutions for diagnosis and problem-solving, and of educational programmes enabling societies to function better through the informed and cooperative action of their members. It did not figure in the initial research scheme of the quest but emerged in the later stages as an alternative to comprehensive planning and as a complement to pragmatic social ameliorism. It was first given a name in a 1974 report prepared by UNRISD, which will be discussed later.

According to this report:

> development planning first arose in connection with material production ... In the last few decades, planning has spread to more and more fields of development activity, including social fields, but in this process, objectives have become less amenable to direct measurement, causal relations have become more complex and obscure, and control of the future has taken on a different complexion. [Moreover,] conventional planning leads to an over-emphasis on capital investment in physical structures since these objectives are easier to handle under the methodology of planning (and are likely to be more in demand politically) than are various other kinds of activity that may be equally or more desirable for development and possibly also much cheaper.

Another kind of rational approach to development is therefore needed:

> The doctor or the teacher does not make plans or blueprints of the future but is equally rational. Similarly, at the societal level, it is desirable to think in terms of a 'capacitating' operation which does not try so much to define or control the future as to establish present conditions or capacities which will permit a given society to meet its problems in the future. The emphasis in such an approach is not on setting future output targets but on diagnosing current weaknesses and potentials, finding appropriate policies, and constantly monitoring the course of development.
>
> An example of such a capacitation activity would be the undertaking of structural or institutional change, which conventional planning does not readily deal with through its technical methods.

The implications of a 'capacitation approach' were not further pursued within the quest, and in its bare bones it suggests a faith in the existence of some rational and benevolent entity qualified or qualifiable to direct the capacitating. However, it also suggests a conception of development policy-making as an educational experience in which societal actors learn to cope by struggling with problems under conditions of limited rationality, and this relates it to the contemporary positions of such economists as Albert O. Hirschman and such political scientists as Norman Thomas Uphoff and Michel Crozier.

### Informational enlightenment

Lines of thinking present in the *Report*[s] *on the World Social Situation* since the 1950s envisaged a transformation of the conditions for public action through methods of obtaining, disseminating, interpreting and integrating accurate and relevant information for the diagnosis of social problems and evaluation of progress. The proponents of social development wanted to free their uses of data from domination by economic methodologies and to construct methodologies better suited to their own purposes. They questioned the adequacy of income distribution studies to throw light on levels of welfare as well as the meaning of national aggregate indicators such as the gross national product (GNP).

Several complementary suppositions backed up their emphasis on improvement of information: first, that one important reason why 'development' was so little oriented to human welfare was that policy-makers were poorly informed of needs; second, that informational exposure could generate pressures forcing governments to act – or make way for other regimes that would act. At a more modest level of expectation, timely information would strengthen the hand of forces within national governments (as well as international organizations) disposed to tackle social problems.

These suppositions were clearly legitimate, although they could be qualified by various observations: that governments often did nothing about problems that had become internationally notorious; that governments were often overwhelmed by informational exposure of problems demanding immediate solutions, rather than being short of information; and that governments could use information as an aid to manipulation or repression or as a technique for evading action as easily as they could use it to promote the general welfare. In any case, informational enlightenment was the sphere of action most accessible to the international proponents of social development. It would become an 'approach' on the level of those discussed above only if it were considered a master key to development policy.

The treatment of information in the quest retained certain propositions common to the *Report*[s] *on the World Social Situation* that made the possibility of unified policy depend on the correct manipulation of information and the rejection of certain informational fallacies:

(a) Development had to be measured in a disaggregative way before being 'unified' in policy. 'Diagnosis for unified development involves first an attempt to see if the different factors of development are properly covered in proper proportions.' ('Factors' include the conventional sectoral components – such as education, health, nutrition, housing, conditions of work and employment – and sub-components – higher education, secondary education and so on – around which the *Report*[s] *on the World Social Situation* had been ordered.)

(b) 'Systems for collecting and analyzing information should be designed as far as possible to facilitate understanding of relationships between different phenomena ... one difficulty with most indicators is that they are used as national aggregates or averages and fail to reflect distribution.

Another difficulty is that the indicators that seem to make sense at the national level may not make much sense when examined at the local level ... to diagnose and understand the causal relationships between different developmental factors it is usually necessary to go to the level where the interaction actually takes place rather than deal with abstractions at the national level.'

Development under informational analysis thus becomes a multidimensional jigsaw puzzle, its large pieces divisible into small pieces fitting into each other vertically as well as horizontally. A unified approach must aim at techniques expressing the full complexity of their relationships, but they remain pieces with distinct contours susceptible to meaningful quantitative description once sufficiently disaggregated and combinable by the well-informed governmental player into a coherent whole at the 'national level'.

### Institutionalized Marxist socialism and 'far-reaching structural change'

This was the first in the series of approaches under discussion that questioned the possibility of development responding to the minimum criterion of acceptability and viability within the framework of capitalist or mixed economies. It did so, however, in a peculiarly ambiguous and stereotyped fashion that derived from the role of the 'real socialist' camp in the United Nations and the ways in which policy-making bodies and the Secretariat simultaneously paid respect to and evaded its ideological position.

In the UN debates, the representatives of the countries identifying themselves as socialist, in which the state controlled the means of production and the sources of investment and exercised power in the name of the working class, asserted that these societies could offer to the rest of the world lessons in a functioning unified approach. The fruits of this unified approach were full employment, a relatively even income distribution, and universalization of access to social security and the major social services. The preconditions for these achievements could be labelled 'far-reaching structural changes', a formula covering many kinds of change, from revolutionary seizure of power and dismantling of previous institutions to programmes of agrarian reform or popular participation in developmental decision-making, to which most governments had committed themselves through their votes in the UN.

It had to be assumed that governments could carry out such structural changes if they wanted to and that they had recognized the duty of doing so. The question whether abolition of private ownership of the means of production were not the key structural change could be left unanswered. The traditional Marxist-Leninist hypothesis on the necessity of the destruction of the bourgeois state and seizure of power by the proletariat as preconditions for such structural change remained in the shade.

Its terms of reference and institutional setting inhibited the unified approach quest from trying to decide whether socialism (under whatever definition) or any other comprehensive system of economic and political organization was a necessary condition for a unified approach.

### Neo-Marxist, participationist, self-reliant socialism

This complex of approaches, for which it is particularly hard to find an adequate label, entered the unified approach debate at a late stage, introducing a combination of propositions deriving from dependency theory, Maoism and other recent currents in Marxism, 'conscientization' doctrines and so on, that had come to the fore during the 1960s, mainly outside the inter-governmental debate over development. The proponents accepted the areas of choice deriving from the 'minimum criterion' set forth in the *Preliminary Report* but brushed aside the legitimacy of different styles of development:

> Third world countries are faced with an alternative. Either they accept their dependence or they pursue the path of their own self-reliant autonomous development. In the first case, they are bound to increased polarization, inequality and mass poverty. They continue to accept the mobilization of their resources primarily in function of foreign requirements. The mobilization of the immense reservoir of dormant productive and creative potentialities of the mass of their people will remain unutilized or underutilized ... It is proposed that the countries of the third world can only overcome their poverty and stagnation if and when they decide to pursue a new alternative and original path to development which qualitatively differs from that followed by the industrially advanced countries.[5]

Since the dominant forces of the 'industrially advanced' countries are responsible for the 'underdevelopment' of the rest of the world and depend on its exploitation, the latter cannot look to them for 'aid' and still less take them as models for development. In fact, their style of development is ethically indefensible and will become practically untenable once the Third World has taken another path; their real need for transformation is just as urgent and ineluctable as that of the Third World.

Market incentives cannot guide the transformation, nor can bureaucratized centrally planned versions of socialism, in which strategies decided from above seek to speed up capital accumulation by depressing levels of popular consumption and wringing a surplus from the peasantry. The arousing of the creativity and active participation of the masses of the people is both a central end and a central means of a unified approach to development.

In the version that entered into the unified approach debates, this position, in spite of its radical challenge to more accommodating approaches, retained an ambiguity that was practically a condition for its entering at all. According to its premises, existing governments and the world system of states present in the UN reflected relationships of domination and exploitation. For authentic development, the liberation of popular creativity must sweep away these relationships. Yet it suggested that 'countries' represented by their governments could 'choose' such a transformation and that the offering to them of detailed advice on how to do so was a legitimate activity. The nature of the catalytic force enabling the masses to change from objects of exploitation, cowed by repression and blinded by the lures of the consumer society, into creative participants in control of their own destiny remained obscure.

### *Ecodevelopment*

This approach centred attention on objectives of bringing production, consumption, population size and human settlement patterns into harmony with the carrying capacity of the earth and of reconciling this with an equitable distribution of resources among the world's peoples, implying a drastic lowering of the consumption levels of the richer countries. It had a relatively long history as an organized source of criticism of policies oriented exclusively to economic growth, parallel to but interacting little with the criticisms and prescriptions made in the name of social development.

The initiation of the unified approach quest coincided with the posing by the Meadows Report to the Club of Rome of the problem of 'limits to growth' and with the rapid intensification of international concern over the environmental disbenefits of technological innovations in production and of artificially stimulated consumption.

In the later stages of the quest, theories of 'ecodevelopment' were considered for introduction as an important 'missing ingredient' in a unified approach. Such theories, identified in particular with the work of Ignacy Sachs at the Centre Internationale de Recherche sur l'Environnement et le Développement in Paris, emphasized planning for the management of the natural and social resources of individual 'eco-regions', seeking technologies, settlement patterns, systems of production and distribution adapted to each 'eco-region' and substituting as far as possible the use and husbanding of local renewable resources for non-renewable resources.[6] However, the quest did not foresee the importance that environmental questions were about to assume in international discourse on development or the emergence of 'sustainable development' as a concept as widely accepted and as hard to prescribe for as 'social development'.

### Analysis of political choices and styles

The preceding pages have indicated implicitly the author's preference for an approach different from any of the above, although not radically incompatible with most of them. Such an approach tries to identify and explain political and other factors that condition the character and limits of public intervention in societal change, the circumstances under which policies approximating to the minimum criteria of acceptability and viability might emerge, and the identity of potential social agents for interventions favouring such 'unified approaches'. It rejects the eclectic supposition that national societies can pick and choose among 'lessons' from abroad and put the fragments together as they please, as well as the supposition that there is only One Right Way to develop which national societies must find and adopt under penalty of catastrophe.

Each national society faces a certain limited range of choices, depending on its historically conditioned political, social and economic structures; its productive capacity; its natural and human resources; its dominant values; and its place in the international order. These factors imply differing advantages, degrees of equity or inequity, costs and dangers. Certain choices are either altogether outside the society's reach or feasible only through a revolutionary transformation that cannot be willed deliberately by a regime shaped by current values and power relationships.

Such an approach cannot evade the search for a theoretical framework or set of hypotheses to order its analyses of national societies, but does not expect this quest to be more than partially and provisionally successful. In the version here described, the approach recognizes a permanent danger of becoming ridden by theory, selecting or interpreting facts to fit the theory, and universalizing phenomena that may be conjunctural or local. It finds conspicuous examples of this danger in many attempts to use Marxism as a framework for diagnosis and action.

The approach was open to the criticism that it could lead to the demoralizing conclusion that 'nothing could be done'. While the version that entered into the quest affirmed that many things could and should be done by many kinds of social agents, it remained frankly sceptical about the unified approach conceived as a set of universally applicable pre-scriptions.

Human institutions, from the international order to the local group, were engaged in games so complex and for such varied prizes that attempts to make sense of them and influence them in the name of development called for an exceptional combination of audacity and humility. The quest for a unified approach might contribute something along these lines if it remained iconoclastic, aware of the ritualistic side of the endeavour in which it was engaged, and the ambivalences in all human endeavours. It could not take for granted either that national societies were potentially perfectible, once their shortcomings were diagnosed correctly, nor that their irrationalities and inequities called for root-and-branch destruction and transformation.

### Alternative dichotomies

Several alternative criteria for classifying 'approaches' bring out other tensions and ambiguities in the quest for unified development prescriptions. In terms of polar positions one can distinguish the following.

*Technocratic* vs. *participationist* approaches. The former supposes that properly qualified specialists can find the one correct solution to each problem, adding up to the optimal style of development. Development policy can be unified to the extent to which such specialists can seek and apply the solutions without compromises to meet incompatible demands and resistances. Ideally, then, 'participation' should mean indoctrination in the nature of the optimal solution and corresponding behaviour. The latter approach supposes either that the optimal solution can emerge only from the creativity of the people, in control of its own destiny. or that there is no one optimal solution but that various satisfactory solutions can emerge from democratic political competition. Technocratic imposition, or reliance on policies that do not require popular understanding and cooperation, then, is inherently sterile.

*Centrality of economic or sociological laws* vs. *human-welfare-oriented voluntarism.* The laws looked to might be those of the market, or of the psycho-social conditions for planned modification of human behaviour, or of the socio-economic conditions for transition to socialism. The supposition is that unified development policy depends on a correct understanding of the laws and some combination of submission to and manipulation of the conditions they impose. The latter position denies either the binding nature of the laws or the possibility of their infallible interpretation. Social agents should therefore guide their efforts primarily by their values. The extent to which these values can be realized and human welfare enhanced will be revealed only in the course of struggle and innovation. While the former of these positions seems to have more affinity with the technocratic approach and the latter with the participationist, either can coexist with a predominantly technocratic or participationist outlook.

*Reliance on theoretical or methodological frames of reference* vs. *pragmatic acceptance of whatever works.* This contrast resembles the preceding, but with both polar positions more modest. The frame of reference does not pretend to explain the laws of development or societal change, but those of planning under specified conditions and with specified tools. The pragmatism applies itself to the replication and adaptation of techniques that seem to have proved their usefulness, without aspiring to a voluntarist 'big push' towards the Good Society.

*Universalist* vs. *particularist* approaches. The former position supposes that development must mean approximately the same thing for all national societies, whatever that meaning may be: all societies must become predominantly industrialized, urban and market-oriented; or all societies must become democratically egalitarian; or all societies must become collectivist and frugal in their lifestyles and use of resources. Universalism often combines with catastrophist all-or-nothing positions: unless humankind as a whole achieves certain objectives of productive capacity, technological restraint, social justice, disarmament, freedom, consumption austerity or population limitation, humankind as a whole, or the 'world', or 'civilization' is doomed.

The variants of the particularist position suppose that national societies, or whatever forms of social organization replace them, will continue to develop along many different lines, some more 'acceptable' for their values and some more 'viable' for their internal coherence and efficiency than others. This inevitable diversity has its dangers, particularly of conflicts between national societies and exploitation of the weak by the strong, but also its advantages: the homogenization of humankind is neither possible nor desirable; the wider the range of styles of development, the greater the likelihood that a positive cross-fertilization will take place in the future.

The particularist as well as the universalist position can, of course, combine with a technocratic or a participationist bias, with a belief in iron laws of development or in voluntarism.

## The changing international market for propositions on development during and since the quest for a unified approach

The quest for a unified approach was one manifestation, and a relatively modest one, of the divergence in interpretations of development and the multiplication of attributes of development that had gained momentum during the 1960s and that was to become pronounced and complex at the beginning of the 1970s. 'Development' must stand for something worth striving for, and the goal of increasing productive capacity, particularly industrial capacity, through capital accumulation, investment and technological innovation was still at the core of this something at the beginning of the 1970s.

Experience was making it harder to believe, however, that growth in production by itself, whether guided by the market or by central planning, would bring about equitably distributed gains in human welfare, or that sufficient growth to permit accomplishment of this end was within the reach of the poorer countries without major changes in their internal policies and their place in the world system. Advocates of a very wide range of objectives and policies were arguing that their concerns constituted essential attributes of authentic development, and also that achievement of more conventional development objectives required priority to their concerns.

The unified approach quest was instructed in its terms of reference to find out how to unify what was unifiable in these different positions from the standpoint of one of them: the composite of human welfare objectives and social sectoral programmes that had come to be labelled 'social development'. Before it could accomplish this, however, the range of positions to be unified had widened considerably. As noted above, the 1970s saw, instead of progress towards consensus on a unified approach, a continual diversification of interpretations of development, continually more ambitious international declarations aspiring to reconcile them, and also a mounting criticism of 'development', from several quite different viewpoints, as an outworn and misleading myth.

### Development decades, New International Economic Order, 'another development'

For the present, it will be enough to summarize certain features of the changing international market for propositions on development inside and outside the inter-governmental organizations. Within these organizations the main framework for debate was the Second Development Decade, to be governed by an International Development Strategy approved by the UN General Assembly in October 1970.

The Strategy juxtaposed two main kinds of propositions, the former clinging to the expectations of the first Development Decade, the latter responding to the criticisms of its focus on economic growth. During the 1970s new propositions superseded both kinds:

(a) On international economic relations and on the duty of the richer countries to aid the development of the rest of the world through allocation of a minimum percentage of their national income and through fairer trade policies. The Strategy presented propositions of this kind in considerable detail but in compromise formulations that emerged in bargaining between representatives of governments that wanted binding commitments and representatives of governments that wanted to ward off such commitments without a flat rejection. As the decade progressed the struggle for and against commitments was repeated in forum after forum.

By 1974, the compromises reached in the Strategy were obviously inoperative and Third World governments turned their attention to a Declaration and Programme of Action on the Establishment of a New International Economic Order, for which most of the First World governments, now constituting a small minority in the UN, assumed no concrete responsibility.

(b) On the content of development at the national level. By the mid-1970s, a series of detailed proposals for development approaches focusing on 'redistribution with growth', elimination of extreme poverty and priority to the satisfaction of basic needs, emanating mainly from the World Bank and the International Labour Organization, were disputing the world stage with the UN's New International Economic Order (NIEO), replacing the innocuous juxtaposition of economic and social objectives with a new version of the old controversy over priorities.

The 'basic needs' and related approaches treated policies for production, technological innovation, distribution and employment as central but subordinated their content to immediate human welfare ends. A good many proponents of the NIEO interpreted this as a tactic of the central capitalist countries, intended to justify inattention to trade and aid demands and restriction of the Third World to a second-rate semi-development through labour-intensive technologies. In fact, the new approaches had several variants, some of them envisaging modest reallocations of resources to the poor and gains through aided self-help, others calling for the transformation of structures of production and distribution and an end to affluence for minorities.

Non-governmental institutions were able to carry these ideas farther towards the construction of coherent alternatives for the human future, the most ambitious of these attempts being the proposal of the Dag Hammarskjöld Foundation for 'another development', published in 1975.

### 'Major problems'

An equally striking feature of the international treatment of development during the 1970s, however, was the successive bringing into the foreground of a series of 'major problems' treated with what became a stereotyped ritual: population, the human environment, the status of women, habitat, employment and hunger were all taken up in this way.

The UN General Assembly might proclaim an International Year to recognize the importance of the problem. A world conference or summit meeting, preceded by regional conferences and meetings of 'experts', would approve a Plan of Action, and more regional conferences and specialized meetings would then discuss application of the Plan of Action. A temporary or permanent international secretariat would come into being and a fund to finance practical measures would be set up.

Recognition of the problem would go through several phases. Simple cause-and-effect interpretations and direct remedies would be intensively publicized and then subjected to criticism from many directions. Representatives of Third World governments and ideologists would indicate their suspicion of the First World origins of initial interpretations of the problem and their disposition to recognize the need for action only to the extent that this would not divert attention from economic development and from the duty of the rich countries to help such development. In any case, it could be demonstrated that the problem was complexly related to all other major problems; it could be solved only in the context of development. Thus, all roads seemed to lead back to the unified approach.

But who was to do the unifying? Conceivably, any of the major problems might provide the starting point towards a comprehensive conception and strategy of development around which the other problems and desiderata might be grouped, but they could not all occupy the centre at once. The gap between the capacity of governments and other human institutions in the real world to diagnose, choose and set priorities, and the demand that they advance toward multiple objectives in a unified way, was already wide enough, and the formalization of each 'major problem' threatened to widen it further. At the same time, it could be argued that, overburdened as they were, governments would not act on the major problems unless these were brought to their attention insistently and persistently, backed by organized popular pressures and warnings as to the indispensability of urgent action to ward off catastrophe.

### Other challenges

Meanwhile, outside the international bureaucratic and academic circles of obligatory faith in the rationality and benevolence of governments, several kinds of challenge to the whole structure of international development strategies, new international economic orders and plans of action became more insistent. Each of these challenges included variants ranging from wholesale negation to qualified criticism of the conventional wisdom.

(a) 'Economic development' was reduced to the status of a mobilizing myth, even by some economists prominent in development policy-making, most eloquently by Celso Furtado:

> Myths function as lamps that illuminate the field of perception of the social scientist, allowing him to have a clear vision of certain problems and to see nothing of others at the same time as they give him spiritual tranquillity, since the value judgements that he makes appear to his spirit as a reflection of objective reality.
>
> Today we know irrefutably that the economies of the periphery will never be developed in the sense of becoming similar to the economies that form the present centre of the capitalist system. But how can one deny that this idea has been very useful, to mobilize the peoples of the periphery and induce them to accept enormous sacrifices, to legitimate the destruction of archaic forms of culture, to explain and make them understand the necessity of destroying their physical environment, to justify forms of dependency that reinforce the predatory character of the productive system?
>
> It can thus be affirmed that the idea of economic development is simply a myth. Thanks to this it has been possible to divert attention from the basic tasks of identifying the fundamental needs of the collectivity and the possibilities

that the progress of science opens to humanity, so as to concentrate attention on abstract objectives such as investment, exports and growth.[7]

Such a challenge knocked one leg out from under the declarations of meeting after meeting that wedded the 'abstract objectives' of economic development to basic needs or the 'major problems' listed above.

(b) Faith in the market as arbiter of developmental choices, in the inexhaustibility of natural resources, and in the ability of human ingenuity (spurred by market incentives) to solve problems as they arose, persisted and became more aggressive during the 1970s as the shortcomings of governmental and inter-governmental interventionism became more glaring. According to the proponents of variants of this position, from Daniel Moynihan to Herman Kahn and Milton Friedman, the main danger for the human future lay in the zeal to bind it by regulations and the main stumbling block in the way of the development of poor countries lay in their hankering after welfare state policies and socialist planning, a hankering pandered to by such utopian exercises as the quest for a unified approach.

The dominant forces in a good many Third World countries had clung to such views even during the years of rising prestige for planned and state-managed development. During the 1970s the influence of neo-liberalism on government policies became more pronounced, particularly in certain 'newly industrializing' countries of Latin America and Southeast Asia, although the practically uncontested triumph of this doctrine did not arrive until the 1980s.

(c) The penetration of transnational enterprises in the economies of the Third World, the emergence of 'transnational elites' identified with these enterprises, and the mutation of national cultures and consumption patterns brought about by transnationally manipulated mass communication media and advertising made the vision of autonomous and self-sustaining national development seem obsolete. The relevant development strategies for the future might be those of the transnational enterprises rather than those of the governments.

(d) Two kinds of challenges emerged from alarm over the prospects for resource exhaustion, environmental degradation, potential destructiveness of new technologies and overpopulation. The more direct challenge denied the possibility or desirability of anything identifiable with previous conceptions of development. Some variants of this position derived from it conclusions on the duty of the rich national societies to limit their own consumption and assist the poorer countries in an equitable transition to 'zero population growth' and 'zero economic growth'. Other variants concluded that the rich societies should set their own houses in order and help other societies only if the latter showed promise of viability. Still others concluded that the momentum of current trends and the limited capacity for foresight and rational action made the avoidance of catastrophe unlikely either for humanity as a whole or for the better-off societies.

Variants on the other challenge emerging from this diagnosis affirmed the possibility of solutions to the resource, environmental and population problems, but insisted that these solutions would have to be comprehensive and counter-intuitive. Piecemeal 'practical' responses to problems as they arose would only make matters worse through their impact on other systemically related areas. One variant then questioned the capacity of human institutions to devise and manage such comprehensive solutions; another reasoned that solutions guaranteeing human survival would require a high degree of regimentation and suppression of dissent.

(e) Diagnoses of the inherently exploitative character of the international capitalist order and of the structures of class and power in states supported many variants of the conclusion that both must be destroyed as a precondition for the Good Society. These positions, through their links with the dominant forces in certain Third World countries, with organized revolutionary or terrorist movements, and with international political struggles deriving from the Cold War, on the one hand; and with participationist and 'another development' visions, on the other, had complex and ambiguous relationships to the international debates on prescriptions for development, but logically negated their relevance. The dominant forces in the central capitalist countries could not be committed to end their exploitation of the rest of the world even if the governments they controlled entered into agreements to do so. The most that could be expected was an unacceptable 'renegotiation of the terms of dependence', benefiting only the exploiting minorities in the dependent countries.

The only solution for the latter, once their own people gained control over them, would be to cut all economic and political ties, accept the consequences, and subdue or expel the minorities identified, through their economic roles and their consumption patterns, with the previous ties of dependency. Relations could then be reopened selectively, and mainly with national societies having similar genuinely revolutionary regimes.

The same revolutionary positions denied that existing national governments, whatever the intentions of individuals within them, had any ability to achieve an acceptable social and economic order. Even those labelling themselves 'socialist' were really 'bureaucratic capitalist'. The weakness of their political leaders and bureaucracies in the face of the international order and the transnational enterprises, their inability to identify themselves with the people, and their personal consumerist aspirations ruled them out. A profound and creatively destructive uprising of the masses was called for; and the will of these masses rather than international prescriptions would govern the longer-term future.[8]

# The place of the unified approach quest in the international rethinking of development

## *Resuscitations in the United Nations*

The term 'unified approach to development' retained a certain currency in international circles during the 1970s and a good many of the ideas put forward under this label in meetings or by development advisers can be traced to the quest itself. Variants of these ideas, however, would have circulated in any case. The main feature that distinguished the partial consensus reached in the quest barely received a hearing.

The *Preliminary Report*, as has already been stated, did not pretend to offer either an original theory of development or a set of practical prescriptions. Despite some internal inconsistencies, it tried to propose a flexible way of thinking about development, of confronting its minimum criterion of acceptability and viability with national situations and an international order in which nothing could be taken for granted, in which planning and formulation of norms tended to become ritual activities compensating for inability to influence real trends within the constraints under which social agents, inside and outside national governments, acted.

A study under inter-governmental auspices could not honestly do much more than say: If your society has such-and-such characteristics and the institutions or groups you represent want to achieve such-and-such objectives, you should take into account certain factors, and you may find certain methods more helpful than others.

The Commission for Social Development and the Economic and Social Council to which the *Preliminary Report* was presented naturally wanted more than this, and requested that a final report 'be prepared in such a way as to be of the greatest possible practical use to planners, decision-makers, and administrators'. Since the project team had already dispersed and its budget was exhausted, preparation of a final report on the scale originally envisaged was no longer practical.

UNRISD responded to the request with a brief 'final report' submitted to the 1975 session of the Commission for Social Development. This report spelled out in more detail some of the proposals on development analysis and planning and introduced the idea of 'capacitation'.

The UN policy-making bodies did not allow this answer to be final. They next requested the Secretary-General to 'prepare a report on the application by governments of a unified approach to development analysis and planning', and also to prepare proposals for 'pilot projects' demonstrating the practical application of a unified approach. These requests, in fact, juxtaposed two very different visions of the unified approach that were advanced by the representatives of different governments. The first derived from the thesis that 'far-reaching structural changes' within national societies were the essential precondition for a unified approach. Certain governments of the 'real socialist' camp felt that they possessed the correct specifications for such changes; while they could not expect to obtain inter-governmental consensus on them, they could use the unified approach to keep them in the forefront of attention and demonstrate their own achievements.

The second vision derived from the conception of the unified approach as mainly a question of integrating social and economic programmes, and also from a supposition going back to the beginning of UN social activities that the concentration of advanced methods and integrated services on a local population would provide lessons and achievements that could then be replicated on a larger scale. The unified approach quest had harboured hopes of this kind, particularly in relation to the importance of localized information, but its main emphasis had been on the national level. A unified approach focusing on pilot projects might be expected to appeal to governments that had no intention of sponsoring far-reaching structural changes and preferred to direct attention to the potential of modest but better-integrated incremental changes.

By this time, while UNRISD continued to struggle to bring the research aspect of the unified approach to a coherent conclusion, the responsibility for acting on the new request had fallen mainly to the UN Secretariat's Centre for Development Planning, Projections and Policies, an economic-ally oriented body that had in the past been decidedly cool towards the unified approach. Since the Secretariat was not in a position to decide which governments, if any, were applying a unified approach, however defined, or to evaluate their efforts, it fell back on its traditional method of dealing with controversial mandates. It circulated a request for informa-tion to governments, sorted out the twenty countries that responded into 'countries with centrally planned economies', 'countries with developed market economies', and 'countries with developing market economies', and summarized the information they provided, mainly on their planning systems. The conclusion offered was that 'while many countries have introduced an integrated or unified approach to development planning, clearly there is no unique approach that can be considered applicable to all countries'.[9]

The Secretariat also prepared proposals for pilot projects, but in spite of their cautious formulation these encountered resistance in the Economic and Social Council (ECOSOC):

Several representatives expressed the view that the projects on the unified approach must take fully into consideration the imperatives of the sovereignty of Member States. They emphasized that full account must be taken of the development goals set by each country for itself. Since each country had its own conception of the appropriate economic, social and political systems, development plans and policy measures adopted by Governments could be formulated and implemented only in the context of the actual conditions prevailing in individual countries. A project on integrated development planning should therefore neither seek a universal applicability of its findings nor be used to monitor and pass judgment, based on a single set of criteria, on the development objectives and performance of developing countries.[10]

ECOSOC requested reformulation of the proposals, but by this time the unified approach as a distinct line of inquiry had reached an impasse, surviving only because of the characteristic inability of UN bodies to bring to a clear-cut end any initiative once embarked upon. Moreover, its consideration in the UN policy-making bodies was being submerged in that of several other normative approaches. These were, first, the reformulations of international development policy, in particular the Programme of Action on the Establishment of a New International Economic Order, the Charter of Economic Rights and Duties of States, and the 1975 General Assembly resolution on Development and International Economic Co-operation; second, the various crusades for attention to 'major problems'; and, third, the proposals emanating from the International Labour Organization and the World Bank for development policies focusing on satisfaction of basic needs or elimination of extreme poverty. These last approaches were sometimes identified with the unified approach, and had, in fact, inherited some of that project's central propositions on policy choices.

### In the regional economic commissions

The quest for a unified approach exerted some influence in the regional commissions of the UN and was influenced by currents of thinking already present in them.

In Latin America, a region that was beginning to be labelled 'semi-developed', questions of viable choices between styles of development and the relation of such choices to ideologies and the distribution of political power were in the forefront of attention. Did capitalist 'development' or modernization of peripheral countries such as those of Latin America unavoidably generate increasing dependence on the world centres, increasing inequalities in the distribution of consumption and wealth, increasing insecurity and relative if not absolute impoverishment for large parts of the population, and increasing resort to repressive authoritarian regimes to guarantee the viability of the prevailing style of 'development'? How could the evident gains in productive capacity, economic and social infrastructure, qualifications of the labour force and governmental administrative resources be converted into gains in human welfare and who would be the societal agents of such a conversion?

The experience of different countries of the region suggested that policies concentrated on rapid economic growth through government stimulation of combined public and private investment (as in Brazil or

Mexico), or policies giving priority to structural transformation and social equity (as in Chile or Cuba), could be successful on their own terms, at differing high costs and if backed by sufficient power. The prospects for policies trying to reconcile multiple objectives of growth and welfare under conditions of open political competition, however, were poor. Styles of development meeting the minimum criterion of the unified approach seemed to call for a transformation of values and expectations as well as power structures, but the circumstances of semi-development, in particular the penetration of transnational enterprises and the consumption aspirations of the 'modern' sectors of the population, made the way to such a transformation hard to envisage.

The Economic Commission for Latin America (ECLA) had posed problems of this kind in several studies, and contributed to the unified approach quest the approach labelled above 'analysis of political choices and styles'. The ideas generated in the quest in turn influenced further studies and polemics in the ECLA Secretariat on styles of development.[11]

Moreover, the ideas entered into a series of normative declarations approved by ECLA members at their sessions during the 1970s. The propositions on 'integrated development' in these declarations show a surprising degree of acquiescence by the majority (then governed mainly by military–authoritarian regimes) in what amounted to condemnations of what was visibly happening in the name of development.

Finally, an exhaustive study of development theories and their application in Latin America carried out by the Planning Institute associated with ECLA dismissed the unified approach and the inter-governmental normative declarations associated with it in the following terms:

> The integrated approach is not only the clear expression of a technocratic utopia but also, in spite of its name, it is a utopia made by aggregation of objectives, whose validity by themselves hardly anyone can deny, accompanied by continual reserves to the effect that the particular situation can legitimate their not being achieved and even their being set aside for an indeterminate and indeterminable future. A unified approach to development worthy of the name supposes a unified social science, which does not exist at present and which could only be constructed on certain philosophical postulates, derived from a general theory, which in turn could not count on general support for a long time to come. At the same time, an international declaration of objectives can be possible only through evading philosophical–political differences, so that the only possible base of a unified approach, a common philosophy, is ruled out from the beginning. When such a declaration purports to be a unified approach, the only way to do it that is apparently legitimate is through the aggregation of objectives.[12]

In the Economic and Social Commission for Asia and the Pacific (ESCAP), the unified approach was seen mainly as a new attempt to tackle the previous concerns of the ESCAP Committee on Social Development: better integration of government social and economic programmes, higher priority to the 'social', and more adequate statistical indicators for the social objectives of development. However, the ominous incapacity of urban industrially biased economic growth and social programmes to cope with mass poverty in mainly rural populations, together with the presence of China as a demonstration of the possibility of a radically different style, brought about an openness in ESCAP documents and in advisory missions to the participationist self-reliant approach described above, in a variant deriving directly from the later stages of the unified approach quest.

In Africa, the unified approach entered into discussion mainly through a joint Economic Commission for Africa (ECA)–UNRISD study presented to the Sixth Session of the Conference of African Planners in October 1976, and through visits of ECA–UNRISD teams to seven African countries. The study analysed all available African development plans currently in force in order to:

> determine the degree to which the plan documents represent a systematic attempt to deal with the problem of uneven development, insofar as this could be determined from the range and specification of plan objectives, from the type of planning information and procedures used, and from planned policies and projects relating to the provision of essential services, the composition of production, research and technology, institutional change, and external economic relations.

The visits to countries similarly concentrated on planning objectives and techniques.

The studies and visits found, not unexpectedly, a certain correspondence between the objectives stated in the preambles to plans and the human-welfare-oriented terms of reference of the unified approach quest, but also very nebulous relationships between these objectives and the projects and techniques contained in the body of the plans.

> Several reasons were given to explain these divergences – lack of manpower and finance, inadequate political commitment, unavailability of relevant data, deliberate distortions by executing agencies. Another argument sometimes given was that projects on behalf of the 'little man' are extremely difficult to organize and manage, while big projects involving extensive capital investment can be set up and run much more effectively.[13]

The African study thus started by accepting provisionally the plans as valid expressions of national policy and the planners – the main interlocutors of the study team – as key social agents. By pointing to gaps and shortcomings the study then tried to suggest modest and incremental improvements rather than radically different styles and strategies. How could planners make better diagnoses and influence policy more effectively toward human welfare objectives under conditions of rudimentary information, political instability, and very meagre resources susceptible to allocation by the state? At the same time, the UN African Institute for Economic Development and Planning (IDEP) was diagnosing the existing styles of development of the African countries as neither viable nor acceptable. IDEP was also urging variants of the participationist self-reliant approach. However, the contact between this line of thinking within Africa and the participants in the unified approach quest was slight.

The terms of reference of the unified approach quest had focused on the needs of the 'developing' or 'poor' countries. Its potential relevance to the countries that defined themselves as 'developed' was never clearly specified. According to some of the approaches that entered into the quest these countries figured mainly as sources of aid and of useful lessons for the 'developing' countries; since they were 'developed' it could be assumed that they already had a unified approach or did not need one.

According to other approaches, of course, the 'developed' countries were part of the problem, not part of the solution. Their peoples needed transformations in their styles of development just as much as did the rest of the world, and might find such transformations even harder to achieve, in view of their material and psychological investments in existing patterns of production and consumption.

The contacts of the quest with the Economic Commission for Europe (ECE), however, hardly touched on such questions. The facet of the unified approach of most interest here was that of informational enlightenment: the devising of development indicators and social accounting to supplement the partially discredited GNP and national accounts, in national situations in which statistics were abundant, relatively reliable and capable of providing answers to new questions, presumably including the question of the relationship between economic growth and human welfare.

## The dilemmas of international policy-oriented research

The preceding pages have focused on a few manifestations of the international aspiration to shape the future that, over the past half century, has generated hundreds of meetings and hundreds of thousands of pages of documentation. On the margins of the ceaseless activity generated by the international agencies' cycles of meetings, one finds an even more diverse and complex ferment of theorizing, empirical research, polemics and ideological proselytizing whose practitioners interact with the international normative–prescriptive efforts but scorn their ritualism, utopianism, evasiveness and lack of scientific rigour.

If the quest did not manage to prescribe a 'unified approach to development analysis and planning', it did make more explicit than heretofore certain dilemmas that any international policy-oriented research project would have to face. It also suggested that such dilemmas could not be avoided within the context of such projects. If policy-oriented research were to make any contribution to human welfare it would have to recognize a permanent tension and ambiguity in the demands made on it, and maintain a critical attitude towards its own terms of reference and the suppositions underlying them.

A mandate to reconcile the irreconcilable has at least the virtue of reproducing conditions somewhat similar to those of policy-making in real national societies. The most likely outcome may be evasion, but this is not the only possible outcome. Presumably such an outcome can be guarded against by bringing contradictions out into the open and incorporating them into the hypotheses of the research, a course that should present fewer drawbacks and dangers for a team pursuing policy questions at the international level than for advisers to national political regimes.

What are the dilemmas and tensions that international policy-oriented research must learn to live with? First, there is the tension between the ideal of explicit definition of basic concepts, hypotheses and value premises and the pressures towards a combined eclecticism and 'consensualism' that the heterogeneity of the situations confronted seems to legitimate. It cannot be accidental that the interminable discussions of development have left intact the confusion between development conceived as empirically observable processes of change and growth within social systems and development as progress towards the observer's vision of the Good Society. In the first sense development can be evaluated positively or negatively or judged inherently ambiguous in its implications for the human future. In the second sense development is by definition desirable.

Nor have the discussions overcome the confusion between development conceived as a process subject to uniform laws and development conceived as a wide range of possible real patterns and possible aspirations. Can the term 'development' in the last analysis be anything more than a symbolic stamp of approval for changes that the user of the term considers unavoidable or desirable?

The unified approach quest tried to delimit what was to be approached through the legitimation of different styles of development responding to a minimum criterion of acceptability and viability, but this left room for argument that practically any combination of policies that any regime cared to defend would eventually meet the criterion.

Second, there is the related tension between the ideal of arriving at a comprehensive and coherent theory explaining the phenomena the research confronts and aspires to change, and the pressures towards incongruous marriages of the pragmatic and the universalistic. Theories of development and social change have proliferated in recent years, but the explanatory power and prestige of all of them have waned. The unified approach quest was able neither to make a reasoned choice among the theories already current nor to construct an original theory. It confronted, in addition to the obvious hindrances of inadequate time and disciplinary and other divergences in the team, an inhibiting prejudice against theorizing on the part of the institutional sponsors of the quest.

Theoretical argument is divisive; also, according to oft-repeated views in UN policy-making bodies, it is a luxury that cannot be afforded in view of the urgency of the problems demanding solution. Theoretical explanations are either already available or can be dispensed with. The recurrent superficiality or evasiveness of 'theoretical' generalizations in UN documents, seeking to stay within the limits of the permissible, confirmed this evaluation. The policy-making bodies thus called for the 'concrete' and the 'practical', but with the proviso, explicit or implicit, that the concrete and practical prescriptions must refrain from judging specific national situations and policies. Thus the compilers of reports must aim at prescriptions that appear concrete but are general and conditional enough to be applied by any government that cares to listen.

The result has been a long series of Secretariat responses to demands for 'practical' solutions to urgent problems that were forgotten as soon as presented. This was true of the 'practical applications' proposals deriving from the unified approach quest. However, as noted above, the quest resisted advancing very far along this path.

The well-worn retort that nothing is more practical than a good theory comes to mind but does not take one far towards resolution of the tension. Probably international policy-oriented research will continue to be more a consumer than a producer of theories, and will have to open itself to the possible validity, under defined conditions, of a wide range of theoretical challenges to the relevance of the 'practical'.

Third, there is the tension between the ideal of searching criticism of the conventional wisdom on development and the insertion of the research into a complicated array of institutions and expectations deriving from this wisdom. Policy-oriented research is expected to come up with something new and to criticize the old. There would be no occasion for it if its sponsors thought that existing diagnoses and policies were satisfactory.

Criticism must thus apply itself to a contradictory mixture of conventional suppositions, particularly on the role of the state, of sweeping and apparently radical 'new' objectives – popular participation, elimination of poverty, satisfaction of basic needs and so on – and of terminological innovations giving an air of novelty to policies that have long been current. The 'unified approach' itself began mainly as a terminological innovation for a desideratum previously labelled 'balanced social and economic development'. The most useful corrective should be the cultivation of historical awareness. The history of development as a mobilizing myth is short, but long enough for the observation that those who forget history are condemned to repeat it to have become very pertinent.

The quest for a unified approach to development in terms of norms and prescriptions has been carried as far as it profitably can be, if not farther. The most hopeful direction for the next stages of policy-oriented research lies at levels between the comprehensive theoretical or ideological explanations for societal change, and the local manifestations of change and policies designed to influence change. Comparative studies with a historical perspective focused on the ways in which different social agents of change perceive their roles and act, and the confrontation between their perceptions and the real settings on which they are trying to act, are still relatively few.

Presumably, research in this direction will leave something intact in the aspiration for rationally planned action to bring social change and economic growth into closer correspondence with certain generally accepted values of human welfare, equity and freedom. In all probability, however, it will replace the image of the state, implicit in UN research mandates, as a rational, coherent and benevolent entity, capable of choosing and entitled to choose a style of development, so powerful but so unimaginative that it seeks generalized advice and then acts on it, by a more realistic frame of reference for policy-oriented interpretation of what real states do or evade doing, why, and how.

## Notes

1. Since 1990, the Human Development Index prepared by the UNDP has entered boldly into this path, annually ranking all the countries of the world without, in the opinion of a good many statisticians, dispelling doubts concerning the validity of the exercise. (*Human Development Reports*, 1990-1994.)

2. The Economic Commission for Latin America was probably the first economically oriented UN body to try to incorporate (from the early 1950s) a theoretical sociological approach into its thinking on economic development. This approach, under the intellectual guidance of José Medina Echavarría, gradually escaped from its ancillary role of diagnosing social aspects and obstacles and led to a quite different kind of development dialogue. See, in particular, Medina Echavarría, *Consideraciones sociológicas sobre el desarrollo económico* (1963); and *Filosofía, educación y desarrollo* (1973).

3. These reports, along with other materials on the quest, can be found in UNRISD, *The Quest for a Unified Approach* (1980).

4. The approach derived naturally from the 'programmes of social development' component of the *Report*[s] *on the World Social Situation*, which, in principle, identified programmes that were working in the expectation that they would provide 'lessons' for the governments of other countries confronting similar problems. In practice, the information accessible to the compilers of the reports had been too scanty and the political constraints too confining for them to state with any confidence whether programmes they described, mainly summarizing official documents, really worked or not.

5. UN Economic and Social Commission for Asia and the Pacific, *Premises and Implications of a Unified Approach to Development Analysis and Planning* (UN Economic

and Social Commission for Asia and the Pacific (1975), a text originally submitted for the quest after dispersal of the initial team. This approach is also presented in Kuitenbrouwer, *Towards Self-Reliant Integrated Development* (n.d.).

6. Ignacy Sachs, *Stratégies de l'écodéveloppement* (1980). This approach obviously links with the quest for 'appropriate technogies' and similar initiatives that flourished during the 1970s.

7. Furtado, *El desarrollo económico: Un mito* (1975). (Author's translation.)

8. The summary of these positions, like the preceding summaries, is unavoidably oversimplified, and it might be invidious to identify it with individual participants in the unending debates over development and revolution, many of whom have modified and enriched their diagnoses since the 1970s. However, the writings of Samir Amin and André Gunder Frank are among the more cogent and accessible arguments for the views here summarized.

9. *Application by Governments of a Unified Approach to Development Analysis and Planning, Report of the Secretary-General* (E/CN.540, 22 September 1976).

10. *Projects on the Practical Application of a Unified Approach to Development Analysis and Planning, Report of the Secretary-General.*

11. See, in particular, the papers by Raúl Prebisch, Anibal Pinto, Jorge Graciarena and Marshall Wolfe in *CEPAL Review*, 1 (First Semester, 1976).

12. Solari et al., *Teoría, acción social y desarrollo en América Latina* (1976).

13. *Report on Recent Progress and Current Status of Work on the Unified Approach and Related Projects* (UNRISD internal paper, 1977).

# CHAPTER 3

# STATES AND SOCIETIES AS AGENTS OF DEVELOPMENT

## Universalization and crisis of the 'nation-state'

The 'nation-state', unavoidably, has constituted the principal frame of reference within which development objectives have been defined and policies applied. The 'modern' state, with its internationally recognized attributes, sources of legitimacy and problematic identification with the conception of 'nation', emerged from a specific conjuncture of political, economic and cultural factors in one of the major world regions, Europe. It has been linked throughout its historical evolution with two mutually contradictory but equally conflict-engendering drives: towards imperialist expansion and dominance over weaker peoples, and towards assertion of 'national' self-determination in defiance of existing boundaries and claims of sovereignty.

Over the past two centuries the formal institutions of the nation-state have been transplanted throughout the world, among peoples having quite different pre-existing systems of political organization and conceptions concerning the sources and functions of authority, or in some cases no power structure or tradition of allegiance wider than the tribe, local community or family.

Direct imposition by the empire-building states, and the borrowing by local elites of political conceptions and institutions that offered hope of more effective resistance to such imposition, both contributed to the process. From the 1940s it took on new dimensions as unprecedented numbers of newly independent countries tried to adapt the only available models for political organization within the world system of interdependence. The transplantation involved not only institutions directly concerned with the functioning of the state, but also a formidable intellectual baggage concerning the nature of social classes, the roles of political movements and the determinants of economic growth.

Local elites, as well as social scientists of the dominant or 'developed' countries, advanced 'nation-building' and 'modernization' as self-evident and nearly synonymous desiderata or requisites for 'development', although the latter have admitted to a good deal of difficulty in defining these desiderata.[1]

A historically unprecedented system, comprising practically the whole of the world's population, of nearly 200 formally independent states has emerged from the liquidation of colonial systems and multinational empires. They include rich and powerful states as well as poor and weak ones; states governing hundreds of millions of people as well as microstates of a few thousands; ethnically, culturally, linguistically and religiously homogeneous states as well as states whose peoples are extremely heterogeneous in all these respects. They are, in principle, equal in sovereignty and share certain principles and obligations codified through the United Nations and the 'family' of other inter-governmental organizations to which practically all of them belong. It is hardly surprising that the rapid universalization of a system of states supposed to possess common attributes has generated many anomalies, frustrations and conflicts. Cycles of overconfidence by forces controlling states in their ability to manage and accelerate development, impose national unity, transform values or simply use the state to perpetuate their own domination have been followed by cycles of disillusionment, popular resistance or apathy toward state pretensions, ideological denunciations of state overreaching and inherent incapacity to promote the general welfare. For our present purposes, the modern state can be considered to have three dimensions:

1. *The state as symbol of nationhood* As the permanent expression of a national political community, the state demands the loyalty of members of the community, acts as final arbiter of class and group conflicts, monopolizes the legitimate use of force, etc., according to well-known formulas. Ideally, in pluralist democracies majorities would decide what the state should do or refrain from doing, within generally accepted and codified rules protecting the rights of minorities. The forces controlling most of the newer states have asserted wide autonomy in relation to the society, extending even to creation of collective social actors, but have been weak in representativeness and accepted hegemony. Attempts to mobilize the 'nation' behind the state have contributed to populism and the aggrandizement of the military as symbol of the nation and guarantor of the state. Up to a point, states throughout the world gained strength in recent decades through the weakening or elimination of local power centres and oligarchies and, more ambivalently, through widening expectations in most of the population that solutions to problems of livelihood and protection against injustice depended on the state.

2. *The state as 'public sector'* States constitute aggregations of institutions and bureaucracies with their own forces of inertia and momentum. Up to the 1970s or 1980s, public sector institutions in most countries, in spite of political purges and other vicissitudes, were gradually becoming 'modernized', entrusted with wider responsibilities and staffed by better-qualified functionaries. The enhanced capacity of the public sector to manage the economy and provide social services was commonly pointed to as one of the more positive aspects of 'development', a means of

making this disorderly and precarious process more dynamic and more harmonious in the future. It became evident, however, that even under authoritarian regimes parts of the state apparatus were becoming increasingly detached from central control. They evolved their own techniques for self-defence and expansion, and became more closely linked to external interlocutors (governments, inter-governmental organizations, transnational enterprises, professional peer groups) than to the state as arbiter of national policy.

In a good many countries, the educational upgrading of public employment became entangled with its inflation in order to absorb the output of the universities. In the fragmented autonomization of the state apparatus the military became even more of a special case than before, with their own political culture and conception of state responsibilities, and their unrivalled capacity to impose their own criteria on the state and society.

More recently, particularly in Africa and Latin America, states, whatever their policy stance, could no longer afford the bureaucracies they had acquired piecemeal. Shrinkage of resources combined with public frustration at the shortcomings of public sector activities and ideological attacks on the legitimacy of state social and economic interventions. Thus governments generally could not avoid striving to make the state apparatus less costly, more flexible, more responsive to central directives as well as to democratic principles, and more concentrated on major immediate needs rather than spread over a multiplicity of programmes originating in separate past motives and pressures. Simplification of regulations and controls in order to stimulate private initiative and reduce the costs of the 'nursemaid state' was obviously desirable but hard to achieve in the midst of debt crises and conflicting external and internal demands.

Democratic regimes could not afford to reduce public employment drastically, but neither could they afford to maintain salaries and resources so that the public services could meet their responsibilities. The result was demoralization and 'survival strategies' (multiple jobs, bribe-taking, pressure-group alliances with clienteles) that further discredited or fragmented state authority.

3. *State and regime* Finally, one comes to the government or political regime as the expression of dominant forces in the society or of a compromise between different forces, expected to convert into reality the ideal attributes of the state and harness the public sector institutions for this purpose. Many studies have demonstrated how governments are constrained in these tasks by the traits of the state apparatus, the nature of political support or resistances from within the societies, and their own ideologically biased visions of reality. 'Expert' advice on what must be done invariably exceeds the political leadership's ability to digest, select and act on it.

The chief of state or national executive has been the conventional target for such advice, the modern successor of Machiavelli's Prince. A good deal of socio-political discourse has addressed the problem of how to give him advice he can use, on the supposition that he is playing a difficult game with limited 'political resources' and inadequate information. In practice, the Prince may turn out to be elusive, even in authoritarian settings. His formal representation decides very little and absorbs hardly any of the advice showered on him; the real sources of decisions are dispersed and hidden.

Democratic leadership, in particular, must continually try to balance contradictory principles for action: to feel and inspire confidence in the correctness of its policies while remaining open to criticism; to seek policy consistency while being prepared to compromise so as to broaden political support; and to undertake urgently needed and controversial actions while respecting rules of the game that enable adversaries to block or distort such actions. If the political leadership accepts the full implications of pluralist democracy it must also accept permanent uncertainty as to the outcome of its policies and their endorsement by the society.[2]

At present, the contradiction betwen political conformism or realism in the sense of recognition of narrow constraints on governmental action, on the one hand, and apprehension that major changes in economic and social policy and the role of the state cannot be evaded, on the other, is particularly acute. A number of object lessons throughout the world demonstrate the depths of economic chaos and political ungovernability to which countries can fall either through evasion of choices or through voluntarist strategies that disregard limited control of relevant factors.

## National situations: a sketch of relevant factors

Political structures and development policies have not depended in any direct or consistent fashion on national historical experience, the geographic or demographic setting or the economic structure. The correspondences that might be expected in more slowly and autonomously evolving situations have been blurred by the processes of transplantation and adaptation of or resistance to dominant world patterns. The recent apparent triumph of economic and cultural globalization, market doctrines and democratic principles has not brought correspondences any closer. Nevertheless, the above factors do impose certain limitations and imply differing potentialities for the nation-states and states supposed to be on their way to nationhood. The present chapter is only peripherally concerned with these questions, and it would be beyond its scope to set up a typology, but a brief summary of factors that differentiate or establish similarities between the countries that have been successively labelled 'underdeveloped', 'developing', 'Third World', and 'South' may be helpful.

*Historical*

The countries in question include:

— Countries that attained formal independence in the early nineteenth century after a long period of colonial rule by European powers, in which a relatively protracted process of national self-identification and adaptation of imported political institutions has led to systems with some degree of internal consistency, however wide the gap between their formal character and their real functioning. This group includes most of the Latin American countries.

— Countries with a long independent history, never subjected to colonial rule except for brief periods of military occupation, in which traditional monarchical political institutions have gradually adapted to the circumstances of incorporation into the world system. In a few countries in Africa, Asia and the Middle East ( Jordan, Morocco, Saudi Arabia, Thailand), the adaptations have thus far preserved the institutions. In other countries (Cambodia, Ethiopia, Iran, Yemen), similar monarchies came to violent ends despite or because of their modernizing tactics.

— Countries with long histories as centres of advanced culture and of organization as states or empires (usually not corresponding to present boundaries), subject to colonial domination since the eighteenth or nineteenth centuries, independent since the 1940s or 1950s, after protracted struggles of nationalist self-assertion. Such countries account for the greater part of southern Asia and parts of Africa and the Middle East. Here monarchical institutions disappeared or were reduced to figurehead functions under colonial rule. China, in spite of its formal independence and unique historical upheavals, has some affinity with this group.

— Countries originating in colonial territories embracing peoples without previous political or cultural ties, or peoples introduced by the colonial power as a labour force, newly independent since the 1950s or 1960s. Such countries embrace the greater part of Africa, the Caribbean, and parts of the Pacific island region.

If the objective of 'nation-building' is accepted as a requisite for development, it is obvious that the different groups of countries have faced quite different tasks. In the first three groups the objective might be posed as 'nation-changing', or the transformation of pre-existing social and political structures so that the masses of the population might become active participants rather than passive subjects. In the last group, the 'building' of nations had to be undertaken in circumstances without historical precedent; the masses of the population were already involved to some degree in political processes, but 'national' boundaries were largely arbitrary and group identifications depended on language, religion, tribe or clan rather than on the new states. State institutions were borrowings from the former colonial administrations or the new system of inter-governmental organizations. Potentially unifying ideologies (pluralist demo-cracy, nationalism, developmentalism, Marxism) had to be imposed on recalcitrant realities and introduced new sources of conflict.

The identification of 'state' and 'nation' generated new versions of contradictions that had been notorious in Europe since the nineteenth century, when the great multinational empires began to disintegrate and doctrines arguing for 'national communities' defined by common culture and historical traditions clashed with doctrines arguing for equal citizenship rights for all residents of territorially defined states. These contradictions grew in complexity with the increase in the number of cases in which statehood preceded a sense of common identity and with the worldwide diffusion of ethnic self-assertiveness that accompanied the universalization of the system of independent states. The broadening of the responsibilities of the modern state disseminated through the world system generated the potential for discrimination between groups in distribution of services, in access to public and private employment, and in access to political power. Policies aimed at cultural integration or obligatory use of a 'national' language, whether through deliberate imposition by a dominant group or through the universalized character of norms and activities of the welfare state, the development state or the socialist state, had consequences quite different from their intentions, even when the latter were benign. Out-comes have ranged from state-negotiated pacts guaranteeing group rights to intransigent ethnic separatisms that have practically disintegrated some states.

### Geographic–demographic and economic

For present purposes these factors can best be treated in conjunction. The countries in question include:

— Countries with densely settled peasant populations (although usually also with internal regions that are sparsely occupied), with rates of population increase not exceptionally high but formidable in terms of the huge absolute increases they imply, the declining capacity of peasant agriculture to absorb more people, and the scarcity of capital and other requisites for absorption of labour in modern non-agricultural activities. The urban population and the labour force employed in modern pro-ductive sectors may be of considerable size in absolute terms and in comparison with the other types of country to be described below, but comprise relatively small fractions of the national population. This pattern is found mainly in Asia.
— Countries with moderate to low population density, with very uneven

spatial distribution of population and very high rates of population increase. The relationships of the rural population to the land are diverse, but the importance of modern agroenterprises and of wage labour in comparison with traditional forms of smallholding peasant cultivation or semi-servile labour relationships is greater than in the first group. Much of the rural population is spatially mobile, responsive to migration stimuli. The urban share of the population is high and rapidly growing, with much of the growth concentrated in the largest cities. Industrialization has been substantial, with many vicissitudes and shifts, particularly since the 1980s, from tariff-protected production for the domestic market to production for export. 'Modern' economic activities and the public sector itself have supported the growth of large urban middle strata, but the supply of labour has risen faster than demand. Incomes and wealth as well as political power in this group of countries have long been highly concentrated and this trait has become more pronounced in recent years. The pattern is found mainly in Latin America and in a few countries of Asia.

— Countries with very unevenly distributed populations, until recently sparse and predominantly rural, but growing and urbanizing rapidly. The economies have become highly dependent on specialized exploitation and export of minerals. These have provided abundant funds for the public sector, permitting a rapid expansion of services and infrastructural investments. The native-born population has benefited from income subsidies and access to services, but contracted professionals and workers from poorer countries have provided most of the labour force both for mineral extraction and the newer services. This pattern is found mainly in the Middle East.

— Countries with sparse and unevenly distributed rural population, little urbanization, moderate rates of population growth deriving from continuing combinations of high fertility and high mortality, traditional forms of peasant smallholding predominant as sources of livelihood, with little production for the market until recently except in zones of plantations or modernized peasant agriculture. In some national situations approximating to this type, the main source of cash income consists of remittances from migrants working abroad. Capacity to support a modern state apparatus and services is correspondingly limited. Governments have tried to overcome this limitation by forcing peasant agriculture to concentrate on export crops, by monopolizing marketing and by controlling remittances from migrant workers. Such policies have generally proved self-defeating by generating disincentives to production, tactics to evade inefficient and corrupt administrative structures, and alienation of the people affected from states perceived as merely exploitative. This pattern is found mainly in Africa.

— Territorially small countries, mainly islands, with densely settled and

rapidly growing populations, largely dependent on wage labour. Plantation agriculture specializing in tropical export crops has dominated the
economy except in a few cases in which mineral exploitation or tourism
has recently come to the fore. In most of these countries the population
is divided ethnically between peoples introduced as a plantation labour
force during the colonial period, or between such groups and an
indigenous people. Different groups have come to dominate certain
occupational sectors, with endemic conflicts over status and access to
the state apparatus. Open unemployment is high unless relieved by
emigration. This pattern is found mainly in the Caribbean, Pacific and
Indian Ocean regions.

— Countries with a concentrated and modernized urban majority, with
moderate overall population growth rates, with considerable industry
and some highly productive zones of commercial agriculture or cattle-
raising, with other rural zones constituting impoverished and economically stagnant reservoirs of peasant smallholders or traditional large
estates. Modern urban occupational sectors predominate in the labour
force and in production, but with production and employment growth
both slow and irregular. A few countries in Latin America approximate
to this pattern.

— Territorially small and highly urbanized countries with moderate population growth, dependent on specialized roles within the international
system, as centres of commerce, financial transactions, light industry
and tourism. A few countries in Southeast Asia, the Caribbean and the
Middle East have achieved such specialized roles, and a few ministates
have become even more specialized as tax havens and bases enabling
international financial transactions to escape national controls.

The above listing does not exhaust the combinations to be found in
reality and, except for territorial size, none of the distinguishing factors is
static. Countries approximating all of the patterns have been entering into
crises through the combined impact of economic globalization, affording
new roles for some countries and excluding others altogether; the world
revolution in informational techniques and consumption stimuli; population
increases; the efforts of many kinds of international organizations and
currents of opinion to impose global norms; and the heterogeneous
reactions and survival strategies of their peoples.

## Social classes, elites, distribution of power

Economic and political analysts have commonly assumed that 'nation-
building', 'modernization', 'industrialization' or 'development' would be
accompanied by — or would depend upon — the emergence of social class
structures similar to those of the countries previously 'developed' or

industrialized, with the classes playing equivalent roles. This supposition had numerous Marxian as well as non-Marxian variants, associated itself with many attempts to identify strategic elites capable of bringing about the transformation of the societies and the economies, and naturally influenced the strategies of political movements aspiring to represent such vanguards.

Trends in the countries euphemistically labelled 'developing' provided some supporting evidence for these hypotheses, but it is evident by now that the interaction between pre-existing structures and the external as well as internal economic, technological, cultural and ideological forces working for change meant that the forms of consciousness and real developmental roles of different classes and elites could not safely be deduced from the past of other countries.

The following societal actors can be identified in most of the countries in question. Their specific characteristics and relative importance, of course, vary widely, and in present national settings some of them may have been removed from the scene in the course of recent political and economic struggles.

### Elite groups and classes

Generally a small, privileged, relatively well educated elite can be distinguished that has 'represented' its country in relations with the rest of the world. More often than not, such elites have derived their position from land ownership and have been largely hereditary, although some have been more fluid and open to new recruits than others. In some cases, thay have been recruited in part from newer commercial–entrepreneurial interests, and in some of the more recently independent countries their position has been based almost entirely on first-generation political–bureaucratic and military roles, with access obtained through the educational system of the former colonial administration.

Whatever the origin of these elites, they have had in common a predominantly urban–cosmopolitan outlook, a reliance on manipulation of the state machinery for enhancement of privileges and income (whether as political leaders and administrators or as landowners and businessmen relying on favourable credit and price policies) and a reliance on higher education as a means of passing on privileged status to the next generation.

In a good many countries, such elites have been dislodged from positions of power in the course of political upheavals, but not from their role as models for cultural and consumption patterns. They have often salvaged a measure of influence, after the deterioration of their previous political and economic base, by associating themselves, as bureaucrats and diplomats, with military regimes or, as managers and professionals, with transnational enterprises. Whatever their importance in the power structure, they have rarely constituted a unified force. In a good many countries, in fact, national politics has been structured around conflicts between rival elite factions and families. At the same time, members of elites have acted as spokesmen and introducers from abroad of a wide range of ideologies. Descendants of privileged families have sometimes become protagonists of revolution.

Secondary elites, predominantly rural and local in their interests, can also be distinguished, particularly in the countries in which traditional forms of land tenure and local power structures have persisted. Depending on local circumstances, such an elite can derive its position from land ownership, money-lending and commerce, hereditary chieftainship, or extra-legal political domination fostered or tolerated by the central authorities as a means of local control.

Such local elites have shown considerable resilience in coping with economic and political change; even when they are weakened or destroyed or when their descendants shift to the urban–national scene and to higher education as a channel for status advancement, new claimants emerge to play roughly similar roles.

Industrial–financial–commercial entrepreneurial elites attained consider-able importance in some of the larger countries, but for the most part did not assume the strategic roles expected of them on the analogy of the European and North American experience. In most countries such elites remained dependent either on special protection from the state or on association with foreign enterprises. Whether these entrepreneurs emerged mainly from a pre-existing landowning commercial upper class or from immigrants and cultural minorities, they usually had neither the disposition nor the ability to assume political leadership in bringing about the structural reforms prescribed by developmentalists and Marxists to make the societies fully compatible with dynamic industrial development along 'national capitalist' lines.

For many reasons, bureaucratic and military elites, deriving their roles directly from the state, assumed an importance rarely held by their counter-parts in those countries taken as models. In some cases, as indicated above, such elites came to the fore simultaneously with national independ-ence, in the absence of serious internal competitors. In many others, the relative weakness, conservatism or dependence on external interests of the other elite groups, and the inability of national political processes to derive viable development strategies from the struggles of the many groups contending for a share in power, impelled the state technobureaucracy and the military, imbued with international development ideologies and a sense of urgency, to take the lead.

## The military

The upper ranks of the armed forces and police have constituted a distinct type of elite and a distinct channel for upward mobility from the middle strata. A monopoly of the legitimate use of force has been one of the central attributes of the modern state. The armed forces and police through which this monopoly has been exercised have acquired their own institutionalized conceptions of national security and social order, largely through emulation or direct indoctrination from their counterparts in the opposing camps of the Cold War, and earlier in the contending powers of Europe. Their propensity to impose these conceptions on the state and the civil society, or to advance their material interests under cover of these conceptions, is notorious. Where the legitimacy and representativeness of states have been weak and contested by ideological, ethnic or religious sectarian forces, the role of the military has ranged from a veto power over governmental decision-making to assertion of a 'right to rescue the nation from the politicians' through coups. More recently, military claims to a right to take over the state in the name of security, honesty and efficiency have lost plausibility from repeated demonstrations that military regimes in general are no more capable of managing coherent development policies or free from corruption than civilian governments. Military domination of states today usually signifies opportunistic defence of special privileges or defence of a precarious status quo threatened by separatisms or popular resistance to impoverishment.

In a good many of the states in which pluralist democracy has reasserted itself, the armed forces and particularly the police coexist uneasily with civilian regimes and public opinion that resent their impunity for past uses of their monopoly of the 'legitimate' use of force, and their links with certain interests and ideologies in internal struggles. They face popularly supported efforts by governments to reduce their claims on public resources. However, when military forces are reduced or purged without satisfactory alternatives for ex-soldiers, the outcome, depending on the national situation, may be an unsettling augmentation of armed factions, private security guards or banditry.

## The middle strata

The social structures of most 'developing' countries no longer consist of a tiny 'upper class' confronting a very large and mainly rural 'lower class', as earlier stereotypes had it. Intermediate strata have grown and diversified until they are, in at least some respects (recruitment to positions of power, control of major political movements), dominant. In almost all of these countries, however, the 'middle strata' remain minorities (sometimes very small minorities) and have not achieved sufficient homogeneity of characteristics and interests to entitle them to the label of 'class'. The key differences between them and the middle classes in the past of the countries that are now industrialized or 'developed' seem to be the following: first, the much greater importance of the role of formal education in giving access to middle (as well as upper) status; second, the much greater importance of salaried employment, particularly in the public sector, in relation to self-employment in the professions or in small businesses; third, the presence of the 'demonstration effect' from the high-income countries continually tending to stretch consumption aspirations beyond income capacity.

Independent, frugal, entrepreneurially minded middle groups can still be identified, and some of them are coping resiliently with economic globalization and other challenges. However, many factors in the situations in which they have found themselves − technological dependency, the dominance of large-scale enterprises, the bureaucratization of the rules of the game − have generally restricted them to secondary roles in economic evolution. Their educational aspirations for their children have been likely to divert most of these into bureaucratic or professional occupations. Moreover, in many cases, they have belonged to cultural minorities or alien immigrant groups encountering resistance once they become economically conspicuous.

In fact, the characteristics and roles of the middle strata in the countries here considered have been influenced in so many ways by trends among their counterparts in the high-income countries that it would be absurd to expect them to resemble the middle classes of the past of these countries. In the high-income countries also, the salaried middle groups have steadily gained in importance at the expense of the self-employed; the economic relevance of small entrepreneurs has dwindled; the importance of formal educational qualifications has risen concomitantly; and pressures to consume rather than invest have become steadily more elaborate and insistent.

The growth of the middle strata in countries at much lower income levels has been associated, at one and the same time, with the building up of a stock of indispensable human resources, in terms of formal qualifications and capacity to exercise informed leadership, and with disinvestment and instability. Once educational expansion at secondary and higher levels has acquired a certain momentum, it has become increasingly difficult for the economy to support the expected income and status rewards for such education, and increasingly difficult for the political leadership to confront the demand for ever more education of the same kind.

The usual consequence has been the intensification of two kinds of social struggle: first, a struggle between different groups, cliques and individual families to improve the differential educational advantages of their children and to safeguard preferential access to certain sources of income and status; and, second, a struggle against the existing political and economic order as incapable of meeting such demands, or, more radically, a rejection of the demands themselves as incompatible with social justice. The former kind of struggle has been more characteristic of adults in the middle strata, the latter of the educated youth not yet incorporated into the occupational structure, along with a good many academics and intellectuals.

The contradictory roles and attitudes of the middle strata have been particularly evident in the bureaucracies. The characteristics of national bureaucracies differ in many ways, depending on their origins in colonial civil services, revolutionary nationalist movements, or national adaptations of nineteenth-century European administrative structures, but their evolution shows a number of common traits.

On the one hand, a higher technocratically minded bureaucracy has taken shape, aspiring to direct the development process, claiming appropriate rewards for doing so, and attracting the more capable educated youth of the middle strata. The inter-governmental organizations and international voluntary organizations, along with academic and research institutions in the central countries, have become increasingly important for these groups, in inculcating common norms, offering advanced training and providing employment refuges from national vicissitudes.

On the other hand, the combination of continually diversifying state responsibilities and expanding educational output has generated an enormous lower bureaucracy, preoccupied with job security and status, averse to initiative, vulnerable to petty corruption, inclined to conservatism and acceptance of prevailing values like the lower middle strata in general but chronically dissatisfied with the inability of the system to satisfy status and security aspirations.

### Wage workers in 'modern' economic activities

Most of the countries in question had by the 1970s acquired a range of economic enterprises – in mining, petroleum production, transport and power generation, as well as manufacturing industries – that required a skilled and dependable labour force and that had the capacity to pay wages far above the national average. Even with such wages, wage costs might represent only a small part of their costs of operation. The same countries had usually acquired larger numbers of enterprises at intermediate technological productivity levels, comparable to those of the industrialized countries several decades previously; import-substitution policies stimulated the growth of these and assured their survival.

In both types of enterprise a working class took shape that adopted patterns of trade union organization and frequently socialist political orientations similar to those of working classes in the industrialized countries. The leaders and ideologists engaged in continuing interchanges of influence with the union movements and socialist or Marxist political parties of the latter countries. Except in a few of the most urbanized 'newly industrializing countries', this wage-working class constituted only a very small part of the economically active population. Its concentration and organization gave it a strategic importance out of proportion to its numbers. Capitalist–developmentalist and Marxist visions of the future both supported expectations that this importance would continue to increase.

For some time, the fact that the modern industries and other high-productivity employers of labour were either publicly financed or dependent on governmental export–import policies and labour protection policies meant that influence with the state was more important to the organized labour movement than its strength *vis-à-vis* the employers. Employers and workers could find common ground in exerting pressures on the state.

Since the 1970s, expectations and realities have undergone traumatic changes. The discrediting of 'real socialist' models and Marxist doctrines of the vanguard role of the proletariat deprived working-class organizations of an important source of self-confidence as well as a source of illusions, sectarian conflicts and tactical blunders. The abandonment of import-substitution policies along with technological and market changes, particularly in mining, sharply reduced the numbers employed in the most strongly organized sectors and crippled the capacity of the remainder to defend wage levels and other demands. Governments lost much of their capacity to offer significant concessions to organized labour and, under pressure from the international lending agencies, began to shift their social preoccupations to the unorganized poor. In many countries military–authoritarian regimes dealt blows to unions and related political movements from which they could recover only partially, even under subsequent political democratization.

Finally, the processes of economic globalization, the so-called information revolution, and associated phenomena are introducing new challenges (along with apocalyptic visions); some (automation, robotization, computerization) practically divorcing production from labour input; others continually transforming the qualifications required for employment.[3] Labour unions and political organizations in a good many countries have been experiencing some success in organizing new clienteles, advancing broad social demands and recovering their ability to function as inter-locutors of the state, but they must at the same time cope with the above challenges without guidance from their previous ideologies.

The workers described above have coexisted with much larger numbers of workers in small labour-intensive enterprises and of self-employed artisans. These have predominated in food processing, tailoring, manufacture of furniture and domestic utensils, repair of automotive and electrical equipment, and many other activities. Urban public transport and freight trucking have also commonly been, at least partially, in the hands of many small enterprises and individual operators.

As the modernization of the cities has proceeded, some of these activities have declined in relative importance and ability to compete with larger establishments, while others (particularly repair and servicing of equipment) have risen. Even among the more traditional handicraft activities, while some lines of production have suffered, other lines have found new and more lucrative markets among tourists. A good many such activities, with little capital and antiquated equipment, have been able to survive only by evading the labour regulations that governed larger enterprises.

These workers were, on the one hand, closer in outlook to their employers than workers in large enterprises, and had more hope of becoming employers or independent operators. On the other hand, they were more exposed to job competition from an underemployed marginal labour force, largely of recent migrants. Thus, their attitudes might be expected to show ambivalence and resentment towards the organized workers, towards the more marginal strata, and also towards the state. The small enterprises along with their workers have been able to exert only weak pressures on the state for protection of their immediate interests, and since they produced mainly goods and services for direct consumption by the urban population they were adversely affected by public efforts to control prices and quality. Most of these workers were unorganized, but in a few cases of radical or populist political mobilization, as in Chile during the Popular Unity regime (1970–73), their sudden emergence as political actors with urgent claims upon the state have contributed to impasses and renewed exclusion.

In most countries the above description now applies only to part of a much larger and more varied urban low-income labour force. Probably the most important shift has been the enormous increase in the number of workers producing semi-finished goods, garments, toys, electronic components and many other products for export, generally under contracts between local enterprises and transnational corporations. This has involved the emergence of a mainly female labour force in home piecework and sweatshops. Dividing lines between large modern enterprises and small enterprises have become blurred as the former have more and more contracted out parts of the productive process. Dividing lines between the organized and class-conscious labour force and the remainder have also blurred as many of the former have been forced to accept lower wages and relinquish job security, enter unorganized occupations or depend on earnings of wives and children in such occupations.

## *Peasants and rural workers*[4]

When the present-day system of independent states linked by international norm-setting organizations took shape during the late 1940s and the aspiration to 'development' began to become explicit, the large majority of the population in most of the newer and poorer states was rural–agricultural. In fact, the relative size of the rural population came to be used as a rough indicator of 'underdevelopment'. Oppressed peasant majorities were also looked on, whether with fear or hope, as potential sources of revolutionary upheavals opening the way to different, more egalitarian or communitarian styles of development. Mexico and China seemed to point the way. At the same time, a number of governments, that of India in particular, began to devote significant resources to rural 'community development' schemes designed to modernize and raise the productivity of peasants without such upheavals, through technically enlightened guidance to their supposed traditional community organizations.

Since then, rural populations have transformed themselves in ways too diverse to be detailed here, sometimes seeming to justify the revolutionary or communitarian expectations, but more often at cross purposes with their political and social interlocutors in the national societies, trying to defend themselves against 'development' or escape from rural poverty and insecurity. In most countries, the rural population, although more slowly and irregularly than the urban, became increasingly conscious of the state as a source of services, particularly schools and clinics, and of protection against arbitrary violence from local power-holders. Possibilities for exerting pressure for favourable state responses to needs emerged, and in some cases, as in Bolivia and Mexico, the state was able to enlist peasant movements as sources of support and counterweights to urban working-class movements. State policies for extracting a surplus from rural producers to support industrialization, military forces and urban construction, however, continually clashed with these possibilities. So did the clientelistic channels through which the state usually responded to local demands, and the arbitrary or extortionate behaviour of local agents of the state.

Recent trends in relations between rural people and the state have been contradictory. Processes of democratization, competition for rural votes, and the penetration of mass communications have afforded some rural people a more effective voice in national policies. The shrinkage of state resources associated with economic crises and structural adjustment policies have left rural schools and other services even more poorly supported than before, and may have made local functionaries more corrupt. At the same time, policies of targeting social allocations to the poor may have done something to offset this deterioration. The collapse of state marketing monopolies and dictation of crops to be planted has relieved some peasant groups of onerous burdens. Externally financed voluntary organizations that mingle participatory principles with paternalistic principles have increasingly aspired to replace the state as shapers of rural development. Finally, in a good many rural areas state authority has broken down almost altogether through conflict between ethnic or religious factions among rural people, conflict between peasants and armed henchmen of landowners, or competitive terrorization by armed forces and police, guerrilla movements and drug traffickers, leading to mass flight from the land.

The most common element in rural change has been steady population increase and rising geographical mobility, interacting with agricultural modernization and exposure to world markets. One well-known consequence has been massive migration to the cities and even abroad, converting the rural population into a shrinking minority within an ever-growing national population (particularly in Latin America), generating complex links between the 'urban' and the 'rural', and leaving many rural communities alternatively dependent on remittances from migrants and serving as refuges for migrants expelled from urban livelihood. Another consequence has been the replacement of traditional large landholdings, worked by various kinds of semi-servile arrangements, by modern agribusinesses and by modernized peasant holdings worked by a small stable labour force and a much larger seasonal labour force, partly provided by cultivators of dwarf holdings, partly by a landless floating population. Still another consequence is the competitive penetration of large agro-enterprises, loggers, mining prospectors, peasant settlers, and sometimes 'ecotourist' enterprises, into zones previously thinly occupied by indigenous peoples, leading to environmental devastation as well as endemic conflicts over land and other resources. State activities are influential in this penetration, through road building and incentives for settlement, but changing priorities exacerbate conflicts and controls are sporadic and ineffectual.

### Marginalization and social exclusion

The above summaries suggest that economic growth and societal change have failed to make room for large parts of the population that have been irreversibly drawn into these processes. Controversies over the extent and future implications of this failure have continued since the 1960s. In very simplified terms, two main interpretations, each with many variants, can be distinguished.

First, the phenomena of mass poverty, underemployment, underutilization of human resources and incapacity to participate meaningfully in the social order are unavoidable concomitants of stages in the development process that can be superseded, or they are remediable consequences of certain distortions and inefficiencies in the process. These can be overcome by speeding up the rate of economic growth, by depressing the rate of population growth, by expanding and reforming education, by controlling the 'demonstration effect' and slowing down urbanization, and so on.

Second, these phenomena are generated by the nature of present patterns of dependent capitalist development and will continue to grow, whatever the rate of economic growth or the rate of population growth, until the current style of development and the power structures determining it change radically.

In the earlier stages of discourse on development the 'commitment' of people from peasant societies to wage work in industry and other 'modern' activities was commonly singled out as a central problem. It was assumed that the demand for wage labour would continue to exceed supply until a late stage of 'development', and that the supply would be insufficiently committed and of low productivity, owing to lack of appropriate work habits, lack of education, poor physical conditions and various cultural traits, summed up in one version as absence of 'achievement motivation'. Colonial powers and national oligarchies devised various forms of compulsion, such as head taxes and vagrancy laws, to force reluctant peasants or tribesmen to work for hire. At later stages, with substantial urban and plantation wage labour forces already in being, positive inducements came to the fore: education, subsidized food supplies, social welfare and housing schemes linked to industrial employment. Observers who placed themselves on the side of the groups that were being expelled or lured from previous forms of livelihood and incorporated under conditions of exploitation, insecurity and impoverishment into ways of life functional to the 'development process' then focused attention on the terms of their incorporation and on their capacity to influence these terms through organized efforts.[5]

The question of terms of incorporation remains relevant, but the prospect is emerging more clearly that no 'development process' now in sight will incorporate millions of the people now excluded. As one observer summed up this prospect: instead of Marx's 'spectre of the proletariat', the end of the twentieth century is haunted by the 'spectre of superfluous man'.[6] The final chapter of the present text will return to this prospect.

### Youth

The populations concerned are predominantly young, even where a demographic transition to lower fertility rates balancing reduced mortality rates is under way, and high proportions are in the stages of transition from childhood to adulthood. Under present circumstances one might expect the symptoms of disorientation and exclusion to be particularly acute among these groups, with quite different manifestations according to class and urban or rural setting, but linked by some features of a global youth culture and consumer culture and the inability of the preceding generation to offer applicable role models. (In a good many countries, one of the more paradoxical aspects of the present is the survival of an aged political leadership for decades after the upheavals that brought it to power have passed into history and while a population majority born since those upheavals confronts a very different world.)

At least until recently, formal educational qualifications were rising steadily, particularly for youth from the urban middle strata, but in many countries children of working-class and peasant families were gaining access to free public universities. They expected this access to convey concrete advantages in higher social status and access to public and private white-collar employment. Now access has become more restricted while the expected rewards have become illusory. The dominant style of development calls for technological and managerial qualifications that are much more expensive to acquire and the future demand for which may shift unpredictably.

During earlier periods, university-age youth could look to inspiring political visions of the national future and their role in it. While for the most part only minorities of such youth actually mobilized behind the visions, and these became entangled with narrow interest-group demands, the students sometimes became protagonists in national political change. Now political and economic doctrines are less able to offer inspiring explanations of the situations in which the youth find themselves, except, in some cases, for doctrines of extreme nationalism and religious fundamentalism. Educated youth are from time to time in the forefront of mass mobilizations against dictatorships, but once the dictatorship has been replaced by pluralist democracy with its typical constraints the mobilizations fade away.

For youth in general, recent evidence, mainly anecdotal and focused on extremes, does not support generalization. It is evident that some young people are obsessed by artefacts of the competitive consumer culture and that others are obsessed by the potential of computers and the information revolution. It is evident that many show great ingenuity and industry in finding sources of livelihood, licit or otherwise, and in contributing to the subsistence of their families. It is evident that many, in the face of family disintegration and social exclusion, turn to violent gangs for status and companionship.

## Unifying policy conceptions[7]

Long before the recent decades of explosive expansion in numbers of formally independent states and of universal endorsement of 'development' as a central justification for state activities, rulers, dominant classes, intellectuals and political movements were trying to answer the question: what should the state do (or refrain from doing) to promote national power and prosperity? Or (in the case of colonies) to increase their value to the administering power? Or (in the case of countries threatened by imperialist aggression) to safeguard national political and economic autonomy?

During the nineteenth and early twentieth centuries, the political leadership in a good many low-income, 'traditional', predominantly agricultural countries formulated coherent and fairly comprehensive 'development' objectives and policies. The stimulus to the formulation of such policies came from the industrialization and territorial and commercial expansion of the European and North American states. All societies in the rest of the world that had not already fallen under colonial rule faced the challenge of entering the new international network of trade and political relationships without becoming helplessly dependent. In trying to face this challenge, they naturally borrowed ideologies and prescriptions from the world centres and sought to adapt them to their own needs. In at least one case, Japan, the effort succeeded. More often, it led to loss of autonomy through debt traps, as in Egypt, or to prolonged internal conflict through societal resistance to the consequences of modernization imposed from above, as in Mexico.

Most of the earlier policy conceptions are still current, in one form or another, and many new ones have appeared. Researches and polemics have enriched the conceptual bases for alternative development policies and have helped to clarify the range of choices. It is hardly surprising, however, that the conceptions influencing policy or presented as justifications for policy show unresolved contradictions or incongruities with national situations. Nineteenth-century doctrines on the responsibilities of the state coexist uneasily with newer ones, and neither the older nor the newer conceptions correspond to the ways in which most states actually function.

Guiding national policy formulations generally consist of 'packages' whose components have different sources and justifications, different degrees of importance in the eyes of the various participants in the political process, and different degrees of congruence with one another. The main conceptions that combine with or combat each other in the formulation of objectives for the state and other social actors are summarized below. Some of these conceptions entered into the quest for a unified approach and are discussed in more detail in Chapter 2. (Their claims for explicativeness and applicability are, of course, at quite different levels, and the amount of space devoted to them does not necessarily correspond to their relative prominence.)

1. *Nationalism*: affirmation of the enhanced power of the nation-state as a central value and objective; insistence on the nation-state as final arbiter and focus for allegiance; reliance on national symbols and traditions for the mobilization of popular support for development objectives. As was indicated above, different variants of nationalism or 'nation-building'

have entered to some degree into the packages of conceptions that have governed development policy in practically all countries and have clashed violently both with the realities of global interdependence and with the realities of ethnic and other divisions within state boundaries.

2. *Neo-traditionalism*: attribution of high importance to the preservation of existing values, cultural traits, family and community ties, and power relationships, in the course of controlled modernization. While traditionalism by itself would be simply a defensive and static ideology, having no place among the conceptions here discussed, neo-traditionalism is often wedded to other policy focuses as a means rather than an end.

It may be assumed, for example, that development depends on the undisturbed opportunities for enrichment of an economic elite, that the greater part of the population cannot be incorporated into the development process in the short term, and that continued allegiance to traditional values and power structures is essential to keep this majority from disrupting the process. For this purpose, if authentic traditions do not serve, neo-traditionalism can represent a deliberate tactic to invent or revive from the historical past traditions suiting the need.

3. *Modernism and indigenism*: both of these diametrically opposed approaches are found in association with nationalism. Modernism calls for the systematic adoption of the institutions, cultural traits and material attributes of the industrialized countries as a means of competing with them. In some countries in the past, this approach has gone to the extreme of prohibiting traditional costumes and prescribing European styles of clothing. Indigenism constitutes a systematic rejection of such borrowing and a determination to adapt indigenous institutions and lifestyles for a similar end of national autonomy. Both approaches differ from traditionalism or simple imitativeness in that they conceive of the transplanted or indigenous as means to a nationalist, autonomous style of development.

Both have been influenced by social sciences originating in the industrialized countries: indigenism by anthropology with its insistence on the dangers of disrupting unique cultures and the right of such cultures to respect and freedom in developing their own potentials; modernism by sociology and social psychology with their insistence that 'development' requires certain definable changes in values, motivations, forms of social mobility, family structures and so on in order to make them compatible with a societal model featuring continuing absorption of innovations. Some versions of modernism have a socio-psychological emphasis on the role of child-rearing practices in 'achievement motivation'. Others are more concerned with institutions and the opening of institutionalized stimuli towards mobility, entrepreneurship and innovation. Earlier versions of modernism and indigenism have been overtaken by the advances of the global economy and consumer culture, but the conceptions reappear in the clash of positive and negative evaluations of these advances.

4. *Dualism*: 'dualistic' conceptions have focused on the obvious fact that some components of societies and economies have modernized rapidly, while others have seemed to be lagging or static. The term 'dualism' has been used with differing connotations by analysts of development, but for present purposes it has meant that the typical 'developing' country contains two quite different societies and economies, with only limited intercommunication: one modern, innovative, reasonably productive, governed by market incentives, in close contact with the world centres, predominantly urban; the other, traditional, resistant to change, low in productivity, participating little in market relationships, predominantly rural, physically and psychologically isolated from the modern world. With such a picture in mind, a Brazilian economist labelled his country 'Belindia', as containing within its boundaries a population at the economic and social level of Belgium and another at the level of India.

Dualistic conceptions have carried the implication that the main task for development policy is to break down the isolation and raise the productivity of the traditional sector, expanding the modern sector at its expense, until all of it is absorbed into the modern sector. More complex interpretations of 'structural heterogeneity' gradually replaced such simple versions. The idea of a 'traditional sector' needing to be modernized has given way to emphasis on global patterns making for marginalization, exclusion or superfluity of people no longer traditional but in some respects even farther than before from productive incorporation into a 'development process'.

5. *Populism*: this term has been used to identify certain types of political movement as well as the ideas, not necessarily explicit or coherent, that are common to such movements. The ideas, in fact, are rationalizations for certain approaches to the conquest of political power more than conceptions of development, although they have usually posed 'development' as a central objective. They include affirmation of support by the masses of the population, achieved by responses to their felt needs and visions of social justice, as the source of political legitimacy; rejection of tutelage by elites, combined with faith in the ability of a charismatic leader to solve all problems; explicit or implicit acceptance of the compatibility of immediate redistributionist measures with preservation of the main features of existing political structures and systems of production and property ownership.

Populist approaches have typically included in the 'people' all social classes and interest groups with the exception of certain 'oligarchs' and 'exploiters', preferably aliens, against whom the people is to be mobilized. In national situations in which the state has had at its disposal relatively ample resources, populist approaches have been combined with developmentalist or even market-oriented policies. There seems to be no case, however, in which such combinations have proved viable for long. By now, 'populist' has become a term of abuse aimed at regimes whose tactics are judged incompatible with pluralist democracy, with viable allocations of public resources, or with a realistic appreciation of the limits of state interventions.

6. *Welfare-statism*: this approach, having some affinity with populism, achieved a good deal of formal influence, particularly at the level of international and national policy declarations, but reached an impasse with the crises of the 1980s. It concentrated attention on the elaboration and embodiment in legislation and public institutions of universal rights to education, health, social security, employment, minimum level of living and so on. It was assumed either that these rights were applicable irrespective of the level and structure of production and the power relationships in a given society, or that all societies had the obligation to transform themselves so as to convert the rights into realities.

7. *Populationisms*: two opposed points of view have concentrated attention on population growth as a central problem of development: (a) it has been asserted that rapid population growth and larger national populations are essential for the sake of national power, wider internal markets, and more adequate exploitation of the resources of the national territory; (b) the attainment of low rates of population growth has been insisted on as a requisite for full employment, raising of per capita incomes and alleviation of disruptive social tensions. (Other arguments, while attributing less importance to population as a central problem, have turned the above considerations upside down: rapid population growth is then seen as a challenge forcing the society to undertake a more determined development effort and undergo structural reforms, or as a manifestation of contradictions helping towards the destruction of an intolerable economic and social order.)

A positive evaluation of rapid population growth prevailed in most countries up to the 1950s, and still has some influence, particularly in Latin America. The negative view goes back to the arguments of Malthus in the early nineteenth century but exerted hardly any influence on public policies until the last four decades. Since then it has become increasingly dominant, in the midst of continuing controversies as to the importance of population growth *vis-à-vis* other factors, the prospects for spontaneous vs. state-managed demographic transitions, and the legitimacy of state endorsement of contraception and abortion as means of population control.

8. *Messianism and millennialism*: these beliefs, quite different in origins and preconceptions from the others discussed here, can nevertheless be viewed as rational attempts to interpret social change and act on the interpretation for 'developmental' purposes in groups lacking the experience and educational tools needed for a more conventional approach. The beliefs have typically arisen among peasants, tribes recently brought

into oppressive contact with the modern world, and urban or rural marginalized groups faced by deepening insecurity. 'Development', along with the destruction of an unjust social order, has been expected through the miraculous intervention of divinities or ancestors, sometimes to restore a legendary golden age, sometimes, as in the cargo cults of Melanesia, to bestow on the disadvantaged people the wealth and sources of power of the modern world. This result may be sought through spiritual purification or through the performance of rituals or mass acts rejecting the existing order and demonstrating faith in miraculous intervention.

9. *Economic liberalism*: this approach, dominant from the early nineteenth century up to the emergence of a global system of independent states seeking accelerated development in the mid-twentieth century, affirmed the superior efficiency of free markets and private enterprise for the furthering of economic growth and human welfare. It systematically rejected state intervention in economic as well as social life, except for some degree of endorsement of state responsibilities where the market could not be relied on: principally maintenance of public order, infrastructural investment and education. It has notoriously reasserted itself, sometimes in its most doctrinaire variants, with the discrediting of state interventionist policies during the 1970s and 1980s.

10. *Developmentalism*: the conceptions of development now current and their implications for policy were discussed in Chapter 2. The approach here labelled 'developmentalist' represents a distinct family of theories and prescriptions that took shape following the Second World War and that have since undergone continual evolution, broadening and, subsequently, crises of confidence. The distinction between 'developmentalism' and the conceptions next to be discussed lies in its confidence that prevailing patterns of economic growth and economic relationships at the national and international levels are susceptible to planned rationalization and reform, accompanied by major improvements in distribution of wealth, power and participation in the social order, that will not, however, *necessarily* call for basic transformations of societal values, ownership of the means of production, or the nature of the classes dominating the development process.

11. *Communitarianism and socialism based on religious and cultural values*: this family of conceptions has been distinguished by egalitarianism, distrust of centralized state power and rejection of the models for productive organization, bureaucratized social services and conspicuous consumption offered by the high-income industrialized countries. Objectives of industrialization and productivity increases may or may not be considered legitimate, but they are in any case subordinated to values of equity and cooperation. Stimulation of individual entrepreneurship and competititon for material rewards are ruled out as incompatible with the kind of society aspired to.

The strengthening or creation of various kinds of intermediate bodies between the individual and the state, in which citizens can participate directly and autonomously in managing their own affairs, receives high priority. Belief in the viability and desirability of cooperatively organized production and public services under community management is generally buttressed by reference to traits of social cohesion and mutual aid supposed to be present in pre-existing indigenous value systems and social structures.

The basic elements of such approaches can be traced back to utopian social theorists of the nineteenth century and earlier. Influential modern variants have included Gandhism and several versions of 'African socialism'. The conceptions have commonly exerted a subordinate influence on the thinking of political leaders and on some lines of public policy in settings in which they have been quite incongruous with the main directions of economic and social change and with the priorities that might be deduced from public resource allocations. Proponents of the approaches have sometimes been over-eager to find embodiments of their utopias in real national settings, such as China or Tanzania, with subsequent disillusionment. The more recent manifestations of such hopes have centred on the 'new social movements' that will be discussed in Chapter 4.

12. *Neo-Marxism, revolutionary socialism and anti-imperialism*: it is hard to find a satisfactory label for the family of conceptions and policy approaches to be discussed next, because of the polemical uses of the terms available and the multiple meanings assigned to them by different currents of opinion. Their common features include:

— Assessment of development objectives and instruments in relation to determined power structures and class interests, not in terms of abstract desirability.

— Affirmation that prevailing 'dependent capitalist' styles of development, whether or not viable in terms of increasing production, are inherently associated with increasing marginalization and inequality at the national as well as the international level.

— Affirmation that authentic development requires *both* a different combination of objectives *and* a strategy designed for a class or alliance of classes that combines sufficient strength to impose its will with real interests, deriving from its objective situation, in the success of such a strategy.

— Emphasis on the dominant role, in present national processes of growth and change, of international economic and political relationships defined as 'imperialist'.

A number of radically different action strategies for specific national situations have been deduced by political movements and governments from the above general propositions.

*First*, it has been reasoned that all countries must go through a process of industrialization and affirmation of national economic and political autonomy, and must acquire a sizeable industrial proletariat before becoming ripe for socialist transformation. The strengthening of a national bourgeoisie is indispensable for this purpose, even at the cost of extreme social inequalities and a pattern of development that will later have to be shattered and transformed. This reasoning suggests a medium-term strategy almost indistinguishable from developmentalism.

*Second*, it has been reasoned that the modern situation of global financial and technological domination by capitalists of a few countries means that private entrepreneurs elsewhere can expect only a dependent role in the future. Dynamic industrialization can take place only through the efforts of a strong state, able to restrict consumption, maximize saving and investment from domestic sources, particularly from agriculture, and channel such investment into basic industry. 'De-linking' from the global economy and from political ties to the dominant powers may be a requisite for later re-entry on equal terms. These conditions cannot be met without the coming to power of a revolutionary elite able to exert strict control over popular participation so as to reconcile it with investment requirements and the need for disciplined effort.

*Third*, it has been reasoned that national political and economic systems cannot be transformed in the desired directions by either of the first two strategies, nor by relying for leadership in the next stages on bourgeois entrepreneurs, the middle classes or organized industrial workers. Different sources of transformation must be sought in the urban marginalized population, the rural masses or the youth. The mobilization of such collective social actors requires a commitment to raise and equalize rapidly the consumption of the most disadvantaged strata, at the expense of investment if need be, and to meet the most urgent popular demands for land, jobs, housing and so on. This line of reasoning has some affinity with the populist approach, but differs in its emphasis on use of redistributive policies to mobilize support for more far-reaching societal transformation.

*Fourth*, it has been reasoned that the kind of new society wanted requires new motivations, interpersonal relations and forms of participation in the running of the social order. Progress towards these objectives should not be sacrificed to short-term considerations of productive efficiency or political control. Therefore, cooperative organization, workers' management, decentralization and local initiative should be relied on to the maximum extent feasible. All components of the population, including political leaders and professionals, should perform their share of physical labour and undertake socially useful tasks previously of low status. Non-material incentives (creativity, satisfaction in social usefulness and contribution to national aims) should be preferred to material incentives; superfluous private consumption should not be encouraged or used as a stimulus to production. This last line of reasoning, of course, reaches common ground with the conceptions of communitarianism and socialism based on indigenous traditions.

All of these variant approaches to revolutionary socialism are now more or less in eclipse. They have suffered even more than other prescriptions for development from the disillusioning and sometimes horrifying trajectories of regimes that have tried to apply them or that have pretended to do so. However, eclipses by their nature are temporary; new revolutionary challenges trying to absorb the lessons of the past and apply them to the present may already be taking shape.

The various conceptions, approaches and ideological currents summarized above, in their many combinations, underlie national and international policy declarations. Their degree of real influence on what happens, and the degree to which they enter into the survival strategies of the peoples of the world, are other matters, concerning which it is hardly practicable to generalize. Developmental conceptions and ideological appeals interact with and sometimes camouflage interest-group pressures and bargaining, pragmatic or technocratic policy approaches, external dictates and constraints, and voluntarist or opportunist leadership. The contenders in a struggle for power or a charismatic dictator seeking a ready-made justification for his role may take up one conception or another almost arbitrarily.

It has already been emphasized that capabilities for guidance of economic growth and societal change at the national level are circumscribed by pervasive and complex manifestations of world interdependence. This is too obvious to require elaboration and in any case is nothing new. For most of the countries now on the world stage the present external influences and constraints were preceded by even more inhibiting systems of colonial or semi-colonial domination. The contradictory character of the external influences at present and of the internalization of interpretations and ideologies concerning them does deserve some further attention. The countries in question have faced not only an uncontrollable influx of forces from abroad, accelerating with economic globalization and the global information revolution, but also an influx of theories and advice on how to deal with these phenomena, most of the latter based either on the experience of the countries in which the phenomena originated or on standardized and simplified models of 'the developing country'.

The influences and constraints, of course, were never purely external. All of them became internalized in some degree, in that they became identified with the interests and outlooks of domestic classes and interest groups and acted on the national economy and society through them. This has been obvious in the case of ideologies and consumption standards. Contenders for power have relied on identification with certain international commitments and external models for political behaviour. The denationalization of control over the economy has been accompanied by the recruitment of national managers and suppliers who identify themselves with the outlook of their transnational employers. Scholars have identified themselves with and sought the approval of the international academic community. Professionals and technicians have sought training abroad and later internalized foreign standards and preferences for certain lines of work. Scientific researchers have concentrated on problems conferring prestige and likely to attract funding in the world centres. If unable to modify the national environment to suit the external models, members of these groups have been likely to abandon it altogether. The internalization of external influences could be seen even among the social scientists whose task it was to understand and explain the national societies.

At a certain point, as these phenomena became more prominent, 'dependency', often vaguely defined, came to be advanced as an all-sufficient explanation for the shortcomings of national development. Revolutionary denunciations of dependency, however, could serve as rationalizations for passivity and pessimism about national potentialities. It could be assumed that nothing could be done until some international cataclysm removed the weight of external domination. Or that an evolving world system would have to follow its own logic, brushing aside national resistances and quests for alternatives, until it had exhausted its potential and opened the way for genuinely global transformation.

## Notes

1. The bibliography on these questions is, of course, enormous. Recent explorations referring to many others include Hobsbawm, *Nations and Nationalism since 1780* (1991); Skocpol, *States and Social Revolutions* (1979); and Evans et al. (eds), *Bringing the State Back In* (1985).

2. 'Democracy means that all groups must subject their interests to uncertainty. It is this very act of alienation of control over outcomes of conflicts that constitutes the decisive step toward democracy.... If one set of policies is seen as superior for the welfare of the society and this set of policies is assumed to be known, then it seems irrational to introduce uncertainty as to whether this set of policies will be chosen. Even in an economic crisis, when the economic policy of a particular government is recognized to have been mistaken, some other policy always appears to authoritarian bureaucrats as uniquely destined to improve the situation. Recognition of past mistakes does not constitute a demonstration that the authoritarian system is inherently flawed but only that past mistakes must be corrected and a new, proper policy must be followed.' (Przeworski, 'Some Problems in the Study of the Transition to Democracy', in O'Donnell et al. (eds), *Transitions from Authoritarian Rule: Comparative Perspectives* (1986).

3. See, for example, Martin Carnoy et al., *The New Global Economy in the Information Age* (1993); and Drucker, *Post-capitalist Society* (1993).

4. For detailed research findings on some of the questions treated here, see Barraclough, *An End to Hunger?* (1991); and Hewitt de Alcántara (ed.), *Real Markets* (1993).

5. See Chapter 1 in Stiefel and Wolfe, *A Voice for the Excluded* (1994).

6. Intervention by David Apter at UNRISD 30th Anniversary Symposium, July 1993.

7. This term is used here to refer to the whole range of development theories, strategies deriving from them, value systems invoked to justify a given approach to development, and political ideologies.

# CHAPTER 4

# PROBLEMS OF COMMUNICATION AND PARTICIPATION

## Transmission belts and building blocks

Development, however defined, supposes far-reaching changes in the ways in which people relate to each other and to the wider society, represented by the state and many other institutions. Ideally, these changes should be in the direction of a more open, better integrated society, with freer choices for voluntary associational ties and a voice for all in the composition and guidance of local as well as national authorities. The individual and the family become subject to a wider range of obligations to the state and make a wider range of demands on the state for services and protection. Institutional channels are needed, and eventually come into being in response to needs, for an increasingly complex interplay of informing, reasoning, bargaining, pressure, resistance and control between the primary group and the national authorities.

It is obvious that real lines of change have corresponded only in a partial and distorted fashion, if at all, to this ideal picture. Almost everywhere one finds dissatisfaction or alarm at the shortcomings of the transmission belts between the national authorities and the masses of the population, a dissatisfaction that has been most pronounced in the countries whose political leaders have advanced coherent development objectives with a conviction of urgency. At the level of the primary groups one finds, in different national settings or in apparently incongruous combinations within single settings:

— exaggerated faith in the ability of the state to meet group needs;
— pervasive scepticism concerning the good-will and competence of the functionaries who represent the state;
— apathy toward or rejection of the lifestyles and forms of social intercourse that might be expected to contribute to development;
— outbursts of violence, commonly focused on issues that seem irrelevant to the well-being of the people involved;
— narrow concentration on family or group advancement, accompanied by selective appropriation of the services offered by the state, to the neglect of what seem to be minimum requirements of the wider social order.

Attempts at diagnosis and prescription have followed several different directions:

— incompatibility of national and local power structures with more positive participation by the majority of the population;
— incapacity of prevailing lines of economic growth and societal change, with their traits of widening inequalities, exploitation and social exclusion, to open the way to such participation;
— unsuitability of accessible models for institutionalized relationships between local groups and the national centre to the circumstances of the countries that have introduced such models from abroad.
— inability of human beings and their institutions to cope with the continual readjustments called for by technological transformations and the unprecedented widening in range of choice of possible lifestyles, some time ago labelled 'future shock'.[1]

Such diagnoses have been mentioned in different contexts in the preceding chapters, which were mainly concerned with factors bearing on policy at the national level. The present chapter starts with the supposition that national policy is meaningful only to the extent to which it influences and is influenced by what happens within the social units or building blocks of which the society is composed. It will examine the kinds of institutions, organizations and other channels through which communication takes place; then the changing local situations within which it takes place; then the tactics and responses available to the state and the social unit in advancing their respective purposes.

This chapter is concerned with a dichotomy that can be expressed in several ways, each with differing connotations: between the 'national' state and the 'local' group or community; between the 'centre' and the 'periphery'; between power-holders at the national level and the primary groups their power must reach to the extent that it is real.

The dichotomy has a spatial aspect: the state machinery and the power-holders are concentrated in one point of the national territory and the degree of physical remoteness is one factor complicating or weakening their ties with the primary groups. However, cultural distances and forms and degrees of insertion into national systems of production, marketing, employment and communications are more important for present purposes than geographical distance.

On one side of the dichotomy, the following pages focus on situations in which direct interaction between individuals is possible, whether or not it is present, and on the institutions, organizations and informal groupings through which interactions between individuals and the national power centre take place.

These situations and groupings still coincide in large part with geographical localities, but urbanization, increasing spatial mobility of rural as well as urban populations, and the revolution in communication media make the correspondence less and less predictable. The term 'social unit' will be used here, for lack of a better, to avoid over-emphasis on the 'local' dimension of the phenomena under discussion.[2] Throughout, a double perspective will be attempted.

*First*, it will be assumed that everywhere the forces controlling the state, with a greater or lesser degree of coherence and self-awareness, are striving to open and control channels of communication and mobilization and at the same time to weaken or dominate institutions that threaten these purposes or constitute rival claimants to allegiance. It will also be assumed that everywhere this striving is complicated, diverted or paralysed to some degree by the interplay at the national level of different focuses of power or groups able to influence or veto state activities; by the inadequacy of information and understanding within the state concerning real local situations; and by the special characteristics of the bureaucratic agents of the state and other intermediaries (politicians, magnates, leaders of mass organizations) between the state and the social unit.

The national authorities need coherent local institutions and initiatives coming from below as a means of accomplishing objectives that they cannot reach by fiat or by direct allocation of resources; generally they have some awareness of this need. At the same time, they rarely have a clear idea of what can be accomplished in this way and how, and they are inhibited to some extent by apprehension that local initiative will escape from control and present inconvenient demands.

*Second*, it will also be assumed that the members of any social unit, to the extent that they are conscious of a higher power centre impinging on their lives, make some effort to use its agents and resources for their own purposes (which may or may not be compatible) and to protect themselves against state interventions that they perceive as threatening or disadvantageous. This striving may be atomized, with each individual and family trying to obtain the favour of the power centre in competition with the others, or it may divide the units into factions having different aims, or it may lead to a common front *vis-à-vis* the state.

In practice, some issues that involve contacts with higher power centres tend to divide the social units; some are of interest only to a few members, others to the majority; mobilization of the entire unit around a given issue is bound to be infrequent and transitory.

The strivings from below, like the efforts of the state from above, are in large part ineffective or even self-defeating, in typical circumstances of cross-purposes within the unit, of chains of intermediaries distorting the messages that are passed up or down, and of scanty local information concerning the resources at the disposal of the state, the forces controlling the state, and the reasons behind the state activities that are confronted. The ability of different social units to act collectively and purposefully obviously differs widely, and in most national settings the majority of the population is restricted to sporadic, poorly focused and individualistic tactics *vis-à-vis* the state.

As economic modernization and urbanization have proceeded, the social units able to act collectively have usually increased in relative size and range of interests represented; but the absolute size and relative disadvantage of the units unable to do so may also increase. In any case, it should be kept in mind that the functions of any institution or organization impinging on the lives of members of primary social units, whether introduced from above or created by the unit itself, will be seen quite differently by the parties concerned, all of whom will be striving in some way to manipulate the institution and keep it from manipulating them.

### 'Local' institutions, organizations and channels for communication

#### *The 'traditional' groupings: family, neighbourhood, community, tribe, religious congregation*

Once 'development' and 'modernization' have been posed as national objectives, the pre-existing historically determined social groupings have come under examination instrumentally. Do they offer 'opportunities'? Should they be eliminated, reformed or strengthened? The answers to such questions have been determined more by the various ideologies of development than by the nature of the groupings.

From an economic-liberal point of view, the 'traditional' groupings are hindrances to a free market and to mobility of capital and labour. Since the nineteenth century, liberal regimes have sought through legislation to weaken the extended family, eliminate communal land tenure and so on. From a neo-traditionalist point of view, the same ties are indispensable means of braking and controlling social change, although they do not contribute positively to development. The policies of 'indirect rule' followed by many colonial regimes derived logically from this position.

From a communitarian point of view, the same ties offer values and models of social organization that are indispensable components of the preferred style of development. From developmentalist or neo-Marxist points of view, the assessment of the 'traditional' groupings would focus more on their specific characteristics in relation to short-term tactics and the feasibility of specific programmes.

It would be far beyond the scope of the present chapter to try to summarize even the main features of the enormous body of anthropological and sociological literature on primary social units, their trends of change and their implications for development policy. For present purposes, we can single out a few features that seem particularly relevant. The list could easily be extended. In regard to all of these features, recent shocks to previous expectations have reduced the plausibility of the efforts to interpret them instrumentally as aids or obstacles to a given conception of development.

(a) The kinds of external forces to which the social units have been subjected have tended to bring about, rather than a general weakening of 'traditional' ties, an increasing differentiation in their functions and in the capacity of different social strata or sub-groups to make use of them. This has been particularly evident in the extended family or kinship group, as the expansion of public and private salaried employment and education have multiplied the ways in which a kinship network can advance the interests of its members. Even the least influential elements in national societies have tried to attach themselves to these networks through ceremonial kinship ties and patron–client relationships. For the latter elements, however, the nuclear family may become the last precarious source of mutual security, as in the resource-pooling of family members from multiple improvised sources of livelihood. Differential ability to maintain extended kinship networks may become a significant factor in increasing social inequality and exclusion.

Locality-based community ties have come under strains of many kinds. In a few cases, previous traits of solidarity and egalitarianism have been maintained at the price of resistance to innovation (for example, the role of compulsory ceremonial expenditure in preventing community members from accumulating wealth). More often, if it does not disintegrate, the community organization becomes an instrument of the elements best able to adapt to change, seize market opportunities, and link with national power centres. In the case of communities as in the case of kinship groups, differences in ability to establish helpful external ties (for example, through prospering migrants in the capital city or abroad or through voluntary organizations) may be of decisive importance in increasing inequalities, whether within communities or between communities.

(b) The apparent universality of the basic social groupings does not mean that their functions are of equivalent importance everywhere. In some societies they may have had enough vigour (or inertia) to shape a unique pattern of development (as in Japan) or to cripple the national capacity for any style of development (as in parts of southern Asia, in the view of Gunnar Myrdal). Elsewhere, their cohesion may have been more apparent than real, even before the more recent decades of accelerated growth and change.[3]

(c) 'Recent' changes are not necessarily as recent as they appear at first sight and 'traditional' social groupings can be quite recent, at least in the roles they play. Most parts of the world have experienced disruptive external as well as internal forces throughout modern history, although such forces were usually narrower in their impact and more widely spaced in time than those now operating. The policies of colonial regimes on land tenure, taxation, labour recruitment and local administration, and the traumatic processes of insertion of politically independent states into the world market as primary producers, need only be mentioned. Various studies have pointed out that what seem to be static and traditional local institutions are often in reality the product of defences against external forces or even of direct imposition by such forces. Even the apparent isolation and primitive ways of livelihood of certain tribes can be traced to a retreat and impoverishment imposed by external aggression.

(d) The greater part of the rural population in most countries up to the recent past has lived in dominated or 'captive' local groupings whose capacity to exert any initiative has been small. This applies to widely varying local situations; not only to families of resident workers on large estates under systems equivalent to serfdom or peonage, and to families of renters or sharecroppers, but also to apparently self-governing land-holding communities dominated by local urban-based cliques of officials, caciques, merchants and money-lenders. Under such circumstances the tactics of the power-holders have insisted on 'vertical' communication – between the separate families of peasants and rural workers and the landlord, local official, crop-buyer or money-lender – and discourage 'horizontal' communication for collective action among families at the same economic and social level. The individual or family then seeks a patron offering a degree of security in exchange for homage and material rewards. Expectations are conditioned by the outlook anthropologists have labelled the 'limited good'; that is, the amount of resources or benefits is fixed, and whatever is received by others diminishes one's potential share. The unit engaged in the quest for protection may be the whole community as well as the nuclear or extended family without altering essentially the vertical and competitive character of the communications.

In typical systems of this kind, the local power-holders have naturally tried to monopolize the role of intermediaries; they have discouraged or prevented direct vertical communication between the local group and the higher power centres. Under more recent conditions, this has no longer been possible. The individual or group then begins to try to bypass the local power-holders but carries over previous tactics in appealing for aid and protection to the state and its dependencies. Individual petitioners and delegations journey to the national capital, wait in the anterooms of the president and the ministers, bring gifts to potential intermediaries. Tours by national political leaders are seized on to present grievances. The relationships of the local groups with the various 'modern' institutions and organizations discussed later in this chapter remain coloured by the pre-existing systems of domination and vertical communication.

(e) In most of the world until recently, religious congregations served as focal points for local solidarity and as links with the wider society, through shared beliefs and rituals and also through the unifying efforts of the priests and teachers of the sect in question. To varying degrees, religious bodies served as agents of the state and the local elites but also as their rivals and as defenders of certain popular values and needs against the secular power-holders. With the secularization of many national societies and with the assertion by many regimes of the right to exclusive allegiance in the name of revolution, development or nationalism, the ability of religious bodies to control their followings declined and some of them underwent repression or regimentation by the state. More recently, these trends have altered in contradictory ways. The more localistic and traditional manifestations of religion are showing unexpected resilience, but several quite different phenomena have become more prominent in response to the challenges of 'development'.

*First*, new beliefs and rituals, or new variations of traditional beliefs and rituals, messianic, millennialist, Pentecostal and so on, claiming to cope with the forces of change or offering believers otherworldly compensations for impoverishment and insecurity, appear and gain numerous adherents. These movements sometimes alleviate social tensions, sometimes generate violent challenges to the dominant social and political order.

*Second*, the hierarchies of the established religious bodies, particularly in their lower ranks, have become channels for the dissemination of messages quite different from those of the past, including many variants of nationalism, communitarianism and socialism. In some societies these shifts in institutionalized religious allegiances and messages might be of minor importance in the face of a general decline in organized religious participation. In others, their future importance for relations between the national power centre and the primary social units might be at least as great as that of the 'modern' national political parties and interest-group organizations.

*Third*, and most confounding to previous expectations of secularism and pluralism as concomitants of development, the so-called fundamentalist movements are trying to impose their own conceptions of religious orthodoxy on whole peoples and to repress or expel the recalcitrant or groups judged inherently alien to the religious community. Such movements have been characterized as populist responses to the failures of secular developmentalist and revolutionary regimnes. In some multiethnic settings, such as India, they represent tactics by certain groups to improve their access to the fruits of economic growth. In many cases, they act to fill the gap left by shrinkage of the state in providing social services and poverty relief. At the same time, they make use of the most modern techniques of the communications revolution – television, videotapes, etc. – to spread their message, adapting these to the conditions for reception in rural as well as urban localities.

### *Institutions at the local level introduced or taken over by the state.*

In countries with mainly rural populations the state has generally tried to accomplish its objectives of collecting taxes, maintaining roads and other essential public works, preserving public order, and recruiting soldiers, mainly through non-bureaucratic intermediaries: landowners, traditional authorities of peasant communities, tribal chiefs, caciques and priests. The systems of domination described above were accepted by the state as long as their beneficiaries did not challenge directly the national power-holders. (In practice, the beneficiaries often *were* the national power-holders.) Urban populations were subjected much earlier to direct administration by the state, often after protracted struggles by the state against traditions of municipal autonomy. Recent times have seen two far-reaching and nearly universal changes in relations between local groups and the state.

*First*, the proportion of national populations in urban areas and the size of urban agglomerations have increased enormously. The urban population is more readily subject to direct state controls, is more accessible to state services and is more urgently in need of such services. At the same time, the urban population, particularly that located in the capital city, is much better able than the rural to exert concentrated pressures on the state. The circumstances of rapid and concentrated urbanization, however, have commonly overstrained the capacity of the state to expand and reform pre-existing urban administrations and services. Thus, the growth of the larger urban agglomerations has been paradoxically accompanied by new forms of 'indirect rule' and vertical communication through local political bosses, and new forms of *de facto* local autonomy and horizontal communication through defensive neighbourhood organizations, particularly among urban squatters. As the agglomerations have continued to grow and their problems of livelihood, infrastructure and environment have become more desperate, the local institutions have gone through cycles of democratic mobilization; manipulation by political intermediaries; violent spontaneous mass protests against impoverishment; atomization and apathy; and competitive terrorization from police, criminal gangs and extremist political or religious fundamentalist movements.

*Second*, the state has undertaken to extend an increasingly wide range of administrative mechanisms, services and reform programmes to the rural areas. This has been only one aspect of a wider process of economic, cultural and political 'urbanization' of the countryside as the dominance of urban lifestyles has increased. In their formal structures, the new mechanisms and services have had a high degree of uniformity throughout the world. As in the case of the national institutions on which they depend, they have been based mainly on the models offered by the previously industrialized and urbanized countries, disseminated through colonial administrations and, more recently, international experts. They can be classified roughly as follows.

*Local representatives of the general authority of the state* These are governors, intendents, district officers, etc., named by and responsible to the national executive power. These representatives have usually had as their main function the maintenance of public order and have had at their disposal local detachments of a national police force. They have usually also had a formal supervisory or coordinating role in relation to the local activities of sectoral public agencies and elected organs of local government, although such roles might not be well defined or effective.

In most countries, such systems of local representation of the central authority have long histories, but the role of the representatives has gradually changed from reinforcement of the extra-legal power of local magnates to more direct intervention in the affairs of the smaller population nuclei in support of national policies and programmes.

*Local elected organs of self-government* Here the interplay between the national and the local, between 'modern' institutions based on conceptions of democratic citizen participation in public affairs and pre-existing power relationships, traditional allegiances and land tenure systems, has become particularly complicated and confused. In a good many countries, elected local bodies have experienced repeated vicissitudes deriving from political shifts at the national level.

Since their introduction has responded more often to national policy than to a historical evolution of municipal institutions in the direction of democracy, they have had difficulty in surviving when national authorities have lost interest in them. Any real extension of a share in power through the vote to rural workers and small cultivators in general, or to locally subjugated castes, has commonly been incompatible with the pre-existing power structure. The introduction of elected local organs of government might then simply give the dominant groups a better means of legitimizing their control; the rural workers or tenants would vote according to the instructions of the landlord. Or the benefits of local government would be monopolized by the more or less urban municipal centre, excluding a rural majority.

For the most part, it would seem that the supposedly democratic procedures of local elections have been less effective in defending the interests of the disadvantaged strata than have been the administrative structures directly controlled by the national authorities, when the latter have had an interest in curbing local power monopolies and stimulating change. At the same time, when forces of change have been at work locally, the introduction of local institutions of self-government might have important catalytic effects, with various possible outcomes: a wider sharing of power and disposition to cooperate in furtherance of community interests; a reversal of power relationships and emergence of a new local elite; interminable struggles between factions seeking backing from the higher power centres; or renewed subjugation of the disadvantaged strata that have tried to take advantage of the vote.

The consequences of the introduction of elected local organs of self-government thus depend on the setting into which they are introduced and the circumstances of their introduction. One nearly universal aspect, however, is that the resources accessible to such organs are much too small to enable them to carry out the functions with which they are formally entrusted. In most cases, the national authorities have not allocated to them significant taxing powers or, if they have, the locally dominant groups are able to prevent effective use of such powers (in particular, taxes on landed property). Thus, the energies of the local body are absorbed in an endless series of manoeuvres (sometimes including threats of disorder) intended to extract resources from the national government and its dependencies. Once again, vertical communication displaces horizontal communication, and intense rivalry between municipalities for the favour of the state often emerges.

The advances of pluralist democracy in a good many countries have meant livelier political competition and greater likelihood that local elected bodies will come under the control of opposition parties. Meanwhile, the shrinkage of the state through economic crises and structural adjustment policies has led to the devolution of wider social responsibilities on these bodies, while subsidies have disappeared or been replaced by nationally administered anti-poverty programmes. Relations between national governments and the local bodies are thus likely to become arenas for even more complex and frustrating pressures and negotiations.

*Sectoral public service agencies* These are agencies concerned with education, health, agricultural extension, credit, housing, social welfare, social security and so on. The policy aspiration to universalize the services provided by these agencies, the growth of armies of professionals and functionaries employed to this end, the introduction of the services into rural areas and urban slums, and the generation of expectations concerning them in practically the whole population have been among the most widespread modern trends.

For the most part these services have been administered nationally and separately. The content of services at the local level and their distribution have been the product of pressures from many directions, leading to exclusion or token inclusion of the weaker potential clienteles and not uncommonly ending in services that benefited mainly their own functionaries. At present many of them are undergoing traumatic combinations of reform and abandonment by national authorities, with privatization or devolution to local bodies replacing centralization, and with targeting of resources to the needy replacing the ideal of universal access.

*Mobilizing and participatory agencies or programmes* These set out deliberately to change local ways of life and attitudes in accordance with the values or developmental aspirations of the national authorities. The 'community development' programmes that came to the fore during the 1950s and 1960s have been the most prominent examples. Most of these programmes did not respond to the hopes invested in them, whether because of weak or ambivalent support at the national level, excessive concentration on short-term quantifiable changes (construction of local public works, adoption of new productive techniques), evasion of the implications of local power monopolies, or lack of understanding of the ways of life they set out to change. Nevertheless, such programmes contributed, along with the many other forms of state intervention, to bring about irreversible changes in local situations, in particular in local attitudes toward the state itself.

In a good many countries, programmes of this kind either withered away or became routinized channels for distribution of public services and subsidies, no longer clearly differentiated from the local branches of sectoral public agencies. However, to the extent that different regimes seriously envisaged social structural change and popular mobilization as components of their development strategies, they could not avoid seeking more effective institutionalized means to these ends, in some cases learning from the experience of the earlier localized and weakly supported efforts, more often disregarding them.

A few revolutionary regimes, committed not only to changing local production systems and power relationships but also to transformation of the whole system of urban–rural interactions, have gone much farther in the introduction of change agents from outside and in the imposing of new organizational forms. In the case of China, in particular, the whole of the rural population underwent a series of traumatic organizational changes and campaigns of mass mobilization – the violent agrarian reform, the introduction of communes, the Great Leap Forward, the Great Proletarian Cultural Revolution, the transfer of educated youth and professionals to rural localities – only to return to systems of local government and peasant production similar to the starting point except for modernized agricultural techniques and wider participation in markets. Elsewhere, rural people have contended with state-dictated policies of villageization, collective farming, production cooperatives and so on, whose over-standardization, bureaucratic management and unconfessed motives of exploitation contributed over the long term to rural alienation from the state.

*Statistical, record-keeping and licensing agencies* The functioning of modern states has depended heavily upon the willingness of the population to provide information about itself and submit to registration and licensing of many activities and forms of property. The effort to obtain information about the rural population and to persuade it that state demands for information and registration are legitimate has thus been an important component in the overall expansion of state relationships with localities. To both the dominant and the dominated local groups, however, information has been a potential weapon that might be used against them, although some kinds of information (for example, registered land titles) might also be a valued means of self-defence. The local origins of the quantifications on which governments have relied have thus continued to be suspect, and the shrinkage of state resources has affected information-gathering as adversely as other activities.

### Voluntary organizations for mobilization and aggregation of interests

Formal organizations with local branches intended to advance the interests of their members, and sometimes to resist dominant classes or the state itself, have a long history in some peasant as well as pre-industrial urban societies, as in China. In some other peasant or tribal societies, 'factions' have attained a good deal of continuity and formalized status as channels for the structuring of conflicts within social units, with the immediate issues changing over time. For the most part, however, secular voluntary organizations reaching into the masses of the population have been a recent phenomenon, if present at all, and the capacity for such organization remains unevenly distributed.

Membership and degree of activity in formal voluntary organizations have almost always varied according to social status and income level. It is not surprising if, for the majority of the rural population and the urban marginalized population, formal voluntary organizations are either non-existent or are controlled and manipulated by forces other than their members. For present purposes, it is interesting that several types of organization which sprang up locally in the past of countries which were industrialized early, on the initiative of their members, confronting a hostile or indifferent state, and later organized nationally, partly for the sake of dealing with the state from positions of greater strength, have since been introduced or promoted at the local level by the state itself and other national institutions, relying on doctrines and organizational principles that took shape under earlier circumstances of unsupported group initiative. The main types of organization with which we are concerned here are the following.

*Political parties* In many of the newer states and in some that have long been independent entities, a single political movement has arrogated to itself the function of making nationhood into a reality by mobilizing the whole population or certain classes behind a determined conception of development. This has required the setting up of a network of local branches through which the objectives of the leadership could be conveyed to the local following and, at least in principle, the aspirations of the latter could be conveyed back to the leadership. It would seem that in most cases this interpenetration has been superficial. The local party apparatus becomes either an arm or a rival of the local agents of the state, or it is assimilated by the local power structure,, or newly emerging intermediaries use it for their own purposes.[4]

In multiparty systems the apparent effectiveness of the local party branches in opening two-way communication between the national centre and the social unit is sometimes greater, but in these cases also the communication is likely to be narrow and superficial, limited to electoral periods, and sometimes combining with or exacerbating other sources of local factional conflict. In many cases, the decreasing capacity or willingness of the state to respond to local demands for subsidies and services has naturally weakened the capacity of local party branches to mobilize support and function as intermediaries.

*Unions and similar organizations based on livelihood* Unions of workers in industry, transport, electric power, oil production and mining in many of the countries here considered have staked out a significant but limited role as interlocutors of the state through the geographical concentration of their membership, the capacity of the 'modern' occupations to offer incomes above the national average, and the convenience to the political leadership of offering concessions to the unions in exchange for support. In some cases, as in Mexico, the union leadership has achieved a formally recognized place in the ruling political coalition.  Such unions have frequently threatened the internal balance of power but have not been basically incompatible with it, however revolutionary their overt ideology. Since the 1980s they have generally lost ground for the reasons described in the preceding chapter.

The implications of rural unions, in countries with rural majorities and wide gaps in incomes and opportunities for societal participation between urban and rural people, have been quite different. Several types of rural organization can be distinguished:

— Unions of wage workers on modern farms and plantations, whose tactics and demands for better wages, working conditions, job security and social security may be quite similar to those of urban workers. Here, however, only minorities of skilled and stably employed workers have been accessible to the unions.

— Associations of small and medium farmers producing for the market, desirous of obtaining better terms of marketing and credit, as well as protection against extortion from agents of the state, local magnates and cattle thieves or bandits.

— Associations of cultivators of dwarf holdings, tenants, sharecroppers, and landless workers whose basic demands have been for secure access to enough land to provide an adequate family livelihood.

The first and second types of organization, where effective, have implied important shifts in local power relationships and have made it harder to carry out policies, important to many development-focused national regimes, of capturing a larger share of the proceeds of export agriculture and keeping urban food supplies cheap. The third type of organization has been potentially more revolutionary, since its demands could be met only through a direct assault on the property rights of rural elites. For most predominantly rural countries, even those with national regimes committed to agrarian reforms and equal rights for rural people, the autonomous mobilization of the latter has been an alarming prospect. In practice, such mobilizations have usually been localized and easily re-pressed, except in cases in which other social forces (urban parties and unions, religious bodies, youth movements, local counter-elites such as schoolteachers and lawyers) have seen reasons to ally themselves with land-hungry peasants and help them overcome local isolation.

At the same time, it is well known that peasant movements whose minimum demands for land are satisfied can change from a revolutionary force to a relatively conservative or stabilizing one, loyal to the regime to which they attribute their gains.

*Cooperatives* Cooperatives have been promoted in most of the pre-dominantly rural low-income countries by international agencies, national governments and voluntary organizations with widely differing motives. Cooperativism in its industrialized countries of origin became a powerful movement convinced of the universal applicability of its principles and techniques. Cooperativism appealed to the democratic and communitarian values of many religious as well as political movements. It offered a modern equivalent to decaying traditional forms of mutual aid on which some national regimes set a high value. It offered a prospect of peaceful localized social change and improvement in levels of living without direct con-frontation with vested interests or the mobilization of uncontrollable mass movements. It offered a way of getting done inexpensively things that the state could not afford to do otherwise; in particular, encouraging small cultivators to produce for a national or international market. In many respects its appeal was similar to that of community development; in addition, it promised more immediate material gains to the economy. Consequently, many governments adopted elaborate legislation designed to give special advantages to cooperative organizations and to regulate them for their own protection, and set up public agencies offering credits and technical assistance.

In the case of local cooperatives the paradox referred to above is particularly striking: a type of organization that originated among urban workers and independent farmers as a technique for mutual defence against exploiting middlemen was transplanted among rural groups emerging from situations of isolation or dependency with little or no experience of market relationships or of formal organization. A movement that began locally with no expectation of aid from the state or other external institutions, and that consolidated itself nationally so as to use voting strength and other means of pressure to obtain fair treatment from the state, was promoted and controlled from the top down. In spite of many attempts at innovation, the formal organizational structure of new cooperatives followed the original model rather closely.

The results have been disappointing to sponsors who expected a new and better social order or a rapid improvement in the incomes of large numbers of people, but the real achievements, particularly on the economic side, have been significant enough to justify continued support of co-operatives as a component of development policy. In fact, the need for local organizations of this kind has been so compelling that the quest for effective cooperatives has survived any number of failures and even the free-market dogmas of recent years.

The problems of the cooperatives, when they have been envisaged as something more than economic instruments, have been those of relations between specific kinds of national power centres and specific kinds of local power structures and dominated social units. The character of the national authorities and the paternalistic–authoritarian attitudes of the functionaries directly charged with cooperatives have been barely com-patible, at best, with the kind of autonomous initiatives that the earlier cooperatives represented. Where spontaneous and innovative local initi-atives arose they were more likely to be crippled than helped by the bureaucratic requirements they confronted.[5]

In many rural settings the cooperatives almost automatically fell under the control of the local elites who best knew how to manipulate the administrative machinery. In economic terms, these were often the most successful cooperatives. Elsewhere, cooperatives were tolerated by the local power-holders only as long as they confined themselves to marginal functions and refrained from inconveniencing the merchants and money-lenders. In still other cases (for example, Peru in the early 1970s), the urgency with which the regime was determined to bring about controlled societal change and the wholesale introduction of 'cooperative' manage-ment for large-scale expropriated enterprises resulted in cooperatives that were little more than façades for centralized technocratic direction. Such a policy might have satisfactory economic results if the direction were competent and continuity were maintained, but precarious reformist and revolutionary regimes could hardly meet such requisites. In some national settings (for example, Tunisia in the early 1960s) the imposition of 'co-operation' followed by govermental disillusionment and abandonment of the policy brought about the disintegration of peasant economies and enhanced the opportunities for concentration of local power and wealth.

*Urban organizations for the advancement of group interests* The kinds of 'voluntary' organizations discussed above have been mainly of urban origin, but the discussion has centred on their introduction and functioning in predominantly rural settings, characterized up to the present or the recent past by 'indirect rule', communication with the national power centres through chains of intermediaries, and ways of life that made the very conception of specialized voluntary organizations hard to grasp. In the cities, a wide range of specialized organizations representing class interests, occupational interests, and cultural and sports interests might be expected to appear spontaneously and to form networks. An important part of the urban population might affiliate deliberately with several kinds of organized social units calling for different and even conflicting communications with national and local power centres, in roles as citizens, professionals, workers, consumers, parents, religious believers, sports fans or students.

Other parts of the typical urban population, particularly among the poorer strata, might have no formal associational affiliations at all, and the relative size of these parts was likely to be particularly large under conditions of rapid urbanization. To some extent, as in the rural social units, vertical ties and patron–client relationships might substitute for horizontal solidarity, but the more marginalized strata had few opportunities to acquire such ties, unless electoral competition motivated the party machines to seek them out.

Two relatively new types of organized solidarity appeared in the larger urban agglomerations. The more widespread was the defensive organization of urban neighbourhoods. This was particularly prominent in the peripheral settlements that originated in squatting or organized land seizure, but emerged even in middle-class suburbs as the expansion of the urban areas made defence of strictly local interests and competition for municipal financing of services vitally important to all classes. The other was the club of urban migrants based on place of origin or tribal affiliation.

Both types of organization presented difficulties as well as opportunities for authorities trying to impose order and stretch inadequate administrative and financial resources. The neighbourhood-based associations offered potential channels for aided self-help and for integration of marginalized groups into the urban society. They thus received substantial support from various governments as well as from voluntary 'community development' movements. To the extent that they were effective and autonomous, however, the neighbourhood associations compelled the authorities to devote more resources to urban infrastructure and housing than they would otherwise have done, to allocate these resources differently between urban zones, to ignore breaches of property rights by squatters, and to tolerate types of housing and patterns of settlement that clashed with conventional building regulations and urban planning doctrines.

The expectations of the authorities and the local groups were often directly contradictory. The former hoped that the neighbourhood associations would alleviate municipal budgetary problems by self-help. The latter hoped that their organized efforts would exert effective pressure to obtain more resources from the municipal budget. The clubs of migrants in some countries did a great deal to alleviate anomy and provide social services for their members. They also contributed significantly to the modernization of their communities of origin and functioned effectively as intermediaries *vis-à-vis* the state, helping these communities to obtain redress against arbitrary and extortionate functionaries and to obtain state funding for schools, clinics, piped water and roads.

For the most part, neither the neighbourhood associations nor the clubs of migrants could pool their interests towards solving the wider problems of the urban environment. The former were often intensely competitive in their relations with the authorities and sometimes reproduced in the cities the feuds and prejudices typical of rural communities. Neighbourhood cohesion, like national cohesion, was most readily forthcoming against a bordering neighbourhood. In some countries, the clubs of migrants fostered separatist tendencies, through the migrants' simultaneous exposure to competition with other ethnic, linguistic and religious groups and to doctrines of cultural nationalism.

*Youth and youth movements* The special position of young people within ongoing processes of societal transformation, discussed briefly in the preceding chapter, has given them several different potential roles in the interactions between national power centres and primary social units in predominantly rural countries.

*First*, their propensity to migrate from small towns and villages has been greater than that of other age groups. The more formal education they have been able to obtain, the more likely they have been to move, and the possibility of obtaining further education in a city has been one of the more important motives for migration. The results were likely to include a diminished capacity for innovation and autonomous organization in the locality of out-migration, as its more dynamic elements were continually drained away, and a severe strain on the absorptive capacity of the cities. The associated problems of 'educated unemployment' and of unmanageable pressures on the public sector to absorb the youth into the kinds of jobs to which they felt their education entitled them have been often described.

Some of the educated youth, however, have returned to their small town or rural places of origin, or at least have maintained continuing contact with these localities. In some countries the proportion seems to have been relatively high, and the return or maintenance of contacts has not been attributable solely to inability to find a secure place in the urban occupational structure. Under these circumstances, their ability to transmit inquietudes, exercise leadership and challenge pre-existing power relationships should be relatively high. In some countries, moreover, rural conscripts returning from military service have assumed similar catalytic roles.

*Second,* the national authorities of a good many countries have enlisted important numbers of educated youth, mainly of urban origin, in programmes intended to further the social integration and welfare of local groups, while responding to the youths' own demands for meaningful employment. This has been done through paid employment in national programmes, as in the case of the Village Level Workers of India. In China in the recent past it meant mass transfer of educated urban youth to peasant villages; here the main justification was to re-educate the youth rather than to help the peasants. On a more limited scale, many countries have adopted requirements that graduates practise their professions for a certain period in the rural hinterland, or have mobilized students to take part in promotional and welfare activities in villages and urban slums.

The participation of educated urban youth in programmes of this kind seems rarely to have had a profound impact on the 'target' group. Under official sponsorship it has tended to become bureaucratized, so that the programme is seen mainly as another source of public employment; or paternalistic, so that the participating youth assume they are entitled to direct and 'help' the target group; or revolutionary, when the participating youth find local power structures incompatible with their own values and mount an attack going beyond the intentions of the programme's official sponsors. In the last case, the programme has usually come to a sudden end and some of the participants have then taken on the role discussed below.

*Third,* part of the educated youth have tried to act directly and autonomously in furtherance of certain unifying conceptions of national needs. Although this has often been the most conspicuous public role of youth, the activist groups involved have almost always been small competing minorities, able to enlist intermittent support or sympathy from wider circles. Their guiding principles have derived from pre-existing political ideologies, and their leaders have not necessarily been young, although some movements have deliberately rejected 'adult' influences. The activists have included partisans of nationalism, religious fundamentalism, neo-traditionalism and neo-liberalism as well as partisans of radical societal change. All of them have been distinguished from the predominantly 'adult' movements by their greater disposition to take their guiding principles literally and to further them through direct action involving personal danger. (In practice, this has often resulted in them acting as 'shock troops', used but not trusted by the larger political movements.)

For present purposes, the most important characteristic of the activist youth movements committed to radical societal change has been their common aspiration to proselytize and mobilize the most disadvantaged social strata – the peasants and rural workers, the urban poor, the ethnic minorities suffering discrimination and exploitation – sometimes through tactics of legal mass organization, sometimes through guerrilla warfare or terrorism. These efforts have frequently revealed an unbridgeable gap between doctrinaire insistence on rapid and violent transformation of society on the part of the militant youth, and preoccupation with limited practical demands and paternalistic protection on the part of the dis-advantaged social groups the youth have aspired to lead.[6]

It is well known, however, that a few movements starting among handfuls of militant youth have, after many frustrations and defeats, actually led to major revolutions. More generally, it can be expected that movements of this kind will continue to seek contact with disadvantaged social units and that this will have an intermittent but sometimes crucial influence on the evolution of relationships between these units and national power centres.

### Tactics accessible to actors between the state and the social unit

It is an excessive over-simplification to think in terms of a state that adopts certain objectives for the control and mobilization of social units, that devises instruments and allocates resources so as to reach its ob-jectives, and that encounters a coherent response, positive or negative, from the social units concerned.

At all levels the conceptions of what is at stake held by the different actors (political leaders, planners, administrators, security forces, social sectoral professionals, traditional authorities, magnates, official and non-official community mobilizers, interest-group and issue-oriented spokes-men, and the grassroots members of the social units) are at variance. Overt attempts to advance a given objective may camouflage quite different real objectives. The actors at the level of the state, the social unit and in between are continually changing, and tactics at a given level lag behind in adaptation to changes at other levels.

One can imagine a stage on which certain actors, convinced that they need a script to give sense to their performances, try to play roles in dramas of 'development' that are incompatible with the scripts preferred by other actors on the same stage, or who strain to combine incompatible

roles in their own performances. Meanwhile, the majority of the participants improvise and react to changing opportunities and shocks, paying
little heed to the roles that others define for them in the drama.

Nevertheless, for present purposes, it may be worthwhile to accept the
over-simplification and ask two questions. *First*, assuming that the forces
at the head of a given state are determined to pursue a style of development enhancing the well-being of the whole population, how can they
best cope with the problems of local institution-building, mobilization,
participation, resource allocation and quality control of services? *Second*,
assuming that the social units making up the population should have a
voice in determining their own future and adapting the actions of the
state to their own needs, how can they attain sufficient grasp of the
issues, solidarity and communication wiith the wider society to do so?

A few general propositions can be advanced prior to discussion of
more specific tactics:

— For the state as well as the social unit the most baffling part of the
  problem may well be that of achieving a reasonable degree of con-
  sonance between their own values, objectives and tactical preferences
  and those of the intermediaries on whom they must both rely.
— Satisfactory relationships between the state and the social unit depend
  on a reasonable degree of acceptance by the latter of the legitimacy of
  the state and of belief in its capacity to function as an impartial arbiter;
  *and* on a reasonable degree of acceptance by the state of the legitimacy
  of autonomous decision-making by the social unit and of belief in the
  capacity of existing social units to make realistic and equitable decisions.
  In the real world, acceptance of such propositions by either party cannot
  be more than conditional, and under widely prevailing circumstances
  neither party would have good reason to accept them at all. Their
  tactical choices would vary accordingly with the proportion of conflict
  and coercion rising with the degree of mutual distrust.
— The meaning of specific tactics depends on the nature of the parties
  using them and on the situations in which these parties find themselves.
  It is futile to recommend tactics as desirable in the abstract.

### Approaches accessible to the state

The state can 'choose' among the following approaches to accomplishment
of its purposes *vis-à-vis* primary social units. Some of these choices are
mutually incompatible alternatives; others can be combined and have
entered to some extent into most national development strategies. (In
practice, the state's choice is largely predetermined by precedent and by
its sources of support; the ability to choose radically new approaches is
associated with revolutionary situations or with crises demonstrably linked
to the failure of previous approaches.)

(a) Reliance on detailed central directives and controls, continual supervision of the functioning of local institutions in relation to their centrally determined objectives, severe sanctions for non-observance. This approach has been widely deplored as self-defeating. The state is likely to find itself able to paralyse local initiative, but not to keep the social units moving in the desired direction, or even to control the performance of its own agents. The proliferation of controls can actually prevent the state from achieving priority objectives, since the central authorities are forced to devote as much time to the trivial as to the important questions and cannot keep themselves adequately informed as to what is going on locally.

A good many states, once the national authorities became determined to force the pace of development, modernization and national integration, moved in this direction from lack of ability to visualize any preferable alternative and from a justified distrust of existing local institutions and power-holders. Moreover, a high degree of centralization, whatever its disadvantages, might seem the only practicable approach to an equitable distribution of public services and localized investments.

(b) Reliance on local elites for the introduction of 'modern' institutions and services. An approach of this kind might be adopted deliberately, on the supposition that economic growth and modernization might best be furthered by encouragement of the more dynamic local elements, whatever the cost in social injustice. More often, it might be followed without a deliberate decision: the identity of interests between national and local power-holders might be so close as to rule out the possibility of another course, or the national leadership might have no clear idea of the capacity of local elites to capture democratic institutions and nationally financed public services for their own purposes. With the recent discrediting of central controls and shrinkage of state administrative capacity to apply them, a good many states have returned *de facto* to approaches of this kind, although the elites expected to take advantage differ from those of earlier periods.

(c) Training programmes for community leaders, on the supposition that 'leadership' could be inculcated like a technical skill. In such efforts state initiatives have commonly competed with those of voluntary organizations and political movements. Their effectiveness has commonly been limited by incompatibilities between the kind of leadership envisaged and the local situation, and between the motivations of the trained 'leaders' and those of the programme sponsors.

(d) Reliance on local branches of nationally directed political parties or organizations such as peasant unions or cooperatives to control or countervail both the bureaucratic agents of the state and the local elites. Such approaches could be effective only if the national movement were able to keep its network of local affiliates from falling under the domination of the local direct agents of the state or the local elites, or, alternatively, generating excessively costly conflicts with other local power centres. As indicated above, few national political movements, if any, have had sufficient organizational and ideological coherence to fill this difficult role at the local level.

(e) Deliberate mobilization by forces in control of the state of social strata previously disadvantaged or excluded (poor peasants, landless rural workers, the urban subproletariat, youth) to combat bureaucratization of the state apparatus and overturn local power structures. The state might be expected to resort to tactics of this kind only under exceptional circumstances, particularly in the aftermath of a revolution, when both the existing bureaucracy and the local elites represent entrenched enemies of the new order. The Great Proletarian Cultural Revolution in China demonstrated that an established national leadership previously relying on a disciplined party to accomplish its purposes at the local level could take this course when convinced that the dominance of the party and bureaucracy were threatening its own power or its determination to transform human nature. Some regimes have found themselves on this path less deliberately, when mobilization campaigns with limited objectives brought unexpected results, but have quickly changed course.

(f) Reliance on the inculcation of new values, a 'change of heart' within social units, through exhortations by political and religious leaders, and through intensive use of mass communication media, the educational system, local mobilizers and so on. This approach is compatible with any of those described above, but places its emphasis differently; on values and behaviour rather than on manipulation of organizations and power relationships. In principle, this approach might well be an essential element in any policy aimed at healthier relationships between the national centre and the social units, but applications have tended to be superficial, disregarding the real bases of the attitudes whose change is desired.[7] As the former Soviet Union, in particular, has demonstrated, years of exhortations that contradict realities can leave the social units particularly alienated from the state.

(g) Relocation and concentration of local groups, accompanied by the strengthening of communication, servicing and control mechanisms. Some of the pre-existing as well as some of the newer patterns of settlement have hindered communication between the centre and the social units and have also hindered the development of community institutions and organizations. In fact, this has often been the result of deliberate intention: landowners have preferred to keep their workers as isolated as possible from outside influences and sometimes from each other; small cultivators and squatters have scattered to avoid exactions from landowners and local agents of the state; and settlers in urban shanty towns have found solid advantages in their impenetrability to rent collectors, tax collectors and enforcers of building regulations.

Public policies for population transfers and concentration in nuclei of easier access and control are as old as the existence of organized states, and continue to be resorted to, from various motives and in conjunction with any of the other approaches mentioned above. They have usually comprised some combination of incentives for physical concentration of rural popula-tions in larger nuclei (housing, schools, water supply, electrification and so on) with improvement of roads and communications, so that the population of a rural hinterland, whether living in hamlets or dispersed, can be reached from a semi-urban administrative and marketing centre.

In a good many instances in recent times, moreover, one of the main objectives in state policy has been to make it harder for revolutionary movements using guerrilla tactics to mobilize or draw supplies from the rural population, and for this purpose systematic compulsory population concentration and depopulation of the less controllable zones have been resorted to.

In the cities, difficulties of control and servicing have been associated with dense rather than dispersed settlement. The relevant policy approaches have included transfer of population from zones not suited to human settlement or wanted for other purposes (industries, commercial centres and so on); the opening up of slums and irregular settlements through street construction, provision of urban infrastructure and low-cost housing; and establishment of offices of state agencies in the localities.

In principle, policies aimed at closer communications between the national centre and social units cannot disregard needs for changes in settlement patterns making the units more accessible. In practice, this is bound to be a conflictive policy area, in which the social units have good reason to doubt the advantages to themselves of the kinds of resettlement pressed upon them, unless they have had an effective voice in making the policies.

### Approaches accessible to the social units

These approaches have been suggested above in different contexts. They can be recapitulated as follows, in rising order of participation in the national society.

(a) Withdrawal, non-cooperation, denial of information to agents of the state. A considerable share of the world's population still follows this tactic for lack of a convincing alternative. Its consistent use, however, requires that the social unit command its own sources of subsistence, so that it can survive with a minimum of contacts with the wider society. Ability to do this obviously has become rare and precarious, even in remote peasant communities and forest-dwelling tribes, so that the ap-proach now manifests itself as a persistent but subordinate component in the dealings of disadvantaged social units with agents of the state.

(b) Escape from intractable local problems through migration of part of the social unit to the cities, to frontier regions, or abroad. The role of cityward migration as a safety-valve for rural social unrest is well known. This can lead to the disintegration or stagnation of the social unit, but it can also be an eventual source of strength, through remittances from migrants and through the negotiating capacity gained from contacts of migrants with the wider society.

(c) Reliance on personal, paternalistic or clientelistic ties with individuals higher in the national or local power structure, at the price of submission and reciprocal favours. As the local interventions of the state have become more prominent, the quest for protection has tended to shift from the local magnate to the state itself, in the form of the highest official to whom the social unit or individual can gain access. The proffering of votes can partially replace previous offerings of personal services or produce.

(d) 'Representational violence' when consciousness of the possibility of influencing the state has penetrated, but local interest-group organizations and intermediary bodies between the state and the social unit remain rudimentary or ineffective.[8] It is assumed that the state can provide food, housing, jobs, land or stable prices for basic goods if it wants to. If it does not, and if its repressive apparatus is not acutely feared, mass demonstrations, land seizures, occupation of public buildings and destruction of property (particularly transport equipment) may be resorted to so as to prod the state into action and obtain a higher priority for the needs of the group engaging in the violence. As populations have become more urban this tactic has become increasingly formidable, although by its nature and semi-spontaneous manifestations, participants can never be sure how far they can safely go. Various studies have pointed out that violent outbreaks of the urban poor, when not crushed by force, have had the main result of gaining them some limited benefits, including a sense of accomplishment, and have been followed by a decline in politicization. The same thing seems to be true of successful peasant movements. In recent times, representational violence has been a significant, although usually temporary, restraint on the capacity of governments to apply stabilization and structural adjustment policies.

(e) Strengthening and adaptation to new purposes of pre-existing community or tribal institutions. The availability of this approach, of course, has depended on the pre-existence of forms of local solidarity and participation in which the majority has had a stake. This is far from the general rule, but instances can be found in many parts of the world in which such local institutions have retained sufficent vigour to constitute a significant restriction on the options open to the state. Even here, however, their adaptability to new purposes has commonly been limited by their requirement of a high degree of conformity and resistance to innovation among their members; by their exclusiveness in the face of increasing spatial population mobility, so that newcomers are unable to obtain participatory rights; and by their identification with certain patterns of production and exchange, so that the introduction of new crops or market relationships might be enough to disrupt them.

(f) Organization of cooperative systems of production, credit, marketing, construction and maintenance of public works. Use of this approach depends on some combination of cooperative traditions, a consciousness of common interests overriding class or other divisions, a minimum level of education, and a certain amount of legal, technical and material support (unaccompanied by bureaucratic domination) from the state or voluntary organizations. As was discussed above, the imposition by the state of cooperative institutions for its own purposes has met with more frustrations than successes. In fact, successful local cooperative action may require a reasoned rejection of dependency on the state, and this may be harder for the forces controlling the state to tolerate than occasional representational violence.[9]

(g) Interest-group organization for collective bargaining backed by the threat of strikes, boycotts, etc. To the extent that competing economic interests and different relationships to production have been present, such organization has been a universal element in developmental change. Three main limitations to its effectiveness have been pointed to in earlier sections of this and the preceeding chapter: the widely differing capacity for organization of different classes or strata; the accelerating changes in the labour market continually eroding the occupational bases for organization; and the convergence of organized interest-group demands on the state, under circumstances in which the state has had to relinquish the commanding role in the economy to which it previously aspired.

(h) Participation in national electoral politics; choice between movements and candidates based on assessment of their programmes and their ability to carry out these programmes. This requires: first, a reasonable degree of capacity in the primary social units to aggregate their aspirations and act collectively as a class or broad interest-group rather than as localized competitors for political favours; second, a reasonable degree of openness and competitiveness in the national political system, so that different political movements can offer real alternatives; third, a reasonable degree of ideological coherence and realistic appreciation of national capabilities in the political movements; fourth, a reasonable degree of shared confidence in the possibility of deciding on resource allocations through democratic procedures; and, fifth, voting mechanisms reasonably secure against manipulation by power-holders.

Even if some of these requisites are satisfied poorly or not at all, national elections can enable the disadvantaged to get some attention to their needs from political parties competing for their vote.[10] However,

under typical circumstances of scarce and very unevenly distributed resources; intense competition for jobs, education and state subsidies to
localities; and entrenched vested interests at the national as well as the
local level, it is hard for any political movement that relies on mass support
to avoid falling into the populist trap: an escalation of promises combined
with an evasion of the realities of power and resources that rule out easy
fulfilment of even modest promises.

Moreover, in political competition under such circumstances all issues
tend to become politicized. The parties cannot afford to agree even on
the meaning and validity of basic statistical indicators; unavowable motives
are alleged against every administrative decision; and the individual voter
or social unit is left with very little possibility of rational choice concerning
intelligible issues.

(i) Participation in national politics for the purpose of revolutionary
transformation of the society. A social unit can become so convinced of
the radical incompatibility between its aspirations and its place in the
social order that it collectively envisages revolutionary action leading to
the construction of a new society as the only solution. Such a choice can
only under exceptional circumstances be clear-cut and lasting, and the
circumstances depend very little on the more disadvantaged social units.
While revolutionary aspirations can persist for generations, even supporting
sub-cultures within national societies, the members of the social units are
most of the time more concerned with local power relationships and
opportunities for livelihood than with revolution.

To the extent that revolutionary leadership brings about satisfaction of
immediate demands, a revolutionary posture may be replaced by a defensive
one. If, as has been more often the case, it brings about repression, the
social unit may withdraw into the first of the approaches listed above.
Moreover, the competing political movements that try to mobilize the
social units are likely to inculcate a general impression that 'revolution' is
desirable without helping the social units to grasp its content and implications. In a given national setting most of the competing political
movements may claim to be 'revolutionary'. 'Revolution' may be advanced
as a populist slogan, or as an attribute of a regime's development policy,
or as a tactic for the seizure of power, or as a strategy for rapid and
thoroughgoing societal transformation.

One of the most striking features of very recent times has been the
eclipse of the ideologies that generated in a good many disadvantaged
social units coherent and persistent visions of a Good Society. Since the
phenomena of impoverishment and insecurity to which the visions responded are more acute than ever for many of these units it is unlikely
that the visions will be abandoned, but the new versions may be otherworldly, fundamentalist or xenophobic rather than secular revolutionary.

## Bridging the gap

The above discussion points to the conclusion that relations between national power centres and social units will remain conflictive, continually changing, fertile in mutual misunderstandings, and also in valid distrust of the intentions and capacities of the other party. Any expectation of uniform prescriptions for harmonious relations betrays a certain incomprehension of the nature of the problem. Divergent interests, shortages of resources, and growth processes that make for widening inequalities cannot be wished away or overcome simply by constructing better-functioning institutions and channels for communication.

The formulation of relevant guidelines for more satisfactory relationships between national centre and social units really depends on simultaneous definition of the style of development envisaged and the sources of dynamism of this style of development. At present, one finds an excess of internationally endorsed norms coexisting with radically incompatible prognoses of the outcome of 'development', from the catastrophist to the super-optimistic, and with pervasive scepticism concerning the legitimacy and efficacy of state efforts to mobilize societies behind a defined style of development. Under these conditions, it may be helpful to formulate requirements for bridging the gap between national centre and social units or social movements in terms of attitudes or predispositions to be desired in agents of the state, ideologists and intermediaries. The following points are an experiment in this direction, made at the risk of a repellently exhortatory tone.

(a) They should prepare themselves for an indeterminate future of changing crises and conflicting demands on limited public resources. They should try to explain these prospects, as they perceive them, to the people, and (a very hard saying for political leaders under conditions of open competition for power) should restrain themselves from promising more than the state can perform. Even more, they should refrain from promises that the state has performed what it promised, when such claims conflict with realities perceived by the people.

(b) They should recognize and resist temptations to suppress or manipulate the organized strivings of social units in the interests of a technocratic One Right Way to development. They should keep in mind that the people may know their own needs and capabilities better than the state and the technocrats, without falling into demagogic glorification of the people's wisdom or disregarding group conflicts of interests. (The latter delusion can lead to the invention of an imaginary people that is always right, so that by definition any group that deviates from rightness is excluded from the people.) This implies that they should expect and welcome creative resistance from the social units affected by the centralization, bureaucratization and standardization that are unavoidable in the activities of the state.

(c) They should seek to appreciate realistically the potentialities and limitations of present forms of group solidarity and directions of change in these forms. This implies a critical but sympathetic evaluation of the cultural changes and consumption aspirations that are penetrating the societies through the mass media and other channels, neither embracing them wholesale as attributes of modernity nor rejecting them in the name of an impracticable austerity and cultural integrity. They should try to engage the social units in a debate on these questions – a debate given structure by some coherent image of the national future, but not manipulated to a predetermined set of conclusions on what will be required of the people. Such a debate requires that the people have access to a range of sources of information and opinion managed neither by private interests solely concerned to foster consumerism nor by bureaucrats motivated to exaggerate achievements and conceal shortcomings. No national society as yet has found a fully satisfactory way to reconcile the contradictions behind this desideratum, and one must fall back on the evasive formula that the appropriateness of any solution depends on the setting.

An assessment of prospects and priorities may justify the conclusion that radical changes, conflicting with the expectations of large sectors of the people, are necessary and that these changes cannot wait upon the achievement of consensus. It would be idle to advise agents of the state never to harbour this conclusion. When they try to act on it, however, it is particularly to be desired that they resist suppositions that they are infallible or that they have a right to exempt themselves from sacrifices they expect from others.

(d) They should keep in mind that while their policies may rest on the expectation that all actors can benefit and thus should cooperate, the actors themselves may hold 'limited good' or 'zero sum game' suppositions – what one gains another loses.

(e) Whatever the level of resources that the state can devote to social purposes, the agents of the state should strive for equity in their distribution and should envisage vigorous popular participation as a necessary but inevitably troublesome requisite for progress towards this objective. In conditions of overall scarcity, two propensities will always be present: towards distribution of public resources in line with the power of different groups, excluding the weak; and towards 'equitable' distribution of token amounts, too thinly and irregularly to help the recipients. The agents of the state should also guard against a permanent temptation to seize upon participatory schemes for disadvantaged social units as a means by which the poor can be persuaded to provide for themselves services (such as schools and urban infrastructure) that the state provides for the better-off and more influential.

(f) Agents of the state should refrain from making mechanisms of participation into ends in themselves, converting them into rituals, and subjecting them to quantitative targets. Participation *is* an end as well as a means for any society striving to function better for the well-being of its members, but committees and meetings are not legitimate ends in themselves; they are unavoidable but faulty means towards participation. All organized social units and social movements have to contend with a proliferation of meetings, leading to evasion by the majority, opportunities for manipulation by minorities temperamentally at home in meetings and, if agents of the state or a dominant political party organize the meetings, a likelihood of ritualized conformism in discussions. Even if the state or party does not propose to enforce ideological conformity, its inherent standardizing and quantifying propensity makes it liable to mistake the machinery of participation for the reality. Here the contribution of agents of the state must be mainly through self-restraint. They cannot prevent organized groups from making erratic or time-wasting use of their freedom to meet, but they can refrain from imposing norms that require them to do so.

As a corollary, they should take care not to overburden and confuse local groups by too many competing participatory initiatives from sectoral public agencies, as has sometimes happened when a national policy climate of reform has spurred agencies dealing with education, health, land reform and so on to avail themselves of beneficiary organization as a tool.

(g) Exhortations and cautions such as those above, directed to agents of the state and other intermediaries, rather than to the state itself (the Prince) suppose that the former have a certain limited degree of autonomy and also a certain capacity to transform their own consciousness of their place in the web of conflictive–cooperative relationships between national centre and social units. The following quotation sums up the perspective from which even the more progressive agents of the state have commonly viewed their role:

> The planners tended to conceive of 'the people' as the only proper subject both of their own interventions and of the studies related to these interventions; they did not find it comfortable to think of 'the people' and of themselves as parts of a single system which might be investigated … While it is probably disagreeable for most people to think of themselves as subjects of study, it is probably particularly theatening for those who, like planners, exercise power in large part on the basis of authority derived from a role as technical experts. This rationale for authority tends to be undercut if the technician is viewed as one more actor on the social scene, with his own interests, beliefs, biases.[11]

Up to the present, policy-oriented research into the questions dealt with in this chapter has focused on 'the people', either with the aim of helping the state integrate them better into its schemes for development, or helping the social units to awareness of their place on the social scene and what they can do to change it. A last exhortation might well call for participatory research among the agents of the state as well as other intermediaries and mobilizers, to help them view themselves as actors with their own 'interests, beliefs, biases'. And, of course, understanding of the agents in these terms, as actors with ambivalent relations to the state that employs them, the organized forces that make demands on them, and the class and educational backgrounds that have shaped their consciousness, may become crucial to the efforts of the social units to devise more effective tactics of participation and self-defence.

## Notes

1. Toffler, *Future Shock* (1970).
2. The term 'social unit', as used here, covers groups that are large, composed of sub-units and physically dispersed (cities, political parties, etc.), as long as they have some capacity to act self-consciously and collectively, as well as groupings that are small, localized and capable of direct interaction (neighbourhoods, clubs, trade union branches, etc.). The present chapter is mainly concerned with the latter, but cannot avoid some attention to the large composite units. The individual normally belongs to several kinds of social units, the number and complexity of his relationships depending on his place in the system of social stratification and his degree of deliberate integration into the national society. For an extended discussion of 'social units', see Etzioni, *The Active Society* (1968).
3. 'North Africa doesn't even divide into institutions. The reason Maghrebi society is so hard to get into focus and keep there is that it is a vast collection of coteries. It is not blocked out into large well-organized permanent groupings – parties, classes, tribes, races – engaged in a long-term struggle for ascendancy.... These features, which loom so large elsewhere in the Third World, are, of course, present on the surface of life. But it is only surface. Anyone who takes them for more (as do most foreign observers, but hardly any domestic ones) finds the society constantly coming apart in his hands. Structure after structure – family, village, clan, class, sect, army, party, elite, state – turns out, when more narrowly looked at, to be an *ad hoc* constellation of miniature systems of power, a cloud of unstable micro-politics, which compete, ally, gather strength, and, very soon over-extended, fragment again.' (Geertz, 'The Search for North Africa', 1971.)
4. Political parties of this kind in Africa have been assessed as follows: 'The C.P.P. was a political chameleon taking on the colour of any particular part of Ghana where it existed. In other words, the social structure of Ghana tended to absorb the C.P.P. rather than be altered by it in any radical way ... Its membership regarded it, as far as they took it seriously, as a source of favours and promotion rather than as a mobilizing party. ... At the centre it suffered from bureaucratic elephantiasis and at the periphery it often disappeared into the local scene. ... Insofar as it was anything it was a barrier to communication; it was noise in a system already sufficiently noisy.' (Dowse, 'The Military and Political Development', 1969.) 'There is only very indirect communication between levels in the party and little evidence of what political scientists have discerned in African parties as a 'mobilization function'; it is the sous-prefets rather than the general secretaries who are the active evangelizers of modernization and it is they who are habitually most earnest about the political education of the masses.' (Staniland, 'Single-Party Regimes and Political Change', 1969.)

5. These generalizations are supported by a series of case studies of rural cooperatives in Africa, Asia and Latin America carried out under the auspices of UNRISD and published in 1969–72 in a series of monographs under the general heading *Rural Institutions and Planned Change*.

6. Such discrepancies have received particular attention in Latin American studies. See. for example, Silva Michelena, *The Illusion of Democracy in Dependent Nations* (1971); and Stiefel and Wolfe, *A Voice for the Excluded* (1994).

7. 'One of the most familiar signs of a failure to conceptualize the problems of development at all adequately is the extent to which scarce resources are devoted to *exhorting* people to do things. There is no doubt that people do need to be encouraged to try new things, and to be informed of new opportunities; the radio and public meetings are potent instruments of change, and district officers, agricultural officers, block development officers and so on, the massive army of "change agents" who constitute the most expensive part of the development effort in all developing countries cannot help spending a large part of their time making speeches, to large audiences or small ones. But there is no doubt that the means often becomes an end in itself: people are urged to "work harder" for the sake of "national unity" or "progress" when there seems to be no good individual motive for doing so; they are told to sink their differences when these differences concern scarce resources – say land – which the government cannot make plentiful; they are urged to change their habits or ideas because it would be valuable to somebody *else* if they did so. ... At the bottom, this whole cast of mind is not so much failing to get "beyond economics", as failing to begin from an analysis of the social forces determining the behavior that has got to be changed.' (Leys and Marris, 'Planning and Development', 1971.)

8. The term is borrowed from Needler, *Political Development in Latin America* (1968).

9. A study of a Peruvian rural community illustrates the transition from dependency to self-reliant cooperative action, quoting a community leader as follows: 'During fifteen years we sent to Lima delegation after delegation to get the Government to supply us with the materials and technical knowledge we needed for the project. This was a frustrating experience since they continually made us promises that were never carried out. Besides, when we came back to the community without having accomplished anything, some said we spent the money to have a good time in Lima. Finally after fifteen long years, the Government supplied the engineers and the materials we needed to finish the project. Then we calculated how much the trips to Lima had cost us over so many years, and we realized that we could have done the work much faster and at a lower cost if we had bought the materials and hired the engineers on our own account.' (Whyte, 'Dos comunidades serranas', 1969.)

10. In India, 'although the poor are not organized to press their economic interests, they are so numerous that the outcome of elections often depends critically on how they vote. Over the years all political parties have come to recognize and accept that their votes have to be wooed by adopting programmes aimed at responding to their needs ... The resulting sharpening of conflicts in society does increase pressures for reform to address the problem of social exclusion.' (Paul Appasamy et al., 'Social Exclusion in Relation to Basic Needs in India: Some Preliminary Findings', paper presented to International Institute for Labour Studies [IILS] Workshop on Patterns and Causes of Social Exclusion, Cambridge, July 1994.) In the absence of effective organization, however, the 'programmes' are

likely to benefit state functionaries more than the disadvantaged, by enabling the former to obtain illicit payments from employers for non-enforcement of minimum wage and other regulations. (Breman, *Wage Hunters & Gatherers*, 1994; and 'Labour Nomads in South Gujerat', paper presented to IILS Workshop, Cambridge, July 1994.)

11. Peattie, 'The Social Anthropologist in Planning' (1967).

# CHAPTER 5

# POVERTY AS A CENTRAL ISSUE FOR DEVELOPMENT POLICY

## Identification of target groups

Action-oriented ideologies of societal change or 'development' must identify some class or group as central to the kind of change wanted. In an ideology emphasizing consensus, this centrality can mean capacity for leadership and innovation in an ongoing process. In an ideology emphasizing conflict, it can mean an irreconcilable contradiction with the existing order, implying that a different order is both necessary and possible.

In international discourse on development, attention has recurrently shifted between the fostering of the groups expected to perform innovating and stabilizing roles and to reap rewards for performing these roles (such as entrepreneurs, technobureaucrats, the middle classes, progressive farmers) and the redressing of the disabilities of the least dynamic components of the national societies, those left behind or hurt by the ongoing processes of growth and change.

Identification of the disadvantaged as the 'poor' has carried with it certain preconceptions on the nature of the problem and on acceptable solutions, but has also accorded with the blurring of ideological or theoretical distinctions characteristic of utopias devised by committees. The prescriptions for elimination of poverty have implied a consensus view of future development, while the accompanying diagnoses have incorporated conflicting interpretations of the past and present.

The prescriptions for 'another development' that flourished around the 1970s rejected market forces as arbiters of distribution of the fruits of development. They placed enormous responsibilities on the state and on the world community of states as planners and administrators of development in the interests of the poor, and equally enormous responsibilities on the poor for overcoming their disadvantages by organized efforts. Affirmation of the capacity of the different actors to assume these responsibilities relied on moral imperatives and warnings of doom. Continual use of the passive voice (such and such an action 'must be' carried out) evaded precise identification of the *deus ex machina* that was to put down the mighty and uplift the poor.

More recently, market forces have triumphed in international discourse and the egalitarian spirit of 'another development' has fallen into eclipse. 'Poverty', however, has remained a central issue, occasioning an enormous output of statistical studies, horrifying descriptions, polemics and policy proposals. These last now commonly grapple with the probably unanswerable question: How can poverty be eliminated within international and national 'development' processes that generate extreme inequalities and continual shocks to expectations of livelihood and security? Meanwhile, efforts continue to reconceptualize the problem and identify more adequately, for policy purposes, the social classes or groups whose needs are least served by the existing order.

A discussion of various alternative ways in which such social classes or groups have been identified may help to clarify the above points:

### Proletariat, lumpenproletariat, subproletariat

The term 'proletariat' is identified with the most influential conflict theory of development. By Marxist definition, the proletariat has a central role in capitalist societies. This role of seller of labour power prepares it eventually to transform the society, with a little help from revolutionary intellectuals, through consciousness of radical incompatibility betwen the relations of production and further development of the forces of production, and through the capacity for organized and disciplined action forced on the proletariat by its participation in capitalist industry. Poverty spurs it to act, but it is not poverty but a specific form of exploitation that determines its central role in societal transformation.

Marx labelled 'lumpenproletariat' the urban poor lacking any foothold in industrial wage labour, even the precarious foothold of members of an 'industrial reserve army'. The lumpenproletariat were presumably even worse off materially than the proletariat, and their numbers might be quite large, but they constituted merely an ambiguous social force whose future would be determined by the outcome of the struggle between proletariat and bourgeoisie. The lumpenproletariat might in certain conjunctures be a source of revolutionary cannon fodder; more often they would be a nuisance manipulable by the enemy.

Introduction of the term 'subproletariat' was more recent and recognized special conditions in countries at most semi-industrialized, with economies dependent on the world centres. In such settings the numbers of people subsisting precariously became too large to be identified plausibly with an industrial reserve army, and they were not limited to the mainly parasitic sources of livelihood associated with the lumpenproletariat; many of them were engaged in activities that were socially useful or 'productive' but technologically primitive and affording very low incomes. The subproletariat could thus be identified as an essential ally or even replacement for the industrial proletariat in countries in which the latter was small and relatively privileged. The conception of the 'developmental' importance of the class remained the same: that is, the subproletariat is in irreconcilable contradiction with a bourgeois-dominated economic system that cannot help breeding its own gravediggers.

The identification of propertylessness and sale of labour power as sources of the basic contradiction leading to revolutionary transformation made it rational to welcome the 'proletarianization' of self-employed artisans, shopkeepers and landholding peasants, even if this resulted in their impoverishment. Otherwise, their immediate interests and their illusions would predispose them to political tactics destined to failure or manipulation by the dominant forces in the existing order.

The state, under certain conditions, might assume a semi-autonomous role of arbiter between classes (Bonapartism) but it could not be expected to transform class relationships or eliminate poverty until captured and transformed by the proletariat or subproletariat. Under this viewpoint, demonstrations of the ethical unacceptability of poverty and the duty of the state or society to eliminate it, lacking identification of a social class destined to act, could be no more than propagandistic devices or mystifications.

During the years since poverty came to the fore as a central issue of development this position has fallen into nearly total eclipse, partly because of the perverse outcome of the pretensions of 'real socialist' regimes to be acting on it, partly because of the decomposition of the traditional industrial proletariat and the failure of most of the subproletariat to draw revolutionary conclusions from its plight.

### Marginal or marginalized population

These terms have identified population components practically identical with the 'subproletariat', but without necessarily drawing Marxist conclusions on their role. They were associated with attempts, particularly influential in Latin America in the 1960s, to explain and prescribe for apparently new situations coming to the fore in countries still predominantly rural, experiencing relatively rapid urbanization and more halting industrialization, with accompanying disruption or breakdown of pre-existing rural and urban social structures.

The terms emphasized an unsatisfactory relation between the groups in question and the rest of society, and it was easier to define them negatively than positively. The 'marginal' were not altogether excluded from the changing society or they would be irrelevant to it – as in the hypothetical case of completely isolated subsistence cultivators or hunter-gatherers within the national territory. They were not simply poor, since equally poor groups might have central although highly exploited social roles. They were not simply exploited, nor simply an industrial reserve army, since the dominant forces in the society might have no use for their services, even as a means of keeping down wage claims of organized workers, or might prefer not to use them because alternative combinations of capital and manpower presented fewer problems and obligations.

They were linked to the national society economically, culturally and ecologically, but on terms disadvantageous to themselves and also to the rest of the society. They did not constitute a class, in terms of common relations to production or class consciousness, and they had no strategic role qualifying them as candidates to overthrow the existing order, but their presence indicated that the order was functioning badly. Their growth in numbers and their increasing urban concentration might eventually endanger its survival, or at least make its functioning continually more repressive and costly.

The question then arose whether measures directed by the state to the marginal groups (particularly education, job creation and local aided self-help schemes) could overcome their marginality, or whether the social, economic and political orders would somehow have to be transformed to make possible their participation on acceptable terms.

'Marginality' as a label was compatible with either a reformist or a revolutionary conclusion; this might account in part for its popularity in policy-oriented discussions and also for the subsequent waning of this popularity.

## The oppressed

Identification of the disadvantaged as 'the oppressed', in the usage associated in particular with Paulo Freire's *Pedagogy of the Oppressed* (1972), placed an ethical emphasis on the injustice of relations between oppressors and oppressed, irrespective of the roles in production of the two categories. It brought to the forefront of attention a requisite for societal transformation that was implicit or secondary in the terminologies discussed above: the spiritual liberation of the disadvantaged through systematic 'conscientization' concerning their own situation and their capacity to change it. It gave an essential role to 'pedagogy' from outside the oppressed group (from dedicated intellectuals or activists) but attributed ultimate responsibility and initiative to the oppressed themselves. The transformation of consciousness and achievement of group solidarity had priority over the raising of consumption levels or the organized representation of interests *vis-à-vis* national political and economic systems. The latter objectives should follow logically upon the former, but their pursuit would be self-defeating or futile unless preceded or accompanied by authentic conscientization.

Under this conception, the state was normally an instrument of the oppressors and could not be expected to take the lead in conscientization.

The advocates of conscientization seemed to assume implicitly that the state could be expected to tolerate conscientization activities, although this assumption seemed to contradict their diagnosis of the sources of oppression. Even in the case of a revolutionary state committed to the elimination of oppression and poverty, conscientization initiatives directed to autonomous participation by the oppressed would have to come mainly from sources other than the state. They might be expected to encounter permanent tension with the centralizing and mobilizing drives that are inseparable from action by the state. Since the advocates of conscientization of the oppressed distrusted national political and interest-group organizations almost as much as the state itself, and since simultaneous conscientization of the disadvantaged throughout a country was impracticable, their localized initiatives remained highly vulnerable whenever agents of the state or local power-holders took notice of them.

### The people

This term is the broadest and vaguest of the identifications of the disadvantaged considered here, and in its association with movements labelled 'populist' has had the widest political currency. Its users have generally supposed that the 'people' are a majority but not the totality of the national population. They comprise wage workers, peasants, salaried employees and small businessmen as well as 'marginal' and 'subproletarian' strata.

The 'people' confront 'oligarchs', 'elites' and 'exploiters', domestic and foreign. As a majority they have both the right and the power – through the vote and through organized mass action – to make use of the state to achieve a relatively egalitarian income distribution and ample public services. (Or the initiative can come from a charismatic leader who mobilizes the people against the exploiters and wields the power of the state in their name.) The inclusiveness and heterogeneity of the groups belonging to the people imply that all legitimate claims can be met without irreconcilable conflict between different sectors over their share of the pie; there will be enough to go around. It is also supposed, more or less implicitly, that the claims can be met without revolutionary change in ownership of the means of production; the exploiters are to be tamed and milked but not liquidated.

The marriages of populism, welfare statism and technocratic developmentalism have had notoriously disastrous results, particularly in Latin America, leading first to a period of wholesale relinquishment of state responsibilities *vis-à-vis* the disadvantaged, then to the narrower policy focus on poverty that will be discussed later in this chapter.

## The underemployed and unemployed

This identification of the disadvantaged accorded more readily with the conventional non-Marxist image of economic development than did the others. It centred attention on two directly 'developmental' and quantifiable aspects of their plight: (a) failure to contribute adequately to production of goods and services; (b) failure to earn thereby an income adequate for family subsistence or participation in the consumer goods market.

In practice, description and quantification of the unemployed and even more the underemployed proved a good deal more elusive than was hoped when 'employment' was proposed as a central policy focus for poor countries in the 1960s. Gunnar Myrdal effectively demolished the conventional techniques for definition and measurement, in their application to such countries in *Asian Drama*.[1]

Attempts to quantify an 'unemployment equivalent' in terms of sub-utilization of the economically active population lumped together quite different real shortcomings in sources of livelihood, depending on the researcher's judgement of whether certain occupations contributed to 'development' or not. A series of country studies aimed at comprehensive policy recommendations organized by the International Labour Organization (ILO) within its World Employment Programme since 1969 led the investigators back from the objective of creating more productive employment opportunities to the more general issues of poverty and inequality. One of these studies, on Kenya, eventually proposed a distinction between the 'formal sector' of economic activities, in which unemployment could be measurable, and the 'informal sector', generally larger and harder to delimit, ranging from relatively productive micro-enterprises and self-employment in artisanal activities and street-vending to casual labour and precarious survival strategies.

This formulation has remained influential, but economic crises, globalization of markets, the shifting of productive activities to low-wage countries, and migrations across national frontiers in search of jobs have since blurred the dividing lines between 'formal' and 'informal' sectors. These changes have kept employment in the forefront of attention as a policy issue, but have also made it harder to define plausible policy solutions for the underemployed and unemployed. The final chapter will return to this question.

## The (critically, absolutely, extremely, abjectly, relatively) poor

Concern with the 'poor' as a population category manifestly unable to satisfy minimum needs and requiring public assistance on grounds of humanitarianism or maintenance of public order goes back several centuries in certain European countries.[2] Georg Simmel summed up thus the role of 'anti-poverty' measures in industrialized societies at the beginning of the twentieth century:

> If we take into account the meaning of assistance to the poor, it becomes clear that the fact of taking away from the rich to give to the poor does not aim at equalizing their individual positions and is not, even in its orientation, directed at suppressing the social difference between the rich and the poor ... If assistance were to be based on the interests of the poor person, there would, in principle, be no limit whatsoever on the transmission of property in favor of the poor, a transmission that would lead to the equality of all. But since the focus is the social whole − the political, family, or other sociologically determined circles − there is no reason to aid the person more than is required by the social *status quo*.[3]

This approach to poverty has by no means been superseded in the conceptualizations and the real policies identifiable in many countries. International declarations on human rights and social development since the 1940s, however, have called for the *elimination* rather than the *mitigation* of poverty. This objective began to come to the forefront of the international debate over development somewhat later, along with the objective of full employment, as part of a reaction against the conventional economic wisdom on development priorities and on the 'blessings' of high growth rates. The term 'poverty' and the accompanying data on extreme consumption deficiencies served to dramatize the failure of prevailing patterns of economic growth to contribute to the well-being of a large part of the population in developing countries. They did not commit the user to a precise definition or policy conclusion, beyond the limited economic argument that in populations living in extreme poverty higher consumption is a precondition for higher production.

Gunnar Myrdal's *Asian Drama: An Inquiry into the Poverty of Nations*, a landmark in the rethinking of development in the late 1960s, in spite of its sub-title did not include a heading for poverty in its subject index. Moreover, while this work placed considerable emphasis on inadequate consumption as a reason for the inability of the Asian poor to 'develop', it placed even more weight on institutional factors, values and social inequality:

> Thus it may well be the case that the upper strata of a poor village in India do not have a significantly higher income than sharecropping tenants and landless peasants. Yet there is an important difference between these groups: the former often receive incomes without working while the latter do not ... The inequality in social status creates major incentives to withdraw from productive activity, especially if its pecuniary rewards are minimal ... The fact, therefore, that everyone in a village may be almost equally poor does not imply that everyone is equal; on the contrary they are all so poor because they are so unequal.[4]

By the mid-1970s, 'elimination of poverty' as a central objective of development and identification of the 'poor' (qualified by some intensifying adverb) as target group were common to the appeals for 'another development' and to formulations viewing poverty elimination as compatible with less radical reforms and reallocations of resources. Proponents of the two approaches sought common ground in innumerable meetings and declarations. Both were concerned with the political viability of their prescriptions and the importance of mobilizing world public opinion. Thus, it remained unclear whether the poor were to be protagonists of social transformation or beneficiaries of enlightened state policies.[5]

The following suppositions were given different weight in the various policy-oriented studies of the poor, but were common to most of them:

— A dividing line can be drawn by means of statistical indicators between the critically poor and the relatively poor and policy should concentrate on the former.
— The basic problem and reason for preoccupation with the critically poor is their inadequate consumption, particularly their inadequate intake of food.
— The critically poor can and must be 'helped' by public programmes and the allocation of public funds (including allocations by well-to-do countries for the poor of other countries) to overcome their deficiencies.
— Superfluous consumption of the better-off should be curbed to the extent that it conflicts with meeting the consumption needs of the critically poor.
— The critically poor manifest cultural adaptations to their plight that help to make their poverty self-perpetuating.
— The overwhelming majority of the critically poor are in rural settings and 'urban bias' in development policies and resource allocations is responsible. This calls for a rethinking of policies and priority to rural programmes.[6]
— The movement of rural poor to the cities does not bring them real gains and is dangerous to the social order; this a further reason for relieving rural poverty *in situ*.

Under these suppositions, the relation of the critically poor to production was viewed mainly in terms of the provision of jobs, training, land or tools enabling them to produce more so that they could earn more and consume more. The broader questions of whether they could in reality produce more or keep a larger share of what they produced, or take initiatives, or participate in decisions that affected their livelihood, without a transformation of their relationships with the rest of the society or a transformation of the society itself, were not ignored but were treated with a certain reluctance or evasiveness, suggesting compromises between different ideological positions.

The proposals assumed that the dominant forces in the existing order could help the poor if they really wanted to, or if the threat to political stability presented by the frustrated poor alarmed them sufficiently[7] *and* if sufficient international aid with the right strings attached were forthcoming.[8]

While the proposals commonly recognized that power structures and vested interests *might* be incompatible with improvement of the lot of the poor, they left the impression that these hindrances were mainly local, rural and traditional. The possibility that national or international power structures were also stumbling blocks might be admitted, but with the implication that these were remediable cases of political shortsightedness.

The documents in question referred repeatedly to the 'providing' of aid from above, the stimulation of participation from above, and the curbing of selfish local interests by benevolent restraints from above. If the political will at the national centre could not be counted on to carry out any of these functions, nothing could be done other than pilot projects from which the locally dominant forces might permit a little to trickle down to the critically poor.[9]

The documents – with a few exceptions such as *Another Development: The 1975 Dag Hammarskjöld Report* – presented the possibility that the neglected poor would eventually upset the applecart partly as a warning to shortsighted governments and partly as a disaster equivalent to the collapse of 'civilization', this last in spite of the high marks given to Maoist China by practically all the documents arguing for a policy focus on critical poverty. The expectation of a developmental solution generated precisely by the contradiction between the target group and the unsatisfactory existing order associated with use of the terms 'proletariat', 'subproletariat' and 'oppressed', is absent or slips in as an incongruous element in compromise formulations.

With the 1980s, statistical studies of poverty and debates over definitions of poverty continued to proliferate, but policy preoccupation with the poor as an impediment to development declined sharply, in some regions because of rapid economic growth, in others because debt crises, structural adjustment policies and the discrediting of the state left no room for anti-poverty measures, even if much of the population was visibly becoming worse off. Concentration of incomes and diversified consumption became generally accepted engines of growth. The previous emphasis on redistributive measures, livelihood security and state-managed social services came to seem counter-productive, conducive to economic stagnation and bleaker futures for all, especially the poor. The World Bank, along with the International Monetary Fund, imposed stabilization and structural adjustment policies that, whatever their justifications, were very far removed from the proliferation of anti-poverty initiatives in the previous decade. The poor themselves, while some of them mounted violent challenges to new dimensions of impoverishment and insecurity, for the most part adapted as best they could, far from assuming the apocalyptic roles that some advocates had predicted if their needs were not met.

With the 1990s, poverty has returned to the agenda of the United Nations, the World Bank, the International Labour Organization and other bodies.[10] The apparent triumph of the globalized capitalist economic order and the eclipse of revolutionary ideologies have confined the discourse more than before to 'practical' policy alternatives that will neither threaten existing power structures nor hamper the market forces that are assumed to be working for the long-term good of all. The return of the poor to visibility as a target group responds to a persistent intolerable contradiction between universally professed human values and real processes of economic and social change. At the same time, the nature of international discourse generates inhibitions, evasions and substitutions of promotional devices for objective analysis, to which a focus on the 'critically poor' lends itself better than alternative ways of identifying the groups whose needs are least served by the existing order.

In the discussions by 'experts' of how to eliminate critical poverty without confronting the questions of power, exploitation and inequality, one sometimes catches an echo of the mice discussing how to bell the cat – but also, in meetings at a higher level, of cats discussing how to promote the welfare of mice.

## Some problems of a policy focus on critical poverty in stratified societies

Whatever the shortcomings of the label and the ideological ambiguities of its users, the question of 'critical poverty' is inescapable in any society whose dominant forces profess human welfare values with a reasonable degree of sincerity. Such forces must try to reconcile multiple objectives within political and economic settings that give them only limited room for manoeuvre. In stratified societies whose economies respond to a mixture of market incentives and government intervention, with processes of 'modernization' changing the traits and visibility of the critically poor, one might expect: first, a gradual and intermittent expansion of social measures expected to alleviate their plight, more or less in the spirit summed up by Georg Simmel; second, a continual experimentation with participatory, self-help and job-creation mechanisms that promise to help the poor help themselves at reduced cost to the state; third, consequent changes in their consumption levels, spatial distribution and relations to society and the state; and, fourth, the appearance of various unexpected and unwanted byproducts of the measures and mechanisms. As was indicated above, previous trends were traumatically interrupted during the 1980s, for differing reasons in specific countries and regions. Would-be policy-makers are now returning to the problem within radically changed global and national settings.

The objective of 'eliminating' critical poverty is likely to remain elusive. The realities that stand in the way include the following.

## Power

The critically poor, almost by definition, have less access to power compelling a hearing for their needs than has any other stratum of society. Their labour is in demand only at wages that perpetuate poverty, and recent economic and technological transformations seem to be shrinking even this demand. They are naturally insignificant as a market for consumer goods. They are too heterogeneous in everything except their poverty to to be able to unite other than locally and ephemerally to improve their lot. While they are no longer as isolated and submerged at the bottom of rural power structures as previously, the main forms of protest accessible to them are demonstrations, land seizures, riots and votes for populist candidates, and these expedients are most of the time in most local settings too ineffective or too dangerous to be resorted to.

The critically poor are likely to have an all-too-realistic appreciation of their lack of power and the probable consequences to themselves of militant protest. This leads them to seek dependent clientelistic relations with the state or with local power-holders. One can find no evidence in history or in recent developmental experience that the state, even in a period of revolutionary change, can acquire either the capacity or the will to give the critically poor a share in power or encourage systematically their 'conscientization'; other priorities must be served.

Socialist revolutions, to the extent that they implied genuine transformations of systems of production rather than adoption by elites of a new political label, have commonly converted labour surpluses into labour shortages, thus generating a need for mobilization of the whole of the potentially active population, and have required the rationing of scarce basic goods according to criteria other than ability to pay. Both trends have improved the relative position of the employable poor, who have also received important psychological gains in terms of perceived participation and hopes for the future. In later stages of consolidation, however, special privileges in distribution of goods and concealed unemployment in low-productivity jobs became the rule. Censorious attitudes towards the 'idle' or 'parasitic' poor and attempts to compel them to work then became rather similar to the attitudes toward recipients of public assistance that emerged in capitalist societies. In any case, empowerment of the critically poor through revolutionary class alliances has practically disappeared from future prospects.

Mobilization of the poor, leading to conflicts between public agencies and different levels of government, did enter into the 'war on poverty' proclaimed in the United States in the 1960s, for reasons too complex to be discussed here. Its incompatibility with national and local power structures ensured its eventual curtailing or sterilization; only small minorities among the poor were directly mobilized and these were unable to maintain their impetus once official backing dwindled.

The argument that critical poverty constitutes a threat to the existing order so serious that the dominant forces must eliminate it for their self-preservation is thus in most national settings unconvincing, although the disruptive potential does call for some combination of control and relief. Even major famines do not usually goad the critically poor into anything more than easily repressed local disorders, as long as the national power structure remains intact, as events in Africa and Asia have demonstrated. In the world today, one finds countries with a predatory elite ruling over a majority at the lowest levels of subsistence that are relatively stable to outward appearance. One finds other countries in which rapid economic growth has accompanied widening inequalities, with the uprooting and impoverishment of much of the population and with recurrent disorder, but with dominant forces confident of being able to maintain their control and their advantages. Meanwhile, other societies in which the dimensions of critical poverty are small are chronically enmeshed in conflicts over the distribution of income.

Some of the more recent policy-oriented treatments of poverty that urge targeting of public resources to the critically poor recognize the difficulty of powerlessness but try to get around it as follows:

> Policies that help the poor but impose costs on the nonpoor will encounter resistance whether or not they increase national income. The nonpoor are usually politically powerful and they exert a strong influence on policy. Giving the poor a greater say in national and local decision-making would help to restore the balance. But since political power tends to reflect economic power, it is important to design poverty-reducing policies that will be supported, or at least not actively resisted, by the nonpoor. Sometimes it is possible to build coalitions that bring together the poor and certain nonpoor groups that have an interest in reform … Service providers and recipients may also form coalitions. Pressures on governments to finance social services often come as much from the middle-income providers of services as from the beneficiaries. Teachers, medical personnel, social workers, and other middle- and upper-income service providers themselves benefit when the government devotes more resources to social services, and they often have the voting power and organizational capacity to lobby successfully for greater investments in the development of social services.[11]

The critically poor might well suspect that the lion's share of the benefits from such coalitions would go to their service-providing allies. More broadly, the alliances might lead back to the kinds of clientelistic and populist policies that structural adjustment was expected to rule out.

### Relative vs. critical (absolute, extreme, abject) poverty

The supposition that the 'critically poor' can be distinguished from the 'relatively poor' by means of quantitative indicators and then targeted for public action seems hardly tenable, even if one leaves aside the practical problems, as yet unsolved, of accurate measurement of the levels of living of enormous numbers of people with widely varying patterns of consumption and felt needs, both under assault from economic and cultural globalization. (It can be taken for granted that, for present purposes, per capita incomes expressed in money are a poor makeshift.)

*First*, with the apparent exception of minimum levels of intake of nutrients, poverty is inescapably relative:

> When all is said and done, poverty has nothing to do with ... absolute standards;
> it is entirely a relative concept that can be defined only within a specific context
> of time and space ... A household's poverty, for example, does not exist
> independently of the welfare of other 'reference groups', be they neighbouring
> households, people of other regions or linguistic groups, members of other
> classes or, indeed, other countries. Thus the notion of poverty is intimately
> connected with the idea of inequality, and our views on welfare are closely
> associated with our perception of equality.[12]

*Second*, the poorest of the poor generally represent the worst-off elements of several quite different social groups participating in some kind of gainful activity, along with a residue of social groups with special disabilities that place the entire group in critical poverty: the homeless, families without male breadwinners, vagrant children, aged persons without resources, unemployable drug addicts and alcoholics. Except in countries with relatively high income levels, the 'fully employed poor' are generally in the majority. 'Critical poverty' can hardly serve as an operational definition for a policy package aimed at *causes*, both because of the heterogeneity of the sub-groups and the origins of their poverty, and because the policies other than consumption subsidies that are relevant to the needs of low-income occupational groups cannot be restricted to the part of each group that falls below a quantitative 'critical poverty' line.

*Third*, the 'relatively poor' within a specific social setting – that is, all the groups whose felt needs exceed their capacity to satisfy them – are invariably better able to act effectively, to organize so as to raise their incomes, and to take advantage of whatever services the state offers than are the critically poor. They are understandably unwilling to step aside in favour of the latter. At the same time, communities, neighbourhoods, occupational groups, religious congregations, etc., generally include members on both sides of whatever critical poverty line the statisticians or the state may adopt, and in such bodies solidarity coexists with rivalry.

*Fourth*, while the poor help the poor through informal mutual aid, generally to a much greater extent than the state helps them, the weaker are most directly and visibly exploited by neighbours whose own poverty makes them seek the meagre surplus that can be squeezed out of them: police and other petty functionaries, vendors, liquor dealers, money-lenders, petty criminals, local political intermediaries and so on. While these kinds of exploitation have received relatively little attention from the sectors of opinion aspiring to help or to conscientize the poor, they are probably in many settings so pervasive and so intimidating as to inhibit the critically poor from striving to better their situation. It is also probable that as one moves from larger, more modern cities to the rural hinterland such exploitation becomes even more arbitrary and oppressive. To the extent that the forces controlling the state become preoccupied with unrest and the need for control, this spontaneous preying on the poor by the poor can merge with deliberate recruitment of some of the poor into state-supported apparatuses for informing, intimidation and removal of potential leaders. If, on the contrary, the forces controlling the state want to help the poor, one of the most promising and least costly methods would be through reforms of police and courts and through public defenders offering the poor redress against extortion and intimidation.

One factor setting the 'relatively poor', in a broad sense, against the 'critically poor' has been the inability or unwillingness of states to capture and redistribute part of the rising incomes of the wealthy. Almost everywhere the owners of land and capital, the managers of large enterprises and many professionals have been able to determine their own share of the national income and conceal or export as much of this participation as they see fit. These groups have generally had a symbiotic relationship with political, military and technobureaucratic elites which, however, in some countries have managed to supplant them as chief beneficiaries of 'development'. (Ironically, the trend to concentration of incomes and flaunting of luxury consumption has become as flagrant in the former USSR and in China as anywhere else.)

Some intermediate strata have also gained but, particularly in Latin America and Africa, the organized wage workers, public employees, small manufacturers serving the domestic market, and farmers producing for this market, groups previously confident of their place in development, have lost ground. A good many have fallen into poverty, and larger numbers are acutely insecure and unable to maintain previous levels of consumption.

When international agencies advise governments to give up pretensions to universalized education, health and other social services, of which the relatively poor were the main beneficiaries, and target social resources to the critically poor, they have good reason to expect that they will be the main losers and that the wealthy will be untouched. The only important group among them that might find the argument for an alliance between poor and nonpoor convincing might be the public employees in social programmes.

Authoritarian regimes that have crippled trade unions and resisted wage increases as harmful to development have commonly argued that such increases do not help the critically poor since the latter are self-employed, unemployed or working in activities that are neither organized nor controllable by minimum wage regulations. To the extent that popular pressures influence government policy, then, the 'relatively poor' are likely to gain at the expense of the 'critically poor'. To the extent that a techno-bureaucratic elite determines policy, the critically poor, or some of them, might gain at the expense of the relatively poor, in both cases with no impact on the higher income strata or the overall pattern of inequality.

The difficulties in the way of policy concentration on the needs of the critically poor are thus not limited to the claims of the 'powerful and influential' elements singled out in *The Assault on World Poverty*. Indeed, within the suppositions of the prevailing style of development, these elements are the least likely to be inconvenienced. Meanwhile, where jobs are scarce the groups with access to them will defend this access from intruders and will resist initiatives, undertaken in the name of job creation for the critically poor, to dilute their legal protection of wage levels and job security. The relatively educated will struggle to preserve and extend the income advantages previously associated with differential income qualifications.

In the countryside, a widening gap between critically poor and relatively poor has been visible in most of the world, whether the dominant local trend is towards capitalist modernization of agriculture in medium and large holdings, cooperative organization of producers, or land redistribution to smallholders. In the first case, a minority of permanent wage workers may gain a status equivalent to the urban workers in modern industries. In the latter cases, part of the rural population collectively or individually gains access to land and capital permitting commercial farming, while another part enters into intermediary or specialized managerial and technical functions previously monopolized by landlords or not carried out at all. In all cases the demand for unskilled labour remains stationary, declines or becomes more predominantly seasonal. A residue of small cultivators and landless labourers is left relatively or absolutely worse off than before. Cooperative members and landholding peasants, to the extent that they need additional seasonal labour, exploit this residue in much the same way as the large capitalist agribusinesses.

### Productive livelihood and public assistance

The documents identifying the critically poor as a target group for development policy have invariably emphasized the objective of introducing them to means of livelihood sufficiently productive to afford them satisfactory incomes. However, the definition of the target group in terms of insufficient consumption, and the enormous difficulties in the way of a state-managed transformation of their relations to production, their access to earned incomes and their access to 'qualifying' services such as education above the elementary level, pointed to the probability that the assistance components of anti-poverty policy would predominate in practice.

The assessment of measures practicable within existing political systems in policy-oriented studies from *Redistribution with Growth* (1974) to *Poverty: World Development Report 1990* contrasted with the immediatist and universalist tone of many human-rights-oriented pronouncements. The latter insisted that failure to eliminate poverty would mean world catastrophe. The former suggested that, while many things could and should be done, the really practicable measures were likely to evade the structural aspects of the plight of the critically poor and that their extension to the whole of the target group in the near future was not on the cards.

To the extent that a government could mobilize resources or obtain them from external sources, it was easier for it to distribute free or subsidized food to the poor than to change the structures of employment and land tenure sufficiently to enable the groups most in need to gain an adequate livelihood. The valid argument that better nutrition and health are prerequisites for integration into productive employment helped to justify this kind of targeted assistance approach.

In their early stages, food distribution programmes could count on external contributions meeting a major part of the cost, in view of the need of the United States and some other countries to dispose of food surpluses. They could win political support in the form of votes from the critically poor themselves, or at least reduce the incidence of rioting and crimes against property, while meeting less opposition from other population strata than would alternative measures.

Attempts to combine material assistance with incentives and technical advice enabling the poor to live better by their own efforts have continued through all the vicissitudes of economic crises and globalization, under the auspices of inter-governmental organizations, national governments and many kinds of voluntary associations or NGOs. Local success stories abound, but so do stories of waste and cross-purposes between donors and recipients of aid.[13] Paternalistic and technobureaucratic initiatives share the field with initiatives aiming at conscientization and 'empowerment' of the poor, and sometimes use the same terminologies with different meanings.[14] The most problematic aspect of the initiatives seems to be the effort to promote stable, frugal ways of livelihood and provide access to employment in contradiction to global trends that are so contrary to stability and frugality.

## *Fertility and family planning*

The families of the poor generally have more children than the families of the better off. Thus, either the adult breadwinners must support an inordinate number of dependants with their scanty incomes, or child labour must remain an essential part of the family economy. In either case, the probability that neither the present family nor its descendants will emerge from poverty increases. The conclusion can readily be drawn that, all other things remaining equal, the poor family would be better off if it had fewer children and that persuading and helping it limit reproduction should be an essential component of an anti-poverty policy.

This proposition, advanced with crusading zeal by the family planning movement over many years, ran into a hornets' nest of controversy and attribution of impure motives that need not be returned to here. The upshot was that family planning programmes continued to expand, responding to very real demands among women of urban low-income groups, and a few countries – notably China – made fertility control practically compulsory for all social strata, but the claims for the decisive role of family planning to combat poverty fell into disuse for various reasons. For one thing, family planning programmes had no significant impact on fertility in the mainly rural populations suffering most from critical poverty. For another, the polemical reaction against the implication that the poor should reduce their fertility to make things easier for the well-to-do became so insistent that advocates of development strategies focusing on elimination of critical poverty became inclined to concede the ground or avoid the topic altogether. The more recent international policy declarations – which also constitute utopias devised by committees – assert that the raising of the levels of living of the critically poor must precede or accompany rather than follow upon changes in their fertility levels. Some attempts to quantify possible futures assumed that higher levels of living would be reflected in a determined rate of decline in fertility, while in the absence of improvements in levels of living fertility would not decline.

This supposition was plausible if the improvements in the lot of the poor were to consist in higher and more secure incomes for productive work, more equitable access to educational and health services relevant to their needs, and enhanced capacity for organization and participation in decisions affecting their own lives. To the extent that targeted assistance came to predominate in anti-poverty efforts, however, the effect of improved consumption on the planning of family size and child spacing seemed more questionable. The conditions of subsidized consumption, doles in kind based on availability of food aid and so on, would not enhance the family's capacity to plan for a predictable future, and benefits might increase with the number of dependants.

In such a case, one might expect a revival in official quarters of the hope that some combination of incentives and pressures directed to families or women eligible for public assistance, such as payments for persons undergoing sterilization, might reduce the dimensions of poverty, and a corresponding revival of controversy over the legitimacy of measures that penalize families for reproducing 'irresponsibly'. Such measures, of course, become relevant to the critically poor only to the extent that they do in fact receive benefits that might be withdrawn.

### Quantification and poverty lines

However much one might prefer quality of life and degree of satisfaction with life as central criteria, any attempt to determine the size and location of a 'critically poor' target group must fall back on measurement of the quantity of goods and services consumed. Some policy-oriented studies attribute an almost magical significance to the quest for an adequate combination of consumption indicators, as if the shortcomings of national income or product as yardsticks were responsible for the failure of current development strategies to contribute more unequivocally to human welfare.

Quantitative information on levels and distribution of consumption remains notoriously incomplete and unreliable in most of the world, particularly in the poorer countries. The concern over poverty has been backed up by figures that are plausible but that hardly bear close scrutiny. The main current methods of collecting and tabulating statistical information throw only a dim light on distribution, and for obvious reasons the unreliability increases both at the top and bottom of the income and consumption scales. The deciles or percentages in which the information is usually expressed cannot inform about the patterns of income utilization and consumption in families belonging to real social groups. Nor would information on overall family consumption be sufficient, since it is probable that in many social settings women, children, the disabled and the aged bear the brunt of poverty, whether or not they are incorporated in families. Information on the distribution of consumption wihin families and the consumption of individuals without families, however, is particularly scanty.

The fixing of a 'critical poverty line', in terms of quantitative adequacy of supply of components of the level of living to satisfy minimum physiological needs, *seems* to be practicable only in the case of food intake. Even here the problems of determining minimum requirements and deriving practical policy conclusions are more complicated than they seem at first sight. Minimum calorie and protein requirements differ widely according to climate, physical exertion, stature and so on. People are notoriously disinclined to match their consumption to the dictates of 'experts' on the cheapest way to satisfy their physiological needs. Techniques for measurement of food intake and physiological consequences within families are too costly and time-consuming to be used on a large scale. The statistics now current on food consumption, for all their apparent concreteness, contain about the same proportion of guesswork and the same motivations for problem dramatization as the statistics on income levels and distribution.

Attempts to quantify critical poverty in terms of the components of levels of living that can most readily be measured probably exaggerate the depths of rural poverty and the poverty of groups whose lifestyles are least 'modern'. An urban group, or a group in a relatively modernized rural setting, if its members live in shacks with thatched roofs, dirt floors, lacking piped water and latrines, with no access to schools or clinics, can be assigned to critical poverty without much question. A tribal or peasant population in the same circumstances, if food supplies are adequate, if the 'primitive' conditions of settlement are not associated with high levels of debilitating disease, if local life affords no urgent need for literacy, if community and family relations provide reasonable satisfactions, is another matter. One would need to go beyond the 'primitive' material conditions to consider the people's assessment of their own way of life and the viability of this way of life in relation to change in the wider setting.

Alternative methods of information-gathering and analysis, capable of throwing more light on the real patterns and meaning of consumption in specific settings, are expensive and time-consuming. The anxiety to have better quantitative information about the poor, natural to the economists, sociologists and demographers engaged in debate over the reorientation of development policy, confronts questions of costs and benefits and of linkages between information and action.

If the information that enters into national policy-making consists of separate quantifications of deficiencies in food consumption, housing, sanitation, schooling, etc., the probability increases that the response will be both assistance-oriented and compartmentalized in separate programmes with quantitative targets for subsidized distribution of food, construction of dwelling units and so on. The likelihood that the 'relatively poor' and the 'relatively well off' will benefit more than the critically poor is high. Yet both the information and the action may be governed by political calculations responding adequately to the rationality of the forces controlling the state.

If, on the other hand, the policy-making organs confront exhaustive information on the conditions of each impoverished hamlet and shanty town, each marginal occupational group, and each type of family in the national territory, it is inconceivable that they will be able to digest the information and reconcile it with the kinds of standardized action that the state can carry out. It is also to be expected that the political and issue-oriented movements urging different priorities on them will use their own versions of the information to strengthen their own claims. However much quantitative information may be amassed, it will never demonstrate 'objectively' what can and should be done.

One can envisage an information-gathering strategy that converts the critically poor from a statistical abstraction into groups of people with diverse reasons for underconsumption, exposed to diverse forms of exploitation and discrimination, with diverse potentialities for emerging from poverty. The purposes of such a strategy, however, cannot be reduced to the provision of information to the state on the supposition that the state will use it for the more efficient relief of poverty. Information and the ways in which it is gathered, analysed and disseminated convey more complex and ambiguous advantages and dangers to all the actors in the drama of 'development'. Notoriously, the state can use the information-gathering process for purposes of evasion of action or delay, or of control, identifying potential sources of unrest that it may repress or relieve just enough to render them harmless.

For the disadvantaged, participation in the gathering of information can be a means of conscientization, of presenting their claims more vigorously, and of entering on diversified local action to meet their own needs. The outlook behind the initial definition of the target group may then bias its self-identification. If the group comes to identify itself simply as 'poor', its interest will inevitably centre on demonstration of its poverty to the state or voluntary agencies likely to help. If it identifies itself as part of the 'people', the 'oppressed', or the 'working class', its claims and tactics will be different.

### Self-identification

The present discussion, like many other treatments of poverty as a central issue for development policy, has been unable to emerge from the contradictions inherent in such an effort. At most it has made explicit some of the difficulties that emerge from intellectual attempts to shift the policy focus from helping those best able to help themselves – the entrepreneurs, the modernizers, the strivers – to helping those least able to help themselves without explicitly rejecting previous suppositions on the nature of the development process.

When poverty first came to the fore in international discourse, industrialization, development planning and the continually expanding services of the welfare state offered a framework within which its eventual elimination through enlightened public policies could plausibly be envisaged. 'Another development' and socialism challenged the capacity of existing styles of development to accomplish this but placed even more emphasis on the role of benevolent and rational states within a benevolent and rational international order. The settings and expectations within which the 'elimination of poverty' is addressed today have obviously transformed themselves with the triumph of market forces over planning doctrines and the more precarious triumph of pluralist democracy over authoritarian pretensions of the right and the left. However, contradictions in the interpretations of poverty and how to deal with it retain familiar patterns.

The identification of a disadvantaged target group invariably comes from outside the group itself, from ideologists, political leaders and social scientists, and with instrumental as well as ethical or scientific objectives presents a simplified model of complex realities. In the alternative identifications that were summarized at the beginning of this chapter, two main instrumental–ethical orientations can be distinguished. According to the one orientation, the main purpose of the identification is to help the target group become conscious of its own situation and its own interests so that it can acquire a realistic strategy for transforming its situation and thus transforming the social order as a whole. Different versions lead to quite different strategies, but they agree that the group must free itself through solidarity informed by its own vision of the existing society and of the kind of future society that will meet its needs.

According to the second orientation, the main purpose of the identification is to make *other* elements in the national society and the international order aware that the situation of the target group is unacceptable in terms of their own professed values and incompatible with the perpetuation of their own preferred lifestyles. Differing versions of this orientation also lead to differing strategies, but these are strategies for the state, for the international order made up of states, for the wealthy and powerful, or for all educated persons of good-will, only secondarily for the target group itself. This orientation assumes that the deficiencies of the target group can be overcome only if guidance, policy-oriented research and material support are forthcoming. Such an orientation must be more congenial than the first to external identifiers of the target group, since it enables them to address their natural educated audiences and gives them legitimate leading roles in the strategy to be adopted.

Attempted adherence to the first orientation requires the identifiers either to create the target group in its own image, attributing to it purposes and capacities that it can acquire only under their tutelage, or to discipline themselves, under continual temptations to self-deception and manipulation, to the difficult subordinate roles of 'learning from the people' and 'serving the people'. The Chinese experience shows how readily such precepts can mutate into dictation to the people.

The preceding pages have stressed that the critically poor are objectively an aggregation of different social groups and parts of groups whose main common characteristic is deficient consumption, lumped together on the basis of statistical indicators of dubious reliability and comparability from group to group. However, it is probable that members of some of these groups now identify themselves as 'the poor' and that wider groups will do so if the dominant forces in their societies so identify them and offer them advantages for accepting such an identification.

For all the opinion surveys that have been made one cannot generalize with any confidence as to how the groups identified as 'poor' see themselves and their place in society. The generalizations now current – including those made here – project on them the hopes and fears of educated elites, conservative, reformist or revolutionary. These sectors of opinion cast the same actors alternatively in roles as 'poor' seeking benefits, 'oppressed' seeking liberation, 'people' seeking majority rule, or 'proletarians' seeking to overthrow and replace the existing order. The target groups adopt or adapt one role or another, or identify themselves in ways that are shocking and alien to their external identifiers, as in xenophobic outbreaks and messianic or millennial movements. Their subjective choices among these identifications will have as much to do with their future interactions with 'development' as will their objective situations of deprivation. For all the heterogeneity of the points of view now associated with the focus on 'critical poverty' and equivalent terms, a self-identification of this kind is bound to be closer to conformity, dependency and putting up with small improvements in things as they are than are the alternative self-identifications.

Within the utopias devised by committees the focus on poverty has overlapped with and also competed for attention with other propositions calling for quite different priorities for development policy. Some of these propositions are discussed in other chapters. At this point it may be sufficient to pose the question whether the implications of the focus on critical poverty, at the level of the 'experts' and international bureaucracies now seeking to revitalize the cause of development and justify their own survival, are not somewhat similar to the implications at the level of self-identification of the target group.

## Notes

1. 'The unsuitability of western concepts of unemployment and underemployment', in Myrdal's *Asian Drama* (1968), pp. 1115–24.

2. 'In every city, on the fringes of this working or labouring population, there was also a large sub-group whom the more respectable workers and tradesmen tended to despise and reject. These were the destitute, the beggars, the homeless, the vagrants, the *gens sans aveu*, and the casually employed, who floated in and out of jobs, *dépots de mendicité*, hopitaux, doss-houses and prisons ... In all cities these elements were a matter of constant concern to the police and public authorities ... How many were they? It might be as much as a quarter or a fifth of the urban population ... In Paris, figures published over a twenty-year period between the 1770s and the 1790s suggest that about one-sixth of the population were constantly in receipt of public charity; and ... the proportion in London was probably as high.' (Rudé, *Europe in the Eighteenth Century*, (1974), pp. 90–91.)

3. Simmel, 'The Poor' (1908).

4. Myrdal, *Asian Drama*, (1968), p. 569.

5. *Another Development: The 1975 Dag Hammarskjöld Report on International Co-operation and Development* was the most influential presentation of the first approach. Two World Bank publications were the most authoritative versions of the second: *The Assault on World Poverty* (1975); and *Redistribution with Growth*, a joint study of the World Bank's Research Centre and the Institute of Development Studies at the University of Sussex (1974).The contributors to this last work were more concerned with the relation of poverty to political power and the real constraints on public action.

6. Lipton, *Why Poor People Stay Poor* (1977).

7. 'The real issue is whether indefinite procrastination is politically prudent. An increasingly inequitable situation will pose a growing threat to political stability.' (Address by Robert S. McNamera to Annual Meeting of the Board of Governors of the World Bank, Nairobi, Kenya, 24 September 1973, excerpted in *The Assault on World Poverty*, p. 94.)

8. International resource transfers to the Third World 'should be concentrated on countries whose efforts are or will be directed towards the priority goal of satisfying the needs of the majority poor and which are carrying out or will carry out the necessary structural transformations.' (*Another Development*, p. 18.)

9. 'In many countries, avoiding opposition from powerful and influential sections of the rural community is essential if the program is not to be subverted from within. In cases where economic and social inequality is initially great it is normally optimistic to expect that more than 50% of the project benefits can be directed toward the target group; often, the percentage will be considerably less.' (*The Assault on World Poverty*, p. 40.)

10. See, in particular, World Bank, *Poverty: World Development Report 1990* (1990) and the series of *Human Development Reports* (published for the United Nations Development Programme by the Oxford University Press since 1990). In November 1993, the International Institute for Labour Studies held a Symposium on 'Poverty: New Approaches to Analysis and Policy', at which papers covering a wide range of positions and research interests were presented.

11. *Poverty: World Development Report 1990*, p. 52.

12. Keith Griffin, 'Employment Strategies in World Perspective' (document presented at Symposium on Employment Strategies and Programmes, Commonwealth Youth Programme, Barbados, September–October 1975).

13. For a positive account of such initiatives, see Annis and Hakim (eds), *Direct to the Poor* (1988). For an intensively negative account, see Hancock, *Lords of Poverty* (1989).

14. According to an evaluation based on research in Zimbabwe: 'Terms such as "empowerment", "transformation", and "community" are used without establishing any implicit understanding regarding their meaning. Thus NGOs are vulnerable to manipulation by outsiders who employ the same terms for distinctly different purposes. The use of the term "empowerment" gives the clearest example of the divergence between rhetoric and actual practice ... NGOs call for the "empowerment" of communities. In practice, what this "empowerment" typically consists of is attaining self-reliance, that is, the ability of people to reduce their "dependence" on governments and donors. It does not entail any changes in actual power relationships or in control over resources ... The indications are that "empowerment" was originally used by development NGOs in a much more fundamental sense ... But

the appropriation of the term "empowerment" by the political right wing in some northern countries, and its redefinition to mean "self-reliance", has led to an unacknowledged shift in emphasis by the NGOs which receive funding from industrialized countries.' (Vivian and Maseko, *NGOs, Participation and Rural Development*, 1994.)

## CHAPTER 6

# THE ENVIRONMENT ENTERS
# THE POLITICAL ARENA

### The starting point

This chapter explores the political dimension of the entry of the environment as a missing ingredient into the international debate over development. The greater part of the discussion could apply to other broad themes that have entered similarly; in particular, human rights, gender equality, population growth and poverty.

Our starting point is a period of conflictive mutations in the international political and economic order, strain on the capacity for crisis management in political systems of all kinds, and confusion or disillusionment over 'development' as a central focus for policy. During this period transnationalized or globalized capitalism penetrated and increasingly dominated national societies, even those most incongruous with it culturally and ideologically, making them more interdependent than ever before, excluding options for autonomous national styles of development that seemed viable up to the 1970s or 1980s, but generating contradictions and resistances that made its future appear both precarious and maleficent.

One consequence was a dissociation between utopian–normative strategies for development oriented to human welfare, promoted by international organizations and formally endorsed by many governments, on the one hand, and real trends in structures of production and distribution, in the expectations and tactics of the groups able to make themselves heard, and in governmental actions, on the other. This dissociation had been visible since the 1950s or earlier, but became more pronounced as resource exploitation intensified and consumer societies for minorities entrenched themselves, while internationally endorsed requisites for authentic development became more ambitious and comprehensive. The international declarations and plans of action constituted a protest against the real trends; but they also became a ritualized substitute for effective action to change the trends. In the case of the environment the latest stages have been the highly publicized convening by the United Nations of the 1992 Earth Summit in Rio de Janeiro and the creation of a permanent Commission on Sustainable Development, whose first sessions have been marked by frustration at the continuing failure of national governments to give environmental policies and expenditures an effective priority matching the semi-commitments made at the Earth Summit.

For present purposes, it seems most promising to view what is happening in terms of *processes* of societal mutation that may or may not be perceived as *problems*, and that are imperfectly and precariously susceptible to rational action – rational from the standpoint of some definable social interest or vision of the Good Society. If one accepts the proposition that 'development' must curb its aggressions against the ecosystems of the world, moderate its appetite for non-renewable resources, and prefer enhancement of the quality of life to proliferation of consumer goods, the technical means to this end may not be too hard to elaborate. The question is how such a fundamental challenge to real trends can relate itself politically to our starting point of conflictive mutations, lowered expectations concerning state capacity to solve problems, and precarious ascendancy of economic and cultural globalization.

### Process and problem

Let us define 'process' as any major ongoing evolution in social organization, distribution and use of power, livelihood, exploitation of resources, technology, settlement patterns, capital accumulation, or distribution and content of consumption. Let us define 'problem' as any situation or aspect of the society that some social force or group capable of acting perceives as unsatisfactory. In this sense, dissatisfaction with a given level of consumption or share in power is a problem, as are perceived threats to personal well-being or human survival.

Processes may or may not be perceived as problems, or may be so perceived by some societal actors but not by others. One can expect an unending series of interactions between perception of problems, responses, and modification of ongoing processes. One can also expect a certain lag in the perception of problems and responses to them behind the processes to which they refer, suggested by the saying that generals are always prepared to fight the last war.

Perception of processes as problems, leading to the generation of controversy, pressures for action and policy responses, may be indirectly intellectualized or directly derived from experience. Generally, but not necessarily, strong indirect perceptions are associated with some degree of direct perception. (However, a person may be militantly concerned over the extermination of whales even if he or she has never seen a whale or hopes to see one.) Indirect perceptions reach the individual through the mass media, through organizational affiliations, through contacts with like-minded people and, in the case of small but influential minorities, through activity as scientists, futurologists, planners and publicists. Indirect perceptions will be filtered by the informational channels themselves, which will transmit some messages but not others, and through the ideological perceptions or world-view of the recipient. These preconceptions colour the perception of new problems and may exclude some from consideration; but if the impact of the problem is strong enough it may colour or even transform the ideology.

Since the environment, perceived as a problem, has been a latecomer in international discourse on development, one might expect its reception in different quarters to be subordinated to various preoccupations already on the stage: to economic growth, to access to the consumer society, to social revolution, to national security, to human rights and so on. At the same time, its impact is probably strong enough modify the perception of these other problems.

## Perceptions and responses

The perception of problems and responses to them likely to characterize different collective actors can be distinguished as follows, in a very simplified fashion.

(a) *The state or government facing demands that it 'solve' the problem.* Even if this is an authoritarian state, new problems are bound to be perceived as complications jostling for attention and for scarce resources, to be evaded or put off if possible, or to be dealt with according to the relative strength of political pressures and the feasibility of using the problem as a rallying point for political mobilization. As long as the capacity of states is as overstrained as at present, the forces controlling them must prefer, in regard to most problems, 'satisficing' rather than 'maximizing' solutions; that is, doing just enough to keep the problem from reaching unmanageable dimensions.

The environmental question imposed itself on world attention at a time when governments were already trapped between continually diversifying demands that they solve problems, or transform themselves so as to become able to solve problems, on the one side, and a contradictory combination of rising disillusionment at their failure to act coherently and rising resentment at the costliness and bureaucratic rigidity of the measures through which they try to cope with demands, on the other. In this respect, governments in the industrial or post-industrial countries have resembled governments in the periphery more than might have been expected. Events since the 1970s have cruelly exposed the pretensions of the former to effective economic planning, administrative efficiency and equitable arbitration of the interests of their citizens.

Ideally, environmental concerns, affecting as they do practically all aspects of lifestyles and productive processes, should generate planned responses linking the perceived interests of different groups in the national societies to some coherent common image of a possible and desirable future. In practice, advocates of environmental reforms have had to fight, at the cost of intransigence and exaggeration, to keep their concerns from being submerged each time the state confronts a new crisis, their adversaries find an effective new tactic, or research reveals a hitherto unperceived threat.

(b) *The modern productive and commercial enterprises, national and transnational.* For these, the perception by the state or public opinion of the environment as a 'problem' represents potential hindrances, costs and dangers. Their natural responses are to deny the importance of the problem; to assert that it will eventually solve itself through market mechanisms, technological innovations and the untrammelled growth of production; to shift the costs of whatever solutions are unavoidable to the state and the society; and, finally, if the problem will not go away, to take the lead in devising solutions that will be profitable to themselves.

(c) *Intellectuals, scientists, ideologists and 'concerned citizens'.* This heterogeneous category has a bias towards comprehensive rationalistic long-term solutions and clear priorities. It also has a bias toward solutions that will give leading roles to its own members, as technocrats, planners and mobilizers of public opinion. Within this category of actors, different academic disciplines, professional–technical specializations and movements oriented by political, religious or ethical ideologies naturally perceive the problems and conceive solutions quite differently. These perceptions influence change processes through their reception by the state, organized interest-groups, political parties and the mass media. Generally, as was suggested above, the perceptions are simplified and distorted in transmission and exert influence with a considerable lag.

(d) *Social groups directly experiencing the impact of current processes through environmental degradation and insecurity of livelihood, or suffering more diffuse anxieties without a scientific or ideological frame of reference through which to interpret their origin.* These groups can be classified according to many criteria, the most relevant being their perception of capacity to participate in and benefit from the current style of development, or their perception of exclusion and powerlessness.

For the most part their perception of problems and possible solutions can be expected to be ambivalent, coloured by the state of mind that Alvin Toffler labelled 'future shock'. A generalized feeling of anxiety deriving from the impact of accelerating economic, cultural and technological change can focus on alarm over menaces not directly experienced but encountered through the mass media: for example, nuclear holocaust, climatic changes induced by contamination of the atmosphere and leading to a new ice age or melting of the polar ice caps, and the introduction of noxious extraterrestrial organisms through space exploration. Such indirectly perceived menaces, combining with feelings of powerlessness against manipulation by economic monopolies, politicians or scientists, can generate paranoid fears or movements devoted fanatically to single issues.

The better-off groups in any modern or modernizing society cannot help perceiving a series of environmental problems deriving from the massification of their privileged patterns of consumption: crowded highways, polluted beaches, the deterioration of urban centres and the expansion of suburbs to a point negating the advantages of suburban living.[1] At these social levels, the role of the mass media in linking direct to indirect perceptions is particularly important.

The urban working class is more exposed to easily perceived menaces such as polluted air, overcrowded housing, dwindling access to open spaces for recreation, long journeys to work and job-associated illnessses. It also has fewer possibilities for escape or mitigation. The workers, however, encouraged by their employers, can also be expected to perceive environmental regulations as threats to their jobs and their access to the consumer society. The underemployed and marginalized poor, or their political spokesmen, may perceive environmental concerns and public allocations mainly as competitive with their own immediate needs.

The relative importance of the different actors for the character of the aggregate societal response to environmental problems will naturally differ according to the specific problem. So will their perception of suitable channels for responses. In relation to some problems, the perceptions and actions of technobureaucracies within the state, negotiating with profit-motivated private enterprise, may be decisive, as long as other forces do not perceive environmental measures as problems, or do not perceive any way of influencing the outcome. In relation to other problems, the responses of groups within the society, expressed through the market, the vote, spontaneous or externally-stimulated mass protests, or flight, may determine what happens, at least in the short run.

At this point, it may be worthwhile to introduce two examples of the changing interplay of perceptions and responses in relation to two of the problems that are forcing themselves on the attention of state and society throughout the world.

*First*, let us consider the 'civilization of the automobile'. The privately owned gasoline-powered automobile has prevailed over alternative means of urban transport for various reasons other than its efficiency for this purpose: it gives a wider margin of personal freedom to the individual; it provides a highly visible means of demonstrating social status and income; manufacturers and oil companies seeking new markets have intensively promoted its use. The concentrated expansion of automobile use has generated problems perceived differently by owners, non-owners and city governments.

For the owners, the main problems have been to obtain better highways and more parking spaces, so as to offset the advance of congestion and to keep the vehicle, fuel and maintenance costs at levels they can afford. For the non-owners, the problems have been deterioration of public transport, smog, congestion, accidents and patterns of urban spatial organization and services that discriminate against them. For city governments, at earlier stages, the perceived problem has been how to adapt the city to the needs of the automobile and finance the infrastructure required for this. At a later stage, the problem becomes increasingly one of devising regulations to reduce the disbenefits of concentrated automobile use in the face of resistance from automobile manufacturers, vendors, oil companies and users.

At one stage, market forces determine urban sprawl, deterioration of city centres and predominance of large automobiles with high fuel consumption, without any significant perception of these phenomena as problems. At another, the state begins to intervene to control certain land uses, rehabilitate public transport, hinder the entry of private automobiles into the city centre, and regulate the characteristics of automobiles in the interest of lower fuel consumption, lower emission of fumes, and greater safety. These interventions generally are improvisations intended to reduce the most urgent problems to manageable dimensions. They also represent compromises between the views of urban planners, political leaders and the sectors of the public that are able to make themselves heard.

Eventually, as during the 1970s, sudden and steep increases in the price of oil, making the automobile a much heavier charge on family income as well as on the balance of payments of countries that are not self-sufficient in oil, set in motion new perceptions of the role of the automobile in the consumer society itself, new processes of adaptation and regulation, and new tactics designed to shift the cost and preserve existing privileges and sources of profit. Contradictions between the policies and actions of different public agencies probably become more pronounced. Still later, falling oil prices may relegate the new perceptions and responses to temporary oblivion.

Meanwhile, the greater part of the urban population in poor countries has little or no hope of acquiring an automobile and no coherent perception of the impact of mass automobile use by minorities on its own living conditions. Its one intermittently effective intervention in the contest may be to preserve cheap but uncomfortable public transport by political pressures or by rioting to protest fare increases.

*Second*, let us consider the land deterioration and impoverishment associated with *minifundio* cultivation. Agricultural technicians, planners and bureaucrats have perceived these problems through surveys and have tried to respond to them, according to their own professional backgrounds and values, by trying to expel the cultivators from eroding land and reafforest it, by regulation of grazing, by agrarian reforms to give the cultivators more adequate land resources, by supervised credits, by educational campaigns and by provision of local employment opportunities outside agriculture.

The more modern large landowners and agribusinesses have perceived the problem as one of inefficient land use and immobilization of labour. They have used various tactics to gain control of the land held in *minifundios*, to the extent that this could serve their own production plans, and to convert the cultivators into wage labourers. Alternatively, they have accepted the *minifundio* as a convenient source of seasonal wage labour that can be paid less than its cost of subsistence.

Other sectors of the national power elite have informed themselves to some extent and have responded according to their own priority preoccupations, including ecological or humanitarian values. (For example, the military leadership might be concerned about the poor physical condition and illiteracy of recruits from the *minifundio* population or about its propensity to harbour guerrilla movements; the urban authorities might be concerned about the *minifundios* as sources of ill-adapted migrants. Counter-elites have seen in the contradiction between the interests of impoverished cultivators and those of the forces nationally dominant possibilities for revolutionary mobilization.

The *minifundio* cultivators themselves have perceived the problem through diminishing capacity of the land to give them subsistence, increasing pressure from modernized capitalist agriculture, and decreasing acceptability of their meagre and precarious livelihood in the kind of society growing up around them. They have responded according to the alternatives they could perceive in specific local settings, through further intensification of land use; shifts to cash crops, including illegal crops such as coca and opium poppies; mobilization to demand state aid and better land; temporary migration to obtain a supplementary income; migration to frontier zones; or abandonment of the land through permanent migration to towns and cities.

The accelerating loss of arable land and rural impoverishment are presumably more important to the national future than the trials of urban transport users. It is evident, however, that in this case the combined technocratic, political and popular perceptions of the problem, while of long standing, have not added up to pressure on the state for action on a scale matching this importance. Still less have they enabled the cultivators to participate effectively in determining their future livelihood and place in the national society.

In this case, as in that of the automobile, new factors are forcing various societal actors to revise their perceptions, without necessarily helping the cultivators to make their own views of their interests heard. The increasingly dangerous dependence of the countries on imports of basic foods, combined with the increasing costs and environmental disbenefits of modern large-scale agriculture (fuel, fertilizers, pesticides, heavy machinery) make the dominance of such agriculture and its export-orientation increasingly precarious. Policy shifts towards domestic food production using relatively labour-intensive methods may become unavoidable, and in one way or another the societal actors able to influence policy will have to take the land and labour power of the *minifundio* cultivators into account.

## Perceptions of environmental problems: some lessons from the central countries

It is commonly asserted that industrialized countries and 'developing' countries perceive environmental problems differently. Certainly the configurations of problems differ and so do the dominant perceptions of them, but the formulation can be misleading. 'Countries' as such do not perceive any more than they 'choose' styles of development. Social forces and groups within them have quite different perceptions and choices, and the aggregate national responses to problems, as was argued above, emerge from the interactions of different perceptions, from the channels through which different actors perceive the problems, and from the degree to which these different actors are in a position to act on their perceptions. Even the most powerful and purposeful regime encounters resistances and pressures that it cannot altogether disregard.

One of the most striking features of the industrialized countries during the recent past has been the extent to which conflicting perceptions of environmental problems, ranging from the complacent to the catastrophist, have become explicit, have entered into public opinion, have been debated in the mass media and have been advanced by specialized organizations trying to influence legislation, allocations of public resources and private behaviour. The more organized and articulate sources of perceptions and public positions can be classified roughly as follows:

— Industrial and agricultural enterprises in general.
— Transnational enterprises in particular.
— Energy producers and vendors in particular.
— Trade unions.
— Ecological, conservationist and consumer movements.
— Organizations of sportsmen and campers.
— Journalists.
— Economists.
— Other social and physical scientists.
— Religious bodies.
— 'Enlightened' public opinion (academics and professionals).
— Mobilizers of groups experiencing exclusion or discrimination.
— The state itself (in principle the final arbiter of policy but in practice

a conglomerate of bureaucracies and political factions allied with different social forces advancing their own perceptions and responses).

Naturally, none of these categories is monolithic in its perceptions; most of them are deeply divided. Some are concerned almost exclusively with environmental questions. In others the environment competes with or is subordinated to perceptions of other urgent problems and demands. Several of these latter problems and demands are storm centres of equally complex and conflictive organized perceptions: equal rights for women and ethnic minorities; abortion; consumer protection; employment; enhancement of national military power. In some quarters, also, the environment as well as the other problems may be perceived entirely opportunistically, for their potential in advancing political careers, providing employment for professional mobilizers and publicists, or offering a field for profit-making enterprises.

In the United States, in particular, the various perceptions confront each other through institutionalized adversary procedures. It is expected that the proponent of each position will advance it in the strongest terms – generally in a tone of righteous indignation and warnings of doom – and that policy will emerge from differential capacity to convince, mobilize and overcome the inertia of the political process. Such policy, however, will represent a series of compromises. No contender will achieve all objectives, and interests that do not choose to join in the public contest will influence the result by backstage negotiations.

Some consequences of this way of arriving at policy are a proliferation of regulations originating in legislative compromises; considerable increases in the range of interventions by bureaucracies, not only in the functioning of enterprises but also in everyday life; and a projection of the initial contest, through the courts, into the interpretation of laws and the allocation of public funds. The proliferation of environmental regulations coincides with a proliferation of regulations responding to other problems and arrived at by similar paths of conflictive advocacy and political compromise. In their combination these regulations clash with a general disillusionment with the welfare state as over-regulative, over-costly and incompetent.

Thus, important sectors of public opinion are torn between distaste for environmental degradation, on the one hand, and distaste for bureaucracy and taxes, on the other. Industrial and commercial enterprises now use this factor in their publicity, declaring themselves practising environmentalists, but insisting on the costs of excessive regulation and the intransigence of their opponents. The adversary procedure of policy-making has up to the present generated substantial gains in environmental protection, but there are signs that the overload of perceived problems can lead to paralysis; the contending parties are better able to block or dilute decisions favouring their adversaries than to advance decisions suited to their own perceptions.

This kind of policy-making perpetuates a kind of schizophrenia in government actions: costly programmes that directly contradict each other may be introduced to satisfy different interests and perceptions. One public agency subsidizes tobacco growing and crusades against barriers to wider markets for cigarettes abroad, while another mounts intensive propaganda campaigns against smoking as a menace to health. At the same time, adversary campaigns are only slowly and erratically effective against large public agencies that have linked their self-preservation to the reproduction of activities that arguably have already been carried to excess, as in the case of the dam-building of the Army Corps of Engineers.

To the extent that the perceivers of environmental problems are unable to influence the state through arguments or votes, or question the ability of the state to meet their demands, they may resort to direct action, boycotts, civil disobedience or sabotage. Their expectations from such tactics are generally mixed. The participants may hope to make environmentally hazardous industrial processes or resource exploitation impossible through the intensity of their action, but generally they are more concerned to mobilize wider support, and to convince the state or the entrepreneurs that meeting their demands will be cheaper politically and economically than resisting them. In the industrialized countries, action of this kind long centred on nuclear power installations and drew in sizable minorities of youth disillusioned with more conventional forms of political action.

The last response to environmental preoccupations, in groups sceptical of action by the state and of the effectiveness of extra-legal militancy, is change in personal lifestyles or withdrawal from participation in the prevailing style of development. The withdrawal may be limited, inspired by sentiments of personal responsibility for getting changes under way, as in groups and individuals that try to limit their own use of contaminating energy sources and convert to solar power, regardless of comparative costs, or that scrupulously save waste materials for recycling. It may encompass a systematic effort to make oneself independent of the economic and political order and prepare for survival after the expected catastrophe. In recent years, manuals giving instructions for this kind of preparation have achieved wide circulation. Some religious sects have added an environmental dimension to their conviction that doom is at hand for the unconverted majority.

## Perceptions of environmental problems in the rest of the world

In the 'peripheral' countries that have achieved some degree of industrialization, in a context of continually changing challenges and shocks from economic and cultural globalization, perceptions have also been diverse and difficulties in the way of coherent policies have been formidable, as the two examples described above indicate. However, the social forces involved have been more restricted, at least until very recently. The perceptions that have counted for environmental policy have been those of transnational and national enterprises, and those of the circles of economists, engineers, planners and other professionals who advise governments and direct programmes on the basis of their claims to specialized knowledge. The mass media in these countries have begun to pay attention to the environment and middle-class public opinion has become at least uneasy, unable to ignore urban degradation in the pursuit of modernized consumption, but public perceptions have been far from the intensity and organized combativeness of those evident in the central countries.

The transnational enterprises might transfer a certain concern for the environmental impact of their activities from their present forced adaptations in their home countries, and might perceive advantages in keeping such impact within tolerable limits. Their predominant interest, however, has been in preserving as long as possible situations of low costs and freedom from regulations such as those cramping them at home. The record of dangerous products and processes disseminated in peripheral countries after being prohibited in their countries of origin demonstrates no aptitude for environmental self-restraint. National enterprises have been even less likely to view, of their own accord, environmental impact as a problem to which they should subordinate their calculations of profitability.

In rapidly urbanizing and precariously industrializing countries such as those of Latin America and Southeast Asia, however, the widening of political participation has coincided with a very rapid intensification of the kinds of environmental problems that have a direct and evident impact on the well-being of the population, including the parts of the urban population that are able to make themselves heard. Under these conditions, one might expect environmental concerns to penetrate a wider range of social groups, to become formalized in organizations, to seek political expression and, if unable to find relief through governmental actions, to generate violent extra-legal protests. The trend would be speeded up by the ease of borrowing interpretations, slogans and remedies from like-minded groups in the central countries. The state would come under stronger pressures to act, but the diversity of these pressures would continually inhibit action. For a time, as has happened in relation to other major problems, one might expect the undertaking of elaborate surveys and the drafting of comprehensive plans to serve as a means of demonstrating good intentions while postponing the fixing of realistic priorities.

Responses such as these have been visible since the 1970s or earlier, and by now all except the poorest countries and those on the verge of disintegration have an array of environmental movements interacting with the national authorities. However, two quite different features of economic globalization have stunted their evolution and pushed their preoccupations into the background: in most of Latin America and Africa the debt crises of the 1980s and the consequent stabilization and structural adjustment policies forced governments to concentrate on economic viability as defined by international lending institutions, and left most of the public preoccupied by insecurity and impoverishment. In much of Asia, on the contrary, rapid economic growth and rising consumption levels generated distrust in governments as well as the public of any initiatives that might put a brake on growth.

What are the possibilities for the awakening of a wider policy-oriented environmental perception that can escape the domination of privileged minorities and keep within limits the adversary procedures, interest-group tactics and regulative entanglements that now plague the central countries? This amounts to asking whether alternative styles of development recognizing the environmental imperative can become accessible. In seeking a plausible answer, let us examine first the roles of technobureaucrats, then the prospects for popular participation in what is done.

## Technobureaucrats

The label 'technobureaucrat', for present purposes, lumps together specialists with quite different ideological and disciplinary frames of reference who have in common their claim to show the state how to bring about 'development' on the basis of correct theories and professional expertise. The rise of technobureaucrats has been a relatively recent phenomenon, as the range of responsibilities of states and the range of expertise supposed to be needed have widened simultaneously. The technobureaucrats have aspired to a more autonomous and innovative role in policy-making than the more traditional bureaucrats, who based their claim to authority on mastery of precedents, procedures and regulations. As far as they and their political sponsors have been able, the higher technobureaucrats have separated their status and rewards from those of the remainder of the public administration. It was to be expected that when the theme of the environment came to the fore the technobureaucrats already on the scene would try to assimilate it to their prescriptions for development, and that different professional specializations would use it to support a claim to a more prominent place in the technobureaucratic ranks. The ways in which technobureaucrats have intervened in policy suggest the following hypotheses.

(a) The professional or disciplinary specialization and institutional socialization of technobureaucrats largely determine their ability to perceive and assimilate new problems or reformulate the interventions they consider relevant to their policy prescriptions. When a major problem area such as the environment comes to the fore, different categories of techno-bureaucrats may reject it as a dangerous diversion of attention from what is important, transfer responsibility for action to some other professional specialization, or redefine the problem in terms permitting them to in-corporate it into their previous disciplinary terms of reference. In general, technobureaucrats have shown poor capacity to adjust to major shifts in perceived problems, or to foresee the long-term consequences of national styles of development.

(b) Technobureaucrats commonly assume that there must be one optimal technical solution to every problem and that political or other resistances to the application of this solution are to be condemned. The technobureaucratic rationality continually clashes with the rationalities of politicians, administrative bureaucrats and organized interest-groups. Unless the technobureaucrats gain exclusive access to authoritarian sources of power, such as military regimes, their interventions become either in-effective and ritualistic, as in the case of much formal development planning, or deliberately narrow in focus, so as to shield them from the unmanageable wider setting, as in the case of most development projects. In trying to strengthen their influence, technobureaucrats have commonly exaggerated the infallibility of their specialized knowledge and blamed failures on irrationalities elsewhere in the political, administrative and economic systems.

(c) Technobureaucrats generally have been biased towards standardized, universally applicable solutions to problems and large-scale technologically advanced capital-intensive projects. This bias has supported the myth of development as a uniform process going through stages that can be deduced from the past of the 'developed' capitalist countries. A good many environmental disasters have originated in technobureaucratic at-tempts to standardize national policies and introduce advanced technologies without regard to local conditions or real capacity to control execution. In the case of hydroelectric and irrigation dam-building projects, in particular, a fascination with sheer size and ultra-modernity has had perverse results.

(d) The job market for technobureaucrats consists of governments, international agencies, academic and research institutions, and private enterprises, with transnational corporations increasingly dominant within the last market. Many technobureaucrats, especially the more influential, shift frequently from one area of employment to another. Experience in these different settings can be expected to produce different kinds of socialization and different perceptions of developmental and environmental problems.

The following historical sketch of the evolution of bureaucracy and technobureaucracy in Latin America through the 1970s could apply also to other 'developing' regions. First, from the 1930s to the 1950s came a stage of steady expansion in bureaucratic employment, stimulated simultaneously by the creation of new state activities in the name of 'modernization', and by middle-class pressures for jobs, overloading the state with tasks of assisting special groups, in particular the poor, it was unable to carry out efficiently, as yet without a coherent development policy focus.

Second came a stage of confidence in the autonomous capacity of the state to achieve rapid development and reconcile social conflicts through planning:

> if the state wins this autonomy, those who control it, be it only partially, are the political and technical officials of the state who do not directly represent social interests; in other words the technobureaucracy whose power began to take root in the chinks and cracks of the state's margin of liberty, made possible its greater functional diversification and promoted the type of alliances characteristic of the democratic political order in this phase.

Still later, when this order broke down under the pressure of mutually incompatible demands on the state or visions of the Good Society, and military–authoritarian regimes imposed themselves, the technobureaucrats (or other technobureaucrats trained and socialized in different academic settings) gained even more self-confidence. They argued that:

> politics has no meaning or role in the 'technological era'. Politics corresponds to an era of 'trial and error' when solutions were found through successive approximations. In contrast, the Scientific Method brought with it the era of rational planning and the non-political solution of the problems of society, thereby dispensing with the need for any kind of public discussion or collective deliberation. In the technocratic society, the 'specialists' are the ones who decide objectively with the scientific means at their disposal, in the name of the highest national interests and without public responsibility to the people.

Previously technobureaucrats and intellectuals were linked in the aspiration to promote structural changes in the societies. Now, 'intellectuals as well as politicians are the archetypes of disfunctional groups as a technocratic state requires the "unity of the people"'.[2]

The above history could also be summed up as a struggle for influence between different schools of reformist and conformist technobureaucrats. The reformist school that flourished during the 1950s and 1960s fell into eclipse in most countries because of the inapplicability of its policy prescriptions within existing national power structures, the inability of the political alliances on which it depended to overcome internal contradictions, and the ability of external forces to hinder or destabilize policies of which they disapproved. More broadly, the imperatives of the transnationalized world system were able to impose themselves over technobureaucratic efforts to reform the national style of development.

With the 1980s, still another school of technobureaucrats became dominant, through choice by a regime in some countries and through external pressure in others. This neoliberal school aspired to reduce or eliminate the active role of the state in managing development, through dismantling of regulations and privatization of the public sector enterprises and services fostered by their predecessors. Their conviction of a right and capacity to override political resistances to the application of optimal technical solutions was just as strong as that of these predecessors.

Meanwhile, a good many reformist technobureaucrats, after their struggles to reshape public policies led to their own exclusion, took refuge in international organizations, universities or research institutions. The rising perception of environmental menaces since the early 1970s, along with mass impoverishment and other disbenefits of the prevailing style of development, have given them powerful arguments for a rehabilitation of state interventions under their guidance. In fact, the state, whatever forces control it, will have to continue to strive to shape the national future, with the aid of experts who will evolve their own status-enhancing and self-justifying tactics. If styles of development more compatible with enhancement of the quality of life become politically viable, the reallocation of national resources, the drafting and enforcement of environmental controls, and the extension of livelihood opportunities and public services to the masses now excluded will require complex administrative structures and expertise.

In most of the world environmentalist initiatives, like those for assigning priority to the elimination of extreme poverty, are internationally inspired and led by reformist technobureaucrats. These are more concerned to strengthen communication with functioning national technobureaucrats, who remain suspicious of any diversion of attention from economic growth, than to mobilize mass support. The bias towards standardized comprehensively planned solutions to complex problems persists, once more under the label 'integrated approach', although tempered by perplexity at the difficulty of relating such solutions to national societies that are inextricably enmeshed in the consequences of economic and cultural globalization. A major effort of self-analysis seems to be needed if the present perceptions of reformist technobureaucrats are not to be frustrated, like the developmentalist outlook of the past, by misapprehensions concerning their own capacity to plot the course of conflictive societal change.

## Participation

In real political processes, technobureaucrats and political leaders with technobureaucratic inclinations, whatever their ideological frame of reference, can be expected to reject the disorder and hindrances to productive efficiency associated with autonomous popular participation. The doctrinaire extremes to which some egalitarian and anti-market ideological movements have carried their efforts to manipulate such participation are well known. Cycles have recurred of populist or Maoist leaders generating disorder in the name of societal transformation and of technobureaucratically inclined leaders, once they regained the upper hand, imposing the rule of the market or of socialist central planning, depending on the political order in which they found themselves. Campaigns to dethrone the experts have only made the experts more intransigent.

It would be convenient if technobureaucratic prescriptions could be trusted to bring about socially just and environmentally sound development without the conflictive representation of the perceptions of all sectors of national societies. It would also be convenient if the unavoidable tension between technobureaucratic and participationist or pluralist democratic viewpoints could remain within limits, each respecting the other's legitimacy and recognizing its own weaknesses. In the real world, however, the conflictive representation of perceived interests cannot be avoided. If this does not embrace the groups now powerless or otherwise preoccupied, one can expect environmental policy to be shaped by negotiations between national and international or transnational technobureaucracies, with the last holding the advantages of better information, clearer purposes and ability to hire their interlocutors away from the state. One can then assume that the costs of environmental policies and of development policies in general will, as far as is feasible, continue to be heaped on the voiceless and the benefits diverted elsewhere.

No environmental policy or development policy will be politically neutral in its distribution of costs and benefits. In broad terms, this proposition may seem excessively obvious. However, it is worth emphasizing that the real distribution of costs and benefits will depend less on the initial overt purposes of the policy than on its subsequent evolution in specific social and political settings. As long as power and perceptiveness concerning opportunities for self-serving action remain unevenly distributed, new forms of manipulation will continually work upon new forms of state intervention. If the groups affected cannot respond in a reasonably vigorous and well-informed way, the very safeguards introduced to ensure equity may divert the benefits of policy (at least, benefits in terms of power and employment opportunities) to technobureaucrats, lawyers and professional representatives of interest-groups.

In a good many industrialized or post-industrial countries, as was indicated above, environmental questions now constitute one of the more participatory areas of public policy, with participation taking the form of adversary procedures and competitive mobilization, as well as attempted reforms in personal lifestyles. The intensity of participation is unevenly distributed by social class and educational level, but even the disadvantaged groups have some capacity to protest against environmental actions and omissions that affect their perceived needs.

Elsewhere, even in formally democratic countries, this capacity is much more limited, and ideological positions on popular participation have become ritualistic or manipulative to such an extent that it might seem absurd or hypocritical to argue for such participation in environmental policy. The precarious and intermittent interventions of the disadvantaged in defence of their own perceived interests generally focus on access to jobs, basic goods and services, housing, education, health care and land tenure rather than on the environment. Their quest for livelihood and shelter, in urban as well as rural areas, forces them into environmentally damaging activities. These latter eventually come to the attention of technobureaucrats who try to curb them by regulation, exhortation and promotion of environmentally preferable alternatives.

Direct perceptions of environmental changes for the worse are undoubtedly on the rise among the disadvantaged groups, as these changes affect their livelihood, their physical health and their psychological security. Phenomena such as the indiscriminate use of dangerous chemicals cannot be ignored even by the desperately poor, who are most exposed to contaminated food and water, as recurrent press reports of mass poisonings demonstrate. In some cases, technologies damaging to health and livelihood have been deliberately used against them: for example, landowners have forced small cultivators off their holdings by air spraying of pesticides. In other cases, many thousands of peasants have become pawns of shifting technobureaucratic colonization schemes, left stranded when the land once cleared proved unsuitable for permanent cultivation or when public agencies decided to support different lines of production and large-scale 'modern' holdings.

It is probable that less tangible menaces are entering popular consciousness through the now ubiquitous mass media. It may not be too far-fetched to imagine that these combined with other sources of insecurity, in the absence of more adequate channels for perception and response, can stimulate mass rejection of technology and its carriers and fuel new messianic or xenophobic movements.

At best, one can expect that the initial participation of the disadvantaged groups will be defensive, using the tactics of evasion, petition or violence discussed in Chapter 4 to ward off threatening changes and get a hearing from the power centres. One can expect most technobureaucrats and practically all entrepreneurs to condemn such tactics as shortsighted and reactionary. In view of their own record of shortsightedness and disregard of the impact of their activities on popular livelihoods and well-being, however, the emergence of a popular capacity for militant self-defence against the experts seems to be an indispensable, if insufficient, requisite for the formulation and application of more enlightened environmental policies.

## Notes

1. Hirsch, *Social Limits to Growth* (1976).

2. Graciarena and Franco, 'Social Formations and Power Structures in Latin America' (1978). See also O'Donnell, 'Tensions in the Bureaucratic-Authoritarian State and the Question of Democracy' (1979).

# CHAPTER 7

# WHERE TO?

## Policy-making, or Alice-in-Wonderland croquet

The preceding chapters have exposed my scepticism concerning the relevance of prescriptions addressed to humanity at large or governments in general by the international bureaucratic and academic machinery that continually generates meetings and reports and missions around the elusive topic of 'development'. The thorniest problem is not the formulation of better strategies for 'another development', 'human development' or 'sustainable development'. The efforts of dedicated thinkers over the past two centuries seem to have uncovered all possible solutions. Some of these solutions have been tested in practice and some of them have helped to change the course of history. The institutionalized continuation of these efforts during the past half-century has continually rediscovered, without acknowledgement or even awareness, ideas current among utopian socialists in the early nineteenth century and Russian populists in the late nineteenth century. In returning to the pursuit of elusive development I have been haunted by the abundance of inspiring and plausible proposals that reached a peak during the 1970s but that continue to appear and struggle for a hearing in a world order that offers them, at most, a place in the successive utopias devised by committees.

The would-be architects of ideal societies have commonly envisaged social change processes as more manipulable and less ambiguous in their outcomes than has been the case. While their influence has been considerable and has undergone surprising metamorphoses, they failed to identify and enlighten social actors willing and able to apply strategies oriented to human welfare coherently, realistically and flexibly over the long term. This failure, and the exposure of illusions concerning certain regimes that tried or pretended to apply such strategies, helped open the way to the dominion of globalized capitalism and market forces. However, this seems equally calculated for self-destruction through triumphalism, corruption and blindness to phenomena contradicting its dogmas. Can the next stage be a return to scripts rebelling against the economic Kingdom of Necessity but more self-critically than before?

A sympathetic study of the experiences of political leaders and planners who have tried to apply coherent strategies to their own national settings is conducive to humility, and even suggests that the last thing they need is more generalized exhortation on what they ought to do if they could count on an ideal social consensus and an ideal capacity to acquire and digest information. The 'high-level expert' who pontificates on *what* must be done and evades the questions *who* and *how* has justifiably become a figure of fun.[1] At the other extreme, the purveying in international reports of shopping lists of 'practical' techniques and 'pilot projects', on the supposition that policy-makers can pick and choose from sketchy descriptions of what has allegedly succeeded elsewhere, has also reached a dead end of futility.

The situation of the real participants in policy-making is closer to that of Alice in her Wonderland croquet game than to that of the powerful, benevolent, unimaginative entities to which development prescriptions seem to be addressed:

> Alice thought she had never seen such a curious croquet ground in her life; it was all ridges and furrows; the croquet balls were live hedgehogs and the mallets live flamingoes; and the soldiers had to double themselves up and stand on their hands and feet to make the arches ... Alice soon came to the conclusion that it was a very difficult game indeed. The players all played at once without waiting for turns, quarrelling all the while, and fighting for the hedgehogs.

Instead of offering more prescriptions, let us speculate about certain questions that national societies and the international order will be unable to avoid trying to answer *if* the future evolves along lines that seem at least as plausible as the alternatives.

This last point deserves emphasis. If the globalized capitalist economic order maintains its present dynamism, if the present centres retain their hegemony and use it for the same purposes as heretofore, if the contradictions generated by present styles of development in peripheral countries continue to be manageable in one way or another, answers to such questions can, at most, be considered by the dominant forces as 'missing ingredients', to be added to the style of development in order to make it function better, or to forestall criticisms of its inequity, with the likely result of introducing secondary contradictions and anomalies in its functioning. However, if the future should bring generalized and catastrophic breakdown in the global and national orders, we have no way of offering rational guidelines to societies as to how to cope, or even of forecasting what social forces would become dominant in these societies. The following pages will proceed on the supposition that the medium-term future will be one of frequent and traumatic mutations not amounting to catastrophe except locally, of contradictory stimuli from the world centres to the periphery and vice versa, of the increasingly precarious capacity of the centres to exercise hegemony, of challenges for which neither the forces at the head of present governments nor the counter-elites will be any better prepared than in the past.

In the short term, one can expect successive waves of frantic urgency for action subsiding into complacency at any sign of return to the 'normal'. Measures taken piecemeal to cope with disbenefits of the style of development will cumulatively change many traits of this style, probably in unexpected ways. Interventions by states and international institutions will become more vigorous, reversing the trend to shrinkage of the state. These interventions will interact conflictively with the changing demands and values of social forces, and with changing forms of alienation from and resistance to states and other institutions.

It is possible that human societies will prove so dazzled by the promise of present transformations or so intimidated by their inevitability that they will perish rather than change course. It is also possible, unfortunately, that they will find no means of doing so that will not incur such heavy costs – in failed experimentation, substitution of façade achievements and rituals for real achievements, endemic conflict between groups trying to impose their own will, regimentation and manipulation of consensus – that they will respond to the hopes invested in them no better than the variants of 'real socialism' have done.

Can approaches be proposed that recognize the constraints on rational intervention in the transformations that are under way, that eschew utopian prescriptions wanted neither by the forces now dominant nor by most of the dominated, but that point in the direction of the values that inspired 'another development'? If plausible approaches are within reach, what agents are likely to follow them?

Let us try to reach a partial answer by taking a look at three policy questions: satisfaction of basic needs, employment and livelihood, and democratic participation. These questions have been central to discourse on alternative styles of development. They have occasioned an enormous quantity of research and theorizing that is as far as ever from consensus on what is happening and what should be happening. The contradictions between aspirations and realities place them at the centre of political struggle, and other contradictions place them at the centre of development policy debates. Government policies as well as the so-called 'information revolution' influence what is happening in many ways, complicating rather than managing the contradictions. (A fourth question, that of environmental sustainability, presents even more ominous contradictions and incompatibilities with the dominant style of 'development', but we can dispense with rehashing them at this point.)

One might conclude that the contradictions will become more acute until they either bring about the world catastrophe of which proponents of 'another development' have warned or bring about a transformation of values making feasible solutions that at present would be unacceptable and incomprehensible to governments, dominant economic forces and most of the people suffering from the contradictions. However, if such solutions do become feasible it is more likely to be through multifarious experiments, survival strategies, struggles and changes in consciousness than through clear-cut choices between planned transformation and catastrophe.

## Basic needs and consumerism

Proposals for 'another development' during the 1970s insisted on priority to satisfaction of basic human needs. These proposals had the virtue of directing attention equally to the content of production, to consumption (as the main legitimate reason for wanting higher production), and to distribution (as the provision of relevant basic goods and services to all). They pointed to elimination of critical poverty without singling out the poor as a category to be 'helped'. Studies under the auspices of the International Labour Organization, the Dag Hammarskjöld Foundation and other institutions elaborated the implications of basic needs strategies in considerable detail.[2]

The definition of basic needs presented challenging but not insuperable problems. The term had to refer, initially at least, to the goods and services that could be produced and distributed to the whole of a national population, in accordance with realistic expectations, independently of the achievement of a more equitable world order. National definitions should respond to an objective criterion for 'basic' needs (for example, meeting physiological needs), and also to the subjective criteria of the people whose basic needs were in question. It was important to avoid the trap of making definition and measurement ends in themselves, and also to resist the temptation to admit as basic needs the whole range of desiderata that have received international recognition as 'human rights'. Rights to determined levels of consumption were meaningful only to the extent to which national societies were really capable of honouring them for the whole population. Otherwise, affirmation of such rights would unavoidably support tactics for the protection and extension of minority privileges.

The relevant short-term standards for a good many countries might have to be at the 'rockbottom level of physical existence' referred to in the 1975 Dag Hammarskjöld Report. However, Sri Lanka, with a national system of subsidized or free rice distribution in effect most of the time since the 1940s, and with relatively well-developed educational and other social services, demonstrated that a basic needs strategy could be feasible even at a quite low level of per capita GNP. (The Sri Lanka policy seems to have entered into crisis leading to a future of atrocity-ridden ethnic warfare not because of inability to afford the rice distribution and the social services, but because of inability to incorporate these into a coherent style of development affording incentives to productivity and meaningful activity to the educated youth.)

The basic needs proposals obviously assumed on the part of states and civil societies as well as the international order a degree of rationality oriented by values of equity and a capacity to defy the logic of capitalist development that were not forthcoming. They fell under suspicion as devices to divert attention from the just demands of poor countries for aid in achieving conventional economic development. Their potential beneficiaries knew nothing of them, except here and there in the form of local experiments by participation-minded NGOs. Their international promoters turned their attention elsewhere. With the crises of the 1980s, the discrediting of the state as agent of development and arbiter of distribution, the globalization of markets, and the global diffusion of competitive consumerism, 'priority to basic needs' lost credibility even as a slogan.

A more limited version minimizing the challenge to conventional development priorities has indeed recently become current under the label of 'targeting', that is, concentration of whatever resources the state can afford to allocate for social purposes on the neediest strata. The World Bank has urged 'targeting' as a partial remedy for the disastrous social aftermath of stabilization and structural adjustment policies. A number of governments, particularly in Latin America, have embarked on sizeable programmes responding to this criterion, as 'Social Emergency Funds' administered and financed outside the pre-existing structures for social services. Up to a point, such programmes constitute legitimate reversals of previous situations in which overt objectives of universal access masked a real concentratation of benefits on better-off strata, including the functionaries of the programmes. However, targeting as a central criterion for allocation of public resources has more questionable implications for social cohesion than did the earlier proposals for basic needs strategies.

Consciousness of a universal right to public services meeting certain standards, particularly in regard to education and health, is almost a precondition for democratic citizenship, however widely realities may have diverged from this ideal. The middle strata, previously the main bene-ficiaries of many services and now themselves undergoing traumatic re-adjustments of their income and status expectations, naturally resent and resist the implications of targeting. Its political viability would thus be small unless governments were prepared to mobilize the disadvantaged, or some of them, to counterbalance the more influential claimants. At the same time, the intended beneficiaries, to the extent that they could make themselves heard politically, would not be content with meagre and seg-regated services and subsidies based on technocratic calculations of what the state could afford after meeting other priorities or after receiving earmarked funds from abroad.

People throughout the world are now exposed to messages concerning diversified and continually changing norms for consumption. They have internalized such norms to an extent that could hardly have been expected a few decades ago, when the 'revolution of rising expectations' became a current cliché. The present felt needs include packaged foods and beverages that are revolutionizing diets and distribution of family expenditures. They include the durable goods that are largely responsible for spreading the consumerist message: first the transistor radio, then television and various electronic devices. They include the automobile, with its devastating impact on the urban environment and its insatiable demands for roads, parking spaces and fuel. They include many artefacts that are reducing household drudgery and making life easier, particularly for women, and that transform the possibilities for family and community interactions from the local to the global.

They provide major stimuli for participation in innovation and in the quest for more remunerative employment. They have practically eliminated the possibility of popular acquiescence in styles of development emphasizing austerity and capital accumulation, on the one side, and styles giving priority to narrowly defined basic needs, on the other. Under these circumstances, economic liberalization policies have consistently encountered surges in consumer goods imports, outrunning increases in the exports needed to pay for them. Government-sponsored social pacts calling for shared sacrifices in consumption have been unable to restrain the groups committed by their organizations. This has happened repeatedly in Latin America and most recently in China, where pent-up consumer demand has pushed aside the egalitarian and collectivist traits previously admired by advocates of 'another development'. Although hundreds of millions of people remain excluded through extreme poverty, isolation, and cultural resistances, or are being further impoverished by dominant processes of economic concentration, elements of the consumer culture penetrate even these settings of exclusion in incongruous ways, as numerous accounts of present-day village and shanty town life indicate.

Since new lines of consumption quickly become cultural necessities and the possibilities for further diversification are unlimited, consciousness of inability to satisfy felt needs can be strong at any income level. Majorities in the 'rich' countries have achieved levels of consumption that can never be universalized and that are notoriously entering into contradiction with resource limits and environmental sustainability. However, a few years of relative economic stagnation have generated alarm, not only at immediate job and other insecurities, but also by challenging the conviction that each generation has a right to live better than its predecessor.

This is one of the hardest topics to confront realistically and with full appreciation of the momentum of the processes that are under way. The 'right to development', in the sense of the right of all societies to achieve the rhythms of production and consumption of the present high-income societies, and the right of the peoples of these latter societies to achieve higher levels with each generation, are mirages, with consequences inherently incompatible with the satisfaction of basic needs for all, as well as environmentally unsustainable. At the same time, there is no prospect of voluntary acceptance of austere egalitarianism, and since China's recent real cultural revolution no plausible idea as to how a society giving priority to this could function.

There may be no accessible alternative to a flight forward, through permanent revolutions in technology, information and social relationships, to consumer societies that generate equivalent satisfactions without unsustainable demands on resources and with an ebbing of obsession with competitive consumption. Any number of published utopias and dystopias point the way.

## Employment, livelihood, meaningful activity

Up to the 1960s, discourse on development commonly singled out as a major problem the 'commitment' of people from peasant societies to wage work in industry and other 'modern' activities. It was assumed that the demand for wage labour would continue to exceed supply until an advanced stage of development, and that the supply would be insufficiently committed and of low productivity owing to lack of appropriate work habits, lack of education, poor physical condition and certain cultural traits. In the earlier stages of 'development' directed by colonial powers and national oligarchies, various forms of compulsion to work for wages (head taxes, vagrancy laws, corvées) were recommended and applied. At later stages, with substantial industrial, mining and plantation wage labour forces already in being, positive inducements came to the fore: education, subsidized food supplies, social welfare and housing schemes linked to such employment. When it became evident that in most settings the supply of people anxious to work for wages was exceeding demand and that the excess was taking refuge in 'marginal' or 'informal' means of survival it could still be argued that this was a remediable deficiency of the rate or pattern of economic growth, or simply the formation of an 'industrial reserve army' functional to such growth.

In much of the world, the processes that in the past generated a labour force for industrialization are continuing and are fulfilling the same function: expulsion from smallholding agriculture and efforts by peasant youth to escape a life of poverty and drudgery. However, even where rates of absorption into wage labour have been dynamic, as in much of East and Southeast Asia, a precariously subsisting marginal population has increased in numbers.

Excess of labour supply over demand became more clear-cut and extensive during the 1980s in the countries most burdened by debt and forced into structural adjustment policies, mainly in Africa and Latin America. Insecurity of livelihood now struck the salaried middle strata and the previously stable wage workers as harshly as the marginal groups. Import-substitution industries collapsed. Mining was hard-hit by falling mineral prices and rising costs. Governments became unable to support the institutions they had acquired, which had long served as the employers of last resort for university graduates. Inflation reduced the incomes of these latter groups to levels violently excluding them from accustomed lifestyles. Campaigns of privatization and debureaucratization eliminated the jobs of many, or at least threatened their job security. Towards the end of the 1980s similar and even more traumatic changes struck the former 'real socialist' countries. In most of the world, ways of livelihood have since proliferated that represent unresolved mixtures of dependent functional integration into the dominant style of development (sweatshop production, home piece-work, street vending, domestic service), refuge from it through networks of production and exchange among the excluded, and parasitism upon it through begging, theft, drug peddling, prostitution and so on.

Comparable although less traumatic changes have emerged in the high-income countries, partly through economic slowdown and transfer of some productive activities to lower-cost countries, partly through curtailment of welfare state activities, but more ominously through technological and organizational innovations that are increasingly divorcing production from the need for a large and relatively stable labour force. Traditional heavy industries such as steel, automobiles and mining have for a good many years combined rising production with shrinking numbers of workers. More recently, computerization began to eliminate areas of white-collar employment. Industries as well as commercial and financial enterprises fixed on staff reduction as an indicator of efficient management, and turned to the hiring of temporary workers at lower rates of pay, lesser health and social security protection and no job stability. 'Downsizing' now threatened even corporate executives.[3] Shrinkage in opportunities for certain preferred lines of employment derives not only from the creative-destructive logic of capitalism but also from overdue public efforts to modify this logic, particularly by curbing environmentally unsustainable industrial and extractive activities and by winding down military forces and armaments production.

In the high-income countries as well as elsewhere, pressures toward exclusion from livelihood combine inextricably with challenges to seek and qualify for new livelihood opportunities that are undoubtedly emerging. In the well-paid technological and cultural specializations that are expanding, arduous educational qualifications are needed, and demands for such specializations may continue to change as unpredictably as they have in the recent past. The services that are least susceptible to rationalization but indispensable to the consumer society may continue to offer abundant job openings, but with wages and status unacceptable to those displaced from industries and white-collar occupations.

Meanwhile, migrants find opportunities for livelihood and paths to future prosperity in occupations that the recently displaced reject. Women have been able to incorporate themselves into the labour force at all levels, partly through greater independence from traditional family roles, partly through pressure to earn so as to maintain family consumption standards, partly through employers' preference for them in the occupations most susceptible to exploitation. While young people have been most acutely affected by exclusion from industrial work, and for some exclusion has become practically total except for illegal and dangerous activities such as drug peddling, others have benefited from recent education to gain access to the newer and more coveted areas of livelihood.

Within this contradictory picture, it might be premature to conclude that exclusion from livelihood is bound to become more radical and pervasive, qualitatively different from the painful forms of exploitation that all societies have experienced since the industrial revolution. However, according to one dramatic formulation, while nineteenth-century Europe was haunted by Marx's spectre of the proletariat, the world at the end of the twentieth century will be haunted by the spectre of superfluous man.[4]

In this conjuncture, policy debates on issues ranging from free trade to environmental protection, in rich countries as well as poor, continue to be shaped by preoccupation with their consequences in creating, preserving or destroying jobs, whatever the utility or disutility, or even irrelevance of the output of the job-holders. This preoccupation and the associated political promises and denunciations coexist conflictively with continual efforts by governments as well as private employers to get rid of redundant employees. They also coexist with an increasingly overt preference on the part of financial institutions for a relatively high level of unemployment as a curb on inflationary pressures.

The main functions of employment up to the present can be summed up thus:

— to produce goods and services and perform the social roles valued by the society;
— to give individuals and families access to incomes enabling them to satisfy their needs and wants;
— to enable people to enter into relationships with the social order, interpret personal interests in its maintenance or transformation, associate themselves with a class or interest group, and acquire organizational ties;
— to enable the individual to meet psychological needs for meaningful activity, self-realization, creativity and status as family breadwinner.

It hardly needs saying that the ways of livelihood of most people throughout history have combined these functions erratically and contradictorily, as byproducts of economic and political systems that have functioned according to their own laws. In modern times, men and women have had to serve the capitalist system, however irrelevant or even threatening to their own well-being the services demanded and the resulting output might seem to be, in order to make the system serve some of their needs. When public policy has meddled too directly with the system on behalf of human welfare or the curbing of wasteful and destructive activities, the system has functioned badly.

The paradoxical traits of the functioning of capitalism have been exhaustively diagnosed since the nineteenth century. While its gradual compatibilization with welfare state policies managed to raise the satisfaction of human needs and wants to a degree that could not have been expected in the earlier stages, the means remained indirect, wasteful and plagued by unwanted and unexpected byproducts.[5] In the 'real socialist' systems also, objectives of accumulation, armaments priorities, obsessions of infallible leaders, and the suitability of central planning to accomplish some ends rather than others left people servants of the system and the satisfaction of some of their needs a means to their participation in production rather than an end.

An exploration of alternatives for the better-balanced performance of the functions of employment summarized above, setting aside the unrealizable goal of full employment in favour of a goal of meaningful activity for all, seems to be overdue. Such an exploration risks intoxication with dreams of technological abundance and painless transformation of dominant values towards social solidarity and creativity. In principle, nevertheless, the technological and informational revolutions of today should mean almost unlimited possibilities for redistributing the ways in which people spend their time and for broadening their choices.

In some respects this is happening, in the midst of exclusions, forced improvisations, and choices that the observer might well find deplorable. In the better-off countries, globalized economic competition and the widening gap between consumerist aspirations and capabilities pushed aside the gradual shortening of labour time, diversification of work environments and diversification of leisure activities that seemed socially positive trends a few years ago. The present contradictions in job markets and lifestyles are bringing them back to attention. Elsewhere, economic and cultural responses to exclusion and superfluity continue to evolve and innovate, although the promising responses probably are more precarious and reach smaller minorities than their advocates argue. The bringing of a higher proportion of the working-age population into gainful employment is not legitimately an end in itself, although it is understandable that the state, unable to balance the different reasons for wanting employment and with few effective means of making the economic system function for human ends, may not be able to avoid treating it as such.

With the advances of globalization, national policies cannot go beyond striving competitively for changes in production techniques and in products for export that will create more and better-paid jobs and finding resources for education and other social services that will help qualify a labour force for such jobs.[6] However, the policies that count are those of multi-national enterprises. These combine mobilization of low-wage, mainly female labour for simple industrial processes, substitution of robotized and automated techniques for such labour, and flexibility in shifting production from country to country according to wage costs and other comparative advantages. Full employment supporting adequate levels of living remains a mirage. The content of production is ever more divorced from the basic needs of the producers. The imperative of ever more activity for the sake of activity confronts an increasingly uneasy awareness of its contradiction with environmental sustainability and its irrelevance to the plight of the superfluous millions. The solution – at the level of utopian aspirations – should derive from a balancing of the four functions of employment in pursuance of meaningful activity. That is, the social order should enable all adults and youth to engage in activities meaningful to themselves and to the society and at the same time to satisfy their basic needs within limits set by the productivity of the economy, irrespective of gainful employment status.

There is nothing new in the posing of such an objective for human societies. The way to it is now more obscure than it seemed to certain social thinkers of the nineteenth century. Comprehensive strategies aiming in such a direction are obviously far from the intentions of the forces controlling the state in any country today, and also of the counter-elites that aspire to supplant them. Nevertheless, the looming spectre of super-fluous man and the deepening contradictions of employment trends and policies may bring something like it back to the agenda, probably through piecemeal innovations. The incapacity of 'rich' as well as 'poor' states to meet acknowledged social and environmental needs through traditional bureaucratic structures, juxtaposed to the presence of enormous numbers of unemployed and underemployed people endowed with a wide range of skills and motivations, presses toward innovations.

The accessible responses incur differing dangers and drawbacks in specific national settings. One is that of compulsion, as in the 'voluntary' mobilizations of labour on public works in the 'real socialist' countries. Another is that of substitution of otherwise unemployed labour paid subsistence wages for regularly employed workers. Another is that of subordination of the expansion of socially useful public employment to the objective of absorbing the output of dysfunctional systems of higher education. Still another, where offenders are being sentenced to terms of 'community service' in lieu of jail or fines, is the identification of such service with punishment.

Patterns of livelihood and relevant public policies are bound to transform themselves during coming years even more radically than in the recent past. Whether the outcome will be any closer to the ideal of meaningful activity for all depends on many things. From the viewpoint of the present exploration it depends first of all on the capacity of societies to enlist democratic participation to find alternatives to directions of change that now seem both irresistible and unsustainable.

## Democracy and participation

### Pluralist democracy at the national level

Previous chapters have dealt with the precarious and paradoxical triumph of pluralist democracy as the sole legitimate source of state authority. This triumph has coincided with the advance of economic and cultural globalization that has narrowed the possibilities for autonomous choice in the policies that bear directly on livelihood, even in the richest and most powerful countries. The coming into force of the General Agreement on Tariffs and Trade (GATT) purports to penalize choices conflicting with globalization even more systematically. It has coincided with the discrediting of ideologies that offered blueprints for the achievement through organized political action of radically different styles of development. None of the national efforts to apply such blueprints has succeeded and some of them have had horrifyingly perverse outcomes. It has also coincided with a so-called 'information revolution' that has made most of the world's population potential political actors. The capitalist forces impelling globalization dominate but do not monopolize the public discourse emerging from this 'revolution'.

The disadvantaged gain something from electoral participation to the extent that pluralist democracy is more than a façade, but their gains are precarious and far from offsetting the excluding and concentrating impetus of economic processes. In Latin America, where electoral competition has in recent years been more vigorous and open than in most other regions, the previously notorious extremes of concentration of wealth and deepening impoverishment have become even more pronounced; exposure of the weak to arbitrary brutality from power-holders has hardly diminished. Specific national settings show different mixtures of complacency, frustration, alienation and corruption, along with the continual emergence of new political and social movements aspiring to redress the balance of power and refute judgements of the 'end of history' or the 'end of ideology'.

It is evident that the more traditional and structured political parties and interest-group organizations are in crises that derive partly from changes in class and group self-identifications among their clienteles; partly from the discrediting of their ideologies or relinquishment of ideologies;

partly from the impact of the information revolution; partly from the rise of fundamentalist, otherworldly and xenophobic currents; and partly from their internal degeneration through bureaucratization and corruption. Parties that have dominated national scenes for many years have disintegrated into fragments striving to find new rationales and new clienteles. Voting patterns show rejection of discredited regimes more than choice of perceived alternatives.

From the standpoint of the present exploration, strengthening of the capacity of states to offer real political choices and strengthening of the capacity of people to arrive at such choices through 'free, rational, public deliberation' are central questions.[7] The 'national' states within the world system of states now confronting or evading these questions have formally similar attributes, endorse universalist norms, and continually interact with each other through inter-governmental institutions. All of them are constrained by globalization but at the same time they differ in every conceivable respect, including the degree of identification of their people with the state as a political arena and in the kinds of choices that are visible to them.

The nation-state may or may not be the most important arena for such choices in the future, but neither global nor local democratization can replace certain indispensable roles. Some general principles can be proposed to social actors striving to help their states perform these roles better but such principles are more negative (what to avoid) than positive (what to do).

*First*, policy subordination to democratic choice and to uncertainty of outcomes implies that there is no infallible One Right Way to achieve sustainable development or social justice or any other goal. The wonders of the information revolution can bring a wider range of choices within the vision of governments and peoples, and the rules of the game set by globalization can narrow the choices, but neither factor can altogether rationalize the contending forces behind policy-making or transform the absorptive capacities of the executive and legislative bodies that must arrive at decisions. As the press demonstrates every day in diverse national settings, even the pursuit of relatively restricted sectoral policies, in which the executive has a coherent idea of what it wants to do and enjoys majority approval, encounters endless problems in formulation, mobilization of support, overcoming of obstruction, compromise and execution. The effort of the Clinton administration to reform the United States health care system is a case in point. In most states and for most policy issues conditions are less propitious. Proposals for 'integrated' or 'holistic' approaches evade the complexity of the decision-making process in pluralist democracies.

*Second*, ideologies viewing nation-states as organisms with unique laws of development and immutable principles for inclusion and exclusion are dangerous to democracy as well as incompatible with the composition of most real states and the increasing mobility of the world's population. Such views have obviously been most pernicious in multi-ethnic and multi-religious societies, but in more homogeneous societies they can justify a stifling conformism manipulated by power-holders and supportive of stereotyped social class, age-group and gender roles.

*Third*, all 'national' societies contain diverse and overlapping class, interest-group, ethnic, cultural, religious, gender and other sources of conflict, some of them obviously more intractable sources of impasses or disintegration than others. The interplay of these conflicts, the continual emergence of new groups or self-definitions of groups to claim a voice in democratic decision-making are inseparable from the kind of dynamic social integration that can be hoped for. At the same time, to the extent that participants define these conflicts as irreconcilable, zero-sum games, to be resolved only by complete separation or unchallenged dominance of one group or ideology, they become pernicious. A good many recent experiences demonstrate the perverse results of apparently final victories and defeats. Outcomes depend partly on the historical evolution of conflicts, partly on the changing challenges to adapt or suffer exclusion that the global system presents to countries and groups within them. Better understanding of the sources of conflicts, and principled opposition to ideologies that define them as irreconcilable, can presumably contribute to happier outcomes, but this question, like others discussed here, does not lend itself to facile generalization.

*Fourth*, self-limitation of the interventions of the state and the diffusion of responsibilities to other institutions, the market and the civil society do not require replacement of the omnicompetent nursemaid state by the minimal nightwatchman state. This would reduce pluralist democracy at the national level to trivial choices. The cycle of discrediting of the state, stemming from its past overambitious claims and from market-oriented as well as social-movement-oriented ideologies, is no more likely to persist than the previous cycle of technobureaucratic overconfidence. It is legitimate for the forces controlling states to strive to widen responsibilities, and it is equally legitimate for political movements and other institutions of the civil society, as well as international organizations and movements, to keep these efforts under critical scrutiny. (It can be assumed that the complex of multinational enterprises and their ideologists will keep them under scrutiny, whether legitimately or otherwise.) No society can expect the state to reach a permanently satisfactory balance between overregulation and overprotection, on the one hand, and *laissez-faire*, on the other. Recent experiences suggest, however, that state relinquishment of previous responsibilities for social services and for regulation of threats to public welfare is at least as harmful, from the standpoint of equity and democracy, as inefficient and overreaching efforts to meet these responsibilities.

*Fifth*, the capacity of pluralist democracy to widen the range of choices and strengthen popular confidence in choice through political participation supposes transparency on the part of the national political leadership. This is a formidable requirement for agents competing for political support:

> When candidates hide their economic programmes during election campaigns or when governments adopt policies diametrically opposed to their electoral promises, they systematically educate the population that elections have no real role in shaping policies. When governments announce vital policies by decree or ram them through legislatures without debate, they teach parties, unions, and other representative organs that they have no role to play in policy making. When they revert to bargaining only to orchestrate policies already chosen they breed distrust and bitterness.[8]

Policy choices will continue to shape themselves within institutions of the global system and of territorially based states through a permanent interplay of different rationalities trying to make sense of multifarious change processes, relate them to values and perceived interests, manipulate them, build defences against them, or revolt against them. In these efforts a quest for universalistic principles and prescriptions for action is unavoidable and can even be considered one of the constant dimensions of change. However, restraint and even scepticism concerning the quest are advisable. If would-be change agents take seriously the values of democracy they must balance the planning and norm-setting responsibilities of the global system and the state against respect for the right of forces within the societies to make their own choices; organize to advance their perceived interests; and embrace, resist or transform the seemingly overwhelming pressures of globalization.

### Participation: communities, grassroots organizations, social movements

If the capacity of the state and other institutions at the national level to make viable and equitable 'development' policy choices is now questionable, what can be said of the groupings on a scale compatible with participatory democracy? At this level, the expectations of political leaders, administrators, theorists and activists continue to derive from diverse conceptions of development as well as from opportunistic expedients to evade confrontations with the ominous trajectory of globalization. Chapter 4 has discussed some aspects of the contradictory history of participation within development discourse and a recent book has treated it in more depth from the standpoint of the 'hitherto excluded' who are called on to participate.[9]

The localized patterns of organization and solidarity are, like the national manifestations of pluralist democracy, undergoing traumatic changes in representativeness and functions. They include the elected local administrations and sometimes traditional 'tribal' or 'communal' authority systems that are gaining wider formal responsibilities *vis-à-vis* the state. They include groupings based on neighbourhoods, livelihoods, gender, age group, religion, sports and other sources of self-identification, some of which are of long standing, others very recent and possibly ephemeral. All of them are struggling with their own imperatives to adapt or perish. All of them are confronting interlocutors – would-be allies and interpreters as well as would-be exploiters – that are striving to invest them with new responsibilities and make use of them for purposes that may or may not coincide with their own perceived needs. While investigations bearing on their struggles and their contradictory relations with allies and exploiters are by now numerous, they provide only an insecure basis for generalization on the kaleidoscopic scene.

For present purposes, one can distinguish, at the cost of considerable oversimplification, three approaches among their interlocutors that derive from different visions of 'development'.

*Communities* Inter-governmental organizations, national governments and some non-governmental organizations (NGOs) that accept the desirability or inevitability of globalized capitalist development and structural adjustment see decentralization as well as privatization as means of transferring responsibilities that the state cannot afford or handle efficiently to local elected administrations and organizations of the civil society. The devolution of responsibilities, with or without state subsidies and access to revenue sources, can be labelled euphemistically 'empowerment'. Local institutions can also act as transmission belts for aid and advice leading to more vigorous participation in the market economy.

The image of stable local communities open to democratic participation and cooperative endeavours for the common good has clashed with inconvenient realities ever since the community development programmes that flourished during the 1950s. Real local communities have rarely been egalitarian or progressive. Community decision-making has more often than not been in the hands of minorities able to control key resources such as land and to monopolize the use of violence, usually in alliance with local functionaries of the state. Social peace has typically depended on acceptance of the traditional distribution of power and avoidance of issues that might bring conflict into the open. In a good many cases, the assignment of new resources and responsibilities by state agencies has helped to disintegrate the pre-existing conformism. Either the community power-holders have monopolized the new resources and institutions, to the resentment of the majority, or new 'grassroots organizations' have emerged to compete for them.

By now, however, stable communities in which a contest over power and resources can work itself out locally are exceptional, even in rural hinterlands. One pattern of change, studied in the Indian state of Gujarat, could be duplicated in many parts of the world. Here the landowning elite has practically divorced itself from community participation and joined the global society. Its members travel abroad, watch United States television progammes, and send their children to city universities. The middle strata look outside, relying more on contract work in the Gulf states than on local sources of employment. The landless poor, unable to subsist by agricultural work alone, are also mobile, moving to and from the cities in search of casual wage labour. In such settings the possibility of community responsibility has nearly disappeared. Grassroots organization of the poor for self-help and reciprocity is not much more practicable in view of their exclusion from land or other resources and their need to keep moving in search of subsistence. (The researcher labelled them 'wage hunters and gatherers'.) Pluralist democracy at the national level offers somewhat more hope, since parties compete for their votes in return for minimum wage and other protective legislation, but, in the absence of effective organization, enforcement depends on public functionaries open to bribes from employers. Spontaneous violent social protest movements are conceivable, but are likely to focus on symbolic targets of frustration and to end in renewed exclusion.[10]

A study of a town in northeast Brazil, on the other side of the world, gives a similar picture: of a 'modern' upper class operating in a 'world of commercial ventures, finance, interest, travel, newspapers, documents, legality, bureaucracy, rationality'; of an aggressive and insecure middle class continually 'scrambling' to achieve symbols of affluence; and of a remainder that is seen from above as an undifferentiated mass of the 'poor', barely surviving through casual labour, illiterate, with survival tactics including 'individually negotiated relations of dependency on myriad political and personal bosses in town', but inhibited from collective action by many years of helplessness in the face of arbitrary repression.[11]

Patterns of change in many other local settings, of course, are less bleak, but most of them point to 'de-responsibilization' of local communities for meeting of their own collective needs.[12] Such trends may be on the point of reversal through the deliberate decentralization and less deliberate discrediting of national governments, and also through the unprecedented opportunities offered by the information age for interpenetration of local and broader 'community' affiliations. It would be rash to forecast the outcome of such opportunities.

*Grassroots organizations* Some other inter-governmental organizations (or divisions within them), agencies of national governments and issue-oriented organizations see localized expressions of solidarity as means of reforming the dominant style of development, helping the disadvantaged defend themselves against its excesses, bringing basic education and health services into closer correspondence with real needs and wants, combating abuses such as ethnic and gender discrimination and, above all, mobilizing popular understanding and action concerning environmental menaces. This approach is linked particularly to conceptions of 'grassroots organizations'. It assumes that such organizations – with aspirations compatible with those of their interlocutors – are emerging spontaneously but that external help and advice can widen their scope, defend them against their enemies, and enable them to accomplish much more than they could if left to themselves.

Grassroots organizations, while no more consistently defined in current usage than communities, are generally understood to comprise groups within communities or across communities, constituted by their members' choice, in pursuit of common interests. Thus, rural grassroots organizations may be made up of the village poor, landless labourers, tenants, women or people threatened by activities of the state or private enterprise, such as dam construction or deforestation. Urban organizations may be made up of 'informal' microenterprises, street vendors or homeless people attempting collective land occupations. Grassroots organizations ideally function through consensus and reciprocity rather than hierarchical leadership. Entrance and exit are relatively easy. Here the questions most relevant for present purposes are the following.

*First*, their representativeness among the hundreds of millions of people needing collective action cannot be estimated with any confidence. Most of them seem to be short-lived and fluctuating in membership, compared to more structured interest-group organizations such as trade unions. While sympathetic observers argue that their numbers and capacity to benefit their members are increasing, it seems probable that in most settings only very small minorities among the poor and excluded have organizational ties at any one time.

*Second*, most of their activities are defensive, calculated to achieve small gains in livelihood, ward off threats, stretch inadequate resources through mutual aid and take advantage of whatever additional resources are offered by state agencies or NGOs. These tactics can hardly add up to major gains in livelihood or social integration in the face of disintegrating transformations in their economic, political and informational settings, unless, as some ideologists argue, the global order is about to disintegrate altogether, leaving the grassroots organizations as building blocks of a 'new society of castaways'.[13]

*Third*, the grassroots organizations face a permanent tension between their needs for autonomy in solving their own problems and their dependence on aid and protection from state agencies and NGOs. The ideas of these organizations on their own identity, their place within societal transformations, the meaning of 'empowerment' and so on are bound to derive in large part from external interlocutors. This may confront them with divisive choices between radically different interlocutors or lead to conformism with the vocabulary of the most promising sources of aid.[14]

*Fourth*, the leaders and interlocutors of grassroots organizations as well as broader social movements include not only altruistic sources of aid and activists trying to raise their consciousness or fit them into visions of a new society but also mobilizers who are acting for personal advantage, to create clientelistic obligations, or to broaden the following of a political party. Grassroots organizations are vulnerable to exploitation and intimidation. In a good many settings, the more authentic organizations are deeply anti-political because of distrust of the corruption and arbitrariness of state functionaries and political party machines. They cannot expect local and national power structures to keep their hands off once they demonstrate that they constitute potential threats or assets. Political participation and bargaining of votes may then become necessary to protect the internal purposes of the organization. However, to the extent that the organization is localized and limited to the disadvantaged, its political participation will be vulnerable to manipulation or dangerous to its members.

*Social movements* Several schools of theorists and activists, some building on religious doctrines, others seeking to fill the void left by the mobilizing secular myths of the recent past, see mounting human suffering, alienation and future catastrophe in the trends and policies of globalized 'development'. Unlike the earlier proponents of 'another development', who addressed themselves to governments and the international order as potentially rational and open to values of social justice and environmental sustainability, they pin their hopes on the emergence of a new social order from the multifarious survival strategies, networks of reciprocity, collective defences of cultural identity, and other forms of coping among the groups excluded from the dominant style of 'development'.

They generally prefer the term 'social movements', insisting on the spontaneity of such movements and the futility of devising blueprints for the social order that will emerge from their struggles. They look with suspicion on the entry of social movements into electoral politics and organized pressures on the state as conducive to cooptation and conformism. They also commonly argue that would-be interlocutors and allies of the movements are more likely to mislead than help them, although their definition of 'social movement' may become so inclusive that it is evident that some movements (for example, of women or environmental activists) come into being precisely to help more disadvantaged and localized groups to become movements.[15]

Treatments of social movements, unlike most treatments of grassroots organizations, are coloured by hopes of a *general* alternative to the unacceptable reality of globalized 'development'. These hopes struggle with a justified disillusionment with universalized laws of development or revolution. Social movements, as their advocates conceive them, may indeed become more significant actors as the contradictions of such development become more acute. However, it seems unlikely that they will ever encompass the majority of the disadvantaged and excluded, or render obsolete the role of the state and of political parties as arenas for democratic choice.

Affiliation with social movements practising collective self-reliance or 'self-development' is more accessible to some groups among the excluded than to others and in some conjunctures more than in others. Thus far, expectations in various countries that promising small-scale movements would eventually come together in 'national popular movements' have been disappointed. Movements on a national scale, appearing at certain stages of struggles for democratization, as in Chile, the Philippines or Poland, have been inspiring but ephemeral. The movements that have proved most enduring have been made up of ethnic minorities and other groups engaged in long-term defensive struggles against a majority culture.

For the present, at least three 'choices' seem to be more accessible to the majority of the excluded than the choice of self-reliant social movements. One choice, taken by millions of migrants, in particular, is the individualistic or familistic struggle for better livelihood, for entry into the 'culture of opportunity', with complete indifference to the claims of solidarity or environmental sustainability. Another is to enter into the proliferating fundamentalist, xenophobic or otherworldly movements, which combine formidable dynamism with purposes and tactics remote from the hopes of the advocates of social movements. A third is submission to the logic of exclusion and superfluity through opportunistic survival strategies and satisfactions from drugs, alcohol and anomic violence.

## Notes

1. 'A familiar joke on the international scene today is the attempt by the "progressive" economist, domestic or foreign, to sell land reform, or industrialization, or more effective tax collection, or wider educational opportunity, or greater independence from a foreign power to a government whose *raison d'être* is precisely the *prevention* of such developments, or at least limiting them to the greatest extent possible.' (Seers, 'The Prevalence of Pseudo-planning', 1972.)

2. International Labour Organization, *Employment, Growth and Basic Needs* (1976); and Dag Hammarskjöld Foundation, *Another Development* (1975).

3. According to a recent summing up applying to the United States, 'Companies struggling through a weak economy are pushing profits up by pushing employees out. Very few good new jobs are being created to replace the ones that are being lost. All types of workers are being affected, from gung-ho men and women at the

highest levels of the corporate hierarchy to kids fresh out of high school and college.' ('Looking for Work', *New York Times*, 1 August 1993.) See also 'Service Jobs Fall as Business Gains: Automation's Impact Shrinks Employment in New York', *New York Times*, 18 April 1993; 'Temporary Workers on the Increase in Nation's Factories', *New York Times*, 6 July 1993; and 'The Rise of the Losing Class', *New York Times*, 20 November 1994.

4. Statement by David Apter at UNRISD's 30th Anniversary Conference on the Crisis of Social Development in the 1990s, Geneva, July 1993. According to a similar warning: 'Throughout history, masters needed slaves, settlers needed natives and industrialists needed workers ... This is no longer so. Something radically new is happening: rulers – governmental and economic – no longer need so many people. A part of the human species is becoming redundant.' (Nerfin, 'Is Global Civilization Coming', 1992.)

5. 'Keynes did not want anyone to dig holes and fill them. He indulged in a pleasant day-dream of a world in which, when investment had been kept at the full employment level for thirty years or so, all needs for capital installations would have been met, property income would have been abolished, poverty would have disappeared and civilized life could begin. But the economists took up the argument at the point where it had been broken off before the war. When there is unemployment and low profits the government must spend on something or other – it does not matter what. As we know, for twenty-five years serious recessions were avoided by following this policy The most convenient thing for a government to spend on is armaments. The military–industrial complex took charge. I do not think it plausible to suppose that the cold war and several hot wars were invented just to solve the employment problem. But certainly they have had that effect. The system had the support of the corporations who made profits under it and the workers who got jobs, but also of the economists who advocated government loan-expenditure as a prophylactic against stagnation ... So it has come about that Keynes' pleasant daydream was turned into a nightmare of terror.' (Robinson, 'The Second Crisis of Economic Theory', 1972.)

6. See Economic Commission for Latin America and the Caribbean, *Changing Production Patterns with Social Equity* (1990).

7. This formulation is taken from Flisfisch, 'El surgimiento de una nueva ideología democrática en América Latina' (1983).

8. Prezeworski, *Democracy and the Market* (1991).

9. Stiefel and Wolfe, *A Voice for the Excluded* (1994).

10. Breman, *Wage Hunters and Gatherers* (1994); and *Labour Nomads in South Gujerat*, paper presented to International Institute for Labour Studies (IILS) Workshop on Patterns and Causes of Social Exclusion, Cambridge, July 1994.

11. Scheper-Hughes, *Death without Weeping* (1992).

12. The ungainly term 'de-responsibilization' refers to the perceived loss of local capacity to decide how to cope with local social and environmental needs in the face of state centralization combining with unintelligible economic, demographic and cultural transformations. See Amalric and Banuri, *Population, Environment, and De-Responsibilization* (1992).

13. Latouche, *In the Wake of the Affluent Society* (1993).

14. '[N]ew socio-political identities ... stem from the popular movements' continuous interaction with various collaborators. The process can thus basically be seen as a play of mirrors, through which the grass-roots groups construct their self-image so that it reflects their dialogue with different interlocutors'. (Cardoso,

'Popular Movements in the Context of the Consolidation of Democracy in Brazil', 1992.) See also Chapter 8, 'Interlocutors and Allies', in Stiefel and Wolfe, *A Voice for the Excluded* (1994).

15. For provocative denunciations of development mythology combined with variations of this approach to social movements, see Sachs (ed.), *The Development Dictionary* (1992); and Latouche, *In the Wake of the Affluent Society* (1993).

# BIBLIOGRAPHY

Amalric, Franck and Banuri, Tariq, *Population, Environment, and De-Responsibilization: Case Studies from the Rural Areas of Pakistan*, Sustainable Development Institute, Islamabad, 1992.

Amin, Samir, *Maldevelopment: Anatomy of a Global Failure*, Zed Books, London, and United Nations University Press, Tokyo, 1990.

Annis, Shelden and Hakim, Peter (eds), *Direct to the Poor: Grassroots Development in Latin America*, Lynn Rienner, Boulder, CO and London, 1988.

Arndt, H.W., *Economic Development: The History of an Idea*, University of Chicago Press, 1987.

Barraclough, Solon L., *An End to Hunger? The Social Origins of Food Strategies*, Zed Books, London, on behalf of UNRISD, Geneva, 1991.

Bobbio, Norberto, *Democracy and Dictatorship: The Nature and Limits of State Power*, University of Minnesota Press, Minneapolis, 1989.

Breman, Jan, *Wage Hunters and Gatherers: Search for Work in the Urban and Rural Economy of South Gujerat*, Oxford University Press, Delhi, 1994.

Cardoso, Ruth Correia Leite, 'Popular Movements in the Context of the Consolidation of Democracy in Brazil', in Arturo Escobar and Sonia E. Álvarez (eds), *The Making of Social Movements in Latin America: Identity, Strategy, and Democracy*, Westview Press, Boulder, CO, 1992.

Carnoy, Martin et al., *The New Global Economy in the Information Age: Reflexions on Our Changing World*, Pennsylvania State University Press, 1993.

Castells, Manuel, 'The Informational Economy and the New International Division of Labor', in Martin Carnoy et al., *The New Global Economy in the Information Age: Reflexions on Our Changing World*, Pennsylvania State University Press, 1993.

Chenery, Hollis et al., *Redistribution with Growth*, Oxford University Press on behalf of the World Bank, 1974.

Crozier, Michel, and Friedburg, Erhard, *L'acteur et le système: Les contraintes de l'action collective*, Éditions du Seuil, Paris, 1977.

Dag Hammarskjöld Foundation, *Another Development: The 1975 Dag Hammarskjöld Report on International Cooperation and Development*, Uppsala, 1975.

Dowse, Robert E., 'The Military and Political Development', in Colin Leys (ed.), *Politics and Change in Developing Countries*, Cambridge University Press, 1969.

Drucker, Peter F., *Post-capitalist Society*, Butterworth-Heinemann, Oxford, 1993.

Economic Commission for Latin America and the Caribbean, *Changing Production Patterns with Social Equity: The Prime Task of Latin America and Caribbean Development in the 1990s*, United Nations, 14 February 1990.

Etzioni, Amitai, *The Active Society*, Free Press, New York, 1968.

Evans, Peter B., Rueschemeyer, Dietrich and Skocpol, Theda (eds), *Bringing the State Back In*, Cambridge University Press, 1985.

Fals Borda, Orlando, Inayatullah and Apthorpe, Raymond (eds), *Rural Institutions and Planned Change*, Vols I to VI, UNRISD, Geneva, 1969–72.

Flisfisch, Angel, 'El surgimiento de una nueva ideología democrática en América Latina', *Crítica y Utopía*, Buenos Aires, 9, 1983.

Freire, Paulo, *Pedagogy of the Oppressed*, Sheed and Ward, London, 1972.

Furtado, Celso, *El desarrollo económico: Un mito*, Siglo XXI, Mexico, DF, 1975.

Galbraith, John Kenneth, *The Culture of Contentment*, Penguin Books, 1993.

Geertz, Clifford, 'The Search for North Africa', *New York Review of Books*, 16, 7, 22 April 1971.

Ghai, Dharam, *The IMF and the South: The Social Impact of Crisis and Adjustment*, Zed Books, London, on behalf of UNRISD, Geneva, 1991.

Gills, Barry, Rocamora, Joel and Wilson, Richard (eds), *Low Intensity Democracy: Political Power in the New World Order*, Pluto Press, London and Boulder, CO, 1993.

Graciarena, Jorge and Franco, Rolando, 'Social Formations and Power Structures in Latin America', *Current Sociology*, 26, 1, Spring 1978.

Hancock, Graham, *Lords of Poverty: The Power, Prestige and Corruption of the International Aid Business*, Atlantic Monthly Press, New York, 1989.

Hewitt de Alcántara, Cynthia (ed.), *Real Markets: Social and Political Issues of Food Policy Reform*, Frank Cass, London, on behalf of UNRISD, Geneva, 1993.

Hirsch, Fred, *Social Limits to Growth; A Twentieth Century Fund Study*, Harvard University Press, Cambridge, MA, 1976.

Hirschman, Albert O., *A Bias for Hope: Essays on Development and Latin America*, Yale University Press, New Haven, 1971.

— *Exit, Voice, and Loyalty: Responses to Decline in Firms, Organizations, and States*, Harvard University Press, 1970.

Hobsbawm, E.J., *Nations and Nationalism since 1780: Programme, Myth, Reality*, Canto, Cambridge, 1991.

Hughes, Robert, *Culture of Complaint: The Fraying of America*, Warner Books, New York, 1993.

International Labour Organization, *Employment, Growth and Basic Needs: A One-world Problem*, Report of the Director-General, ILO, Geneva, 1976.

Kristof, Nicholas D. and Wudunn, Sheryl, *China Wakes: The Struggle for the Soul of a Rising Power*, Times Books, New York, 1994.

Kuitenbrouwer, Joost B.W., *Towards Self-reliant Integrated Development*, Occasional Paper, Institute of Social Studies, The Hague, no date.

Latouche, Serge, *In the Wake of the Affluent Society: An Exploration of Post-Development*, Zed Books, London, 1993.

Lehmann, David, *Democracy and Development in Latin America: Economics, Politics and Religion in the Postwar Period*, Temple University Press, Philadelphia, 1990.

Leys, Colin and Marris, Peter, 'Planning and Development', in Dudley Sears and Leonard Joy (eds), *Development in a Divided World*, Penguin Books, 1971.

Lipton, Michael, *Why Poor People Stay Poor: Urban Bias in World Development*, Temple Smith, London, 1977.

Medina Echavarría, José, *Consideraciones sociológicas sobre el desarrollo económico*, CEPAL, Santiago de Chile, 1963.

— *Filosofía, educación y desarrollo*, Textos del ILPES, Siglo XXI, México, DF, 1973.

— *La obra de José Medina Echavarría*, Selección y Estudio Preliminar por Adolfo Gurrieri, Ediciones Cultura Hispánica, Madrid, 1980.

Myrdal, Gunnar, *Asian Drama: An Inquiry into the Poverty of Nations*, Pantheon, New York, 1968.

Needler, Martin C., *Political Development in Latin America: Instability, Violence, and Evolutionary Change*, Random House, New York, 1968.

Nerfin, Marc, 'Is Global Civilization Coming?', in Üner Kirdar (ed.), *Change: Threat or Opportunity?*, Vol. I, United Nations Development Programme, New York, 1992.

O'Donnell, Guillermo, 'Tensions in the Bureaucratic–Authoritarian State and the Question of Democracy', in David Collier (ed.), *The New Authoritarianism in Latin America,* Princeton University Press, 1979.

Peattie, Lisa R., 'The Social Anthropologist in Planning', *Journal of the American Institute of Planning,* July 1967.

— *Thinking about Development,* Plenum Press, New York and London, 1981.

Prebisch, Raúl, 'A Critique of Peripheral Capitalism', *CEPAL Review,* 1, First Semester 1976.

— 'Socioeconomic Structure and Crisis of the System', *CEPAL Review,* 6, Second Semester 1978.

— *Towards a Dynamic Development Policy for Latin America,* United Nations, New York, 1963.

— *Transformation and Development: The Great Task of Latin America,* Inter-American Development Bank, Washington, DC, 1970.

Przeworski, Adam, *Democracy and the Market: Political and Economic Reforms in Eastern Europe and Latin America,* Cambridge University Press, 1991.

— 'Some Problems in the Study of the Transition to Democracy', in Guillermo O'Donnell, Philippe C. Schmitter and Laurence Whitehead, *Transitions from Authoritarian Rule: Comparative Perspectives,* Johns Hopkins University Press, Baltimore, 1986.

Rahman, M.D. Anisur, *People's Self-Development: Perspectives on Participatory Action Research,* Zed Books, London, 1993.

Robinson, Joan, 'The Second Crisis of Economic Theory', *The American Economic Review,* May 1972.

Rudé, George, *Europe in the Eighteenth Century: Aristocracy and the Bourgeois Challenge,* Cardinal History of Civilization, London, 1974.

Sachs, Ignacy, *Stratégies de l'écodéveloppement,* Éditions Ouvrières, Paris, 1980.

Sachs, Wolfgang (ed.), *The Development Dictionary: A Guide to Knowledge as Power,* Zed Books, London, 1992

Scheper-Hughes, Nancy, *Death without Weeping: The Violence of Everyday Life in Brazil,* University of California Press, Berkeley and Los Angeles, 1992.

Schuurman, Frans J. (ed.), *Beyond the Impasse: New Directions in Development Theory,* Zed Books, London, 1993.

Seers, Dudley, 'The Prevalence of Pseudo-planning', in Mike Faber and, Dudley Seers (eds), *The Crisis in Planning,* Chatto and Windus, London, for Sussex University Press, 1972.

Silva Michelena, José, *The Illusion of Democracy in Dependent Nations,* MIT Press, Cambridge, MA, 1971.

Simmel, Georg, 'The Poor', originally published in 1908, reprinted in Chaim L. Waxman (ed.), *Poverty, Power, and Politics,* Grosset and Dunlap, New York, 1968.

Skocpol, Theda, *States and Social Revolutions,* Cambridge University Press, 1979.

Solari, Aldo E., Franco, Rolando and Jutkowitz, Joel, *Teoría, acción social y desarrollo en América Latina,* Textos del ILPES, Siglo XXI, México, DF, 1976.

Staniland, Martin, 'Single-party Regimes and Political Change', in Colin Les, (ed.), *Politics and Change in Developing Countries*, Cambridge University Press, 1969.

Stiefel, Matthias and Wolfe, Marshall, *A Voice for the Excluded: Popular Participation in Development, Utopia or Necessity?*, Zed Books, London, in association with UNRISD, Geneva, 1994.

Toffler, Alvin, *Future Shock*, Bodley Head, London, 1970.

Touraine, Alain, *Qu'est-ce que la démocratie?*, Fayard 1994.

United Nations, *International Survey of Programmes of Social Development*, United Nations, New York, 1955.

— *Planning for Balanced Social and Economic Development: Six Country Case Studies*, United Nations, New York, 1964.

— *Preliminary Report on the World Social Situation*, United Nations, New York, 1952.

— *Report on the World Social Situation*, United Nations, New York, 1957, 1961, 1963, 1965, 1967, 1970, 1974, 1978, 1982.

United Nations Development Programme, *Human Development Reports 1990–1994*, Oxford University Press, 1990–1994.

United Nations Economic and Social Commission for Asia and the Pacific (ESCAP), *Premises and Implications of a Unified Approach to Development Analysis and Planning*, ESCAP, Bangkok, 1975.

United Nations Research Institute for Social Development (UNRISD), *The Quest for a Unified Approach*, Geneva, 1980.

Vivian, Jessica, and Maseko, Gladys, *NGOs, Participation and Rural Development*, UNRISD Discussion Paper, Geneva, 1994.

Whyte, William F., 'Dos comunidades serranas', in José Matos Mar et al. (eds), *Dominación y cambios en el Perú rural*, Instituto de Estudios Peruanos, Lima, 1969.

Wignaraja, Ponna (ed.), *New Social Movements in the South: Empowering the People*, Zed Books, London, 1993.

World Bank, *Poverty: World Development Report 1990*, Oxford University Press, 1990.

— *The Assault on World Poverty: Problems of Rural Development, Education and Health*, Johns Hopkins University Press, Baltimore, 1975.

# INDEX